THE
WRITER'S
OPTIONS

THE

WRITER'S OPTIONS

COMBINING TO COMPOSING

DONALD A. DAIKER

Miami University

ANDREW KEREK

The American University in Cairo

MAX MORENBERG

Miami University

JEFFREY SOMMERS

Miami University—Middletown

FIFTH EDITION

HarperCollins*CollegePublishers*

Senior Acquisitions Editor: Jane Kinney
Developmental Editor: Marisa L. L'Heureux
Project Coordination and Text Design: York Production Services
Cover Design: John Callahan
Production/Manufacturing: Michael Weinstein/Hilda Koparanian
Compositor: York Production Services
Printer and Binder: R. R. Donnelley & Sons
Cover Printer: Lehigh Press, Inc.

Library of Congress Cataloging-in-Publication Data

The Writer's options : combining to composing / Donald A. Daiker . . .
 [et al.]. — 5th ed.
   p. cm.
 Includes index.
 Rev. ed. of: Writer's options / Donald A. Daiker, Andrew
Kerek, Max Morenberg. 4th ed. 1990.
  ISBN 0-06-501324-7
  1. English language—Rhetoric. I. Daiker, Donald A., 1938–
II. Daiker, Donald A., 1938–   Writer's options.
PE1408.D13 1993
808'.042—dc20   93-36931
                                                   CIP

     94 95 96   9 8 7 6 5 4 3 2

BRIEF CONTENTS

CONTENTS

Contents

PREFACE

 PURPOSE

The purpose of *The Writer's Options,* Fifth Edition, is to help you become
a better writer. The book assumes that you become a better writer by
practicing writing and by learning to recognize the language options
available to you so that you can choose the best sentence, paragraph, and
essay strategies to make your point. James Joyce, the great Irish writer,
recognized that you have lots of language options to choose from; he
once commented on his writing practice, "What I am seeking is the perfect order of words in the sentence. You can see for yourself how many
different ways they might be arranged." The exercises in *The Writer's
Options* allow you to practice arranging sentences, paragraphs, and essays
in many different ways. Doing the exercises will help you both to master
new constructions and to make writing decisions in terms of context and
purpose. Because there are usually no "right" answers, the exercises
invite you to play with words and phrases, to experiment with language,
and to explore new and exciting ways of expressing your feelings and
ideas.

    You are likely to gain the most from the combining exercises if you at
least occasionally approach the exercises in the spirit of play. Look on the
exercises as a kind of game, and you'll be more willing to take risks and
to try new ways of expressing yourself. You may even have fun in substi-
tuting one word for another, in manipulating phrases and clauses, and in
changing the position of sentences. You'll find that the more you play

with language, the more you will be able to control it. Remember, that's the main purpose of the book: to help you become a better writer by learning to control the vital sentence, paragraph, and writing strategies of written language.

So explore and experiment, We can't emphasize that point enough. You won't improve your writing by reading about language; you will improve your writing by exploring and experimenting with language. The first way you put sentences together is not always the best. See what happens when you rephrase or reorder parts of sentences and when you shift sentences within a paragraph. Only by experimenting and exploring will you increase your writing options, and only by increasing your options will you extend your power over language.

Experimenting with language in the exercises is a means to an end. The end is to improve your writing. If you do the exercises carefully and creatively and then consciously use in your own writing the same structures, patterns, and strategies, you can expect to become a better writer. We have proof of that. A research study at our school showed that first-year college students who practiced sentence combining for one semester wrote better papers than students who had not practiced sentence combining. Few things in life are certain, but it's a good bet that if you transfer what you learn in the sentence-combining exercises to your own compositions, you'll become a much better writer. Your instructor will think so, too.

 ## STRUCTURE

The Writer's Options is organized into three main parts: "Sentence Strategies," "Paragraph Strategies," and "Writing Strategies." Most of the sixteen units in the book consist of an introductory section followed by a series of exercises. The introductory section explains a sentence, paragraph, or discourse strategy and illustrates its use. The introductory sections are important to read and think about. But it is the exercises that are the essence of each unit—and of the book: the exercises give you actual practice in composing and revision. The whole-discourse exercises—those with titles like "Beam Me Up, Cookie Monster" or "How to Get Ahead"—are especially important because they ask you to combine sets of short sentences into paragraphs or essays, and thus they provide a specific context for your writing practice.

The whole-discourse exercise alternate with other types of exercises that help you practice basic sentence patterns, creative patterns, and various constructions or revising strategies. By working out the basic constructing exercise before doing the first whole-discourse exercise in any unit, you can test your mastery of that unit's strategy. The creating exercises take you one step further. They ask you to expand sentences by adding details of your own, following the construction strategy practiced in writing. Creating exercises encourage you to transfer your new skills into actual writing. Additional kinds of exercises both add variety to the book and provide practice in different writing tasks.

 ## THE FIFTH EDITION

The Writer's Options has developed slowly, in three- and four-year cycles, since the first edition appeared in 1978. We have tried to improve it each time. The fifth edition of *The Writer's Options: Combining to Composing* continues to emphasize the rhetorical and contextual elements of the combining and composing processes. But we've made the book leaner and easier to use. We cut it down from nineteen units to sixteen so that it will fit better into a semester course. We simplified explanations and eliminated redundancies. We made the whole-discourse exercises shorter and replaced exercises we thought were out of date or uninteresting. And we rewrote the final section so that it makes a closer link between combining and composing.

ACKNOWLEDGMENTS

We received invaluable feedback for the new edition from the follow-ing reviewers: Carolyn Channell, Southern Methodist University; Ter-rance Flaherty, Mankato State University; Barbara Gable, University of California–Riverside; Mary Meiser, University of Wisconsin–Eau Claire; Margaret Dietz Meyer, Ithaca College; Jane Thompson, Mount Mary College; Ted Walkup, Clayton State College; and Jan Wall, Laney College.

We remain indebted to all those people and institutions named in the previous editions, including Kelly Hunt, Francis Christensen, John Mel-lon, Bill Strong, the English Department at Miami University, and the Exxon Education Foundation. They were our inspiration and support. Dozens of graduate students, colleagues, and friends at Miami and other universities helped us at each step of the way. We'll never forget them. Some of the exercises for the fifth edition were written by Bill Broun, Meaghan Hanrahan Dobson, Vicki Hollon, Holly Roberts, and Erica Scott, Jane Kinney and Marisa L. L'Heureux at HarperCollins pushed and prodded—kindly, carefully, but firmly—until we finished this latest edition.

Donald A. Daiker
Andrew Kerek
Max Morenberg
Jeffrey Sommers

PART ONE

SENTENCE STRATEGIES

PART ONE
AT A GLANCE

UNIT 1

WARM UPS

This unit is not built around one specific structure or strategy. It is simply a set of exercises to allow you to practice combining sentences. We hope that by working on the exercises in this chapter, you will see that sentence combining is not threatening. You can do it and do it well. There are no "right answers" that you have to come up with. For instance, you can combine sentences 8–11 in "Deluxe Pizza" (page 6) like this:

    8. The sauce steams.

    9. The sauce bubbles.

  10. Its smell fills the room.

  11. The smell is slightly sweet.

The sauce steams and bubbles and fills the room with a slightly sweet smell.

You might write instead:

The room is filled with the slightly sweet smell of the steaming, bubbling sauce.

Or you might compose this version:

The sauce bubbles, filling the room with a steamy, slightly sweet smell.

Though there are no right answers, there are lessons to be learned from completing the exercises. The central lesson is that you can put sentences together in lots of different ways. The idea is for you to work with the exercises, trying first this possibility, then that. Do you want to say that **the sauce steams and bubbles** or that **the sauce bubbles**? Perhaps you think that the **-ing** words in **the steaming, bubbling sauce** in the second sentence give a sense of how the pizza looks and smells. Read your sentences out loud, and listen to the differences between one version and another. Think about how the sentence you've written relates to other sentences in the same paragraph; in one context, you might want to end your sentence with the words **slightly sweet**; in another context, it might be more effective to end on **bubbling sauce**.

You do the exercises in this book correctly when you use them to practice the different ways you can compose sentences and paragraphs. Remember to transfer the lessons you learn in this book into your own writing. Practicing and making choices among the options and transferring what you learn from the exercise into your own writing will help you to become a better writer. Good luck. Have fun. And learn a lot about writing.

OPENING FACE OFF

Combine the following sentences into a paragraph that describes the opening of a hockey game. The spaces between groups of sentences indicate possible sentence boundaries, but you may ignore the boundaries whenever you want to make your sentences longer or shorter.

1. The fans leaned forward.
2. The fans were eager.
3. The players leaned forward.
4. The players were eager.

5. The referee skated to center ice to drop the puck.
6. The colors of the players' uniforms reflected from the surface of the ice.
7. The surface was glassy.
8. The ice was newly made.

9. The referee blew his whistle.

10. The referee called to the team captains.
11. The referee dropped the puck.
12. The referee began the game.

LEFT OUT

Combine the following sentences into a paragraph on the plight of left-handers in society. You may add details if you wish to make the paragraph more vivid and personal.

1. Life is difficult.
2. This is true for left-handers.

3. They live in a world.
4. Everything is made for righties in the world.
5. Can openers are made for righties.
6. Zippers are made for righties.
7. School desks are made for righties.
8. Teachers often force them to write right-handed.
9. Coaches often force them to play ball right-handed.

10. Even the words for left relegate lefties to the status of outsiders.
11. This is true in most languages.

12. "Lyft" meant weak and useless.
13. This was in Old English.

14. "Links" means clumsy or awkward.
15. This is in German.

15. "Gauche" means ugly or uncouth.
17. This is in French.

18. But things may be changing.
19. This is true because [of this].

20. Left-handers are organizing.
21. Left-handers are fighting for recognition.

22. Recently, they declared [this].
23. International Left-Handers Day.
24. It will be on August 13.

25. If [this happens], then [this happens].
26. They win their "rights."
27. Southpaws won't be left out anymore.

DELUXE PIZZA

Combine the sentences below into an appetizing description of a pizza.
If you choose, you may add details to make the description more vivid.

1. The pizza sits in the middle of the table.
2. It is fresh from the oven.

3. Its crust rises up.
4. The crust is thick.
5. The crust is golden brown.
6. It is like a wall.
7. The wall surrounds the rest of the ingredients.

8. The sauce steams.
9. The sauce bubbles.
10. Its smell fills the room.
11. The smell is slightly sweet.

12. The pizza is covered with pepperoni slices.
13. They are shiny.
14. They are dappled.
15. They contrast with the sauce.
16. The sauce is dull red.

17. Mushroom slices rest in the sauce.   **7**
18. The slices are shriveled.
19. The slices are soft.
20. Their edges are slightly curved.

21. Green olives are scattered about.
22. Black olives are scattered about.
23. They dot the surface.

24. Cheese melts over the pizza.
25. The cheese is creamy.
26. It enmeshes everything in its weblike strands.
27. The strands trap the taste until someone releases it with a bite.

CABLE CAR

Combine the following sentences into a narrative that shows what happens on a cable car trip to Fisherman's Wharf in San Francisco.

1. The empty cable car approaches.
2. It clangs its bell.
3. It sways as though slightly drunk.

4. The brakes grind.
5. The grinding is harsh.
6. The grinding is metallic.
7. The grinding drowns out the babbling of the people waiting in line.

8. Most of them are tourists.
9. They are adorned with sunglasses.
10. They are adorned with cameras.
11. They press to secure a good view.
12. The pressing is excited.

13. One man refuses to move.

8

14. He has a good vantage point.
15. He is bigger than the rest.
16. He angers the other passengers.
17. He forces them to squeeze past his hulking frame.

18. The tourists are all crammed inside.
19. Then the cable car lurches from the station.
20. The lurching is awkward.
21. The cable car heads down to Fisherman's Wharf.

22. At Fisherman's Wharf, the cable car will pick up another batch of passengers.
23. The passengers will be impatient.
24. It will struggle back up the hill.

WHERE THERE'S SMOKE, THERE'S IRE

Combine the sentences below into an explanation of the recent conflict between the rights of smokers and nonsmokers.

1. This has been true for some time now.
2. A war has raged between smokers and nonsmokers.

3. The smoke of battle is clearing now.
4. The nonsmokers appear to be winning.

5. Legislation protects the rights of nonsmokers over smokers.
6. One piece of such legislation is the Minnesota Indoor Clean Air Act.

7. Many smokers are joining the ranks of nonsmokers.
8. Many smokers are at least abiding by antismoking regulations.
9. Still, other smokers have yet to surrender.

10. This is what happened at Toronto East General Hospital.
11. Patients protested the ban on patient smoking.

12. They rolled their I.V. stands outside.
13. They rolled their wheelchairs outside.
14. They congregated in the cold to enjoy a smoke.

15. It made them especially angry.
16. Staff members could smoke inside the hospital.

17. A Tennessee woman is also angry.
18. A judge told her [this].
19. She couldn't smoke around her four-year-old child.

20. The judge calls passive smoke a form of child abuse.
21. But the woman claims [this].
22. The judge's order violates her civil rights.

23. Apparently this is the case.
24. The war isn't over yet.

"POLLY WANNA RITZ?"

Combine the sentences below into an explanation of why people use brand names rather than generic terms for popular items.

1. You sneeze.
2. Afterward, do you ask for a facial tissue?

3. You cut yourself.
4. Then do you call out for a plastic bandage?

5. You burn yourself.
6. After that, do you ask for white petroleum jelly?

7. If you do, people may look at you strangely.
8. Most people would ask for Kleenex.
9. Most people would ask for Band-Aids.
10. Most people would ask for Vaseline.

11. Kleenex, Band-Aids, and Vaseline are only brand names.

12. Kleenex, Band-Aids, Vaseline, and other brand names are so well known.

13. Kleenex, Band-Aids, Vaseline, and other brand names are so influential.

14. The brand names Kleenex, Band-Aids, and Vaseline have replaced generic names.

15. The generic names are less familiar.

16. The generic names are more awkward.

17. This process has been going on for decades.

18. That is why your grandparents may refer to refrigerators as Frigidaires.

19. That is why your grandparents may refer to men's underwear as B.V.D.'s.

20. So now you know [this].

21. Why do people knit their brows when you say you want to buy denim jeans?

22. Why do people knit their brows when you say you want to play table tennis?

23. Why do people knit their brows when you say you want to consume a gelatin dessert?

RELATIVE CLAUSES

Basketball players have a number of moves that they can use as situations change in a game. Experienced players know how to choose among the moves according to the time remaining on the clock, the defensive alignment, the positions of their teammates, or the number of fouls they've accrued. If Michael Jordan receives the ball near the foul line, he might shoot, fake a pass and then shoot, drive left, drive right, pass off, or call for a time out. Experienced players have more options to draw from and are more apt to choose successful moves than inexperienced players.

The same is true of writers. Experienced writers have a number of moves that they can use as situations change in their writing. If Judy Blume is explaining a point, she might use relative clauses and appositives in her sentence. If she's giving narrative details, she might use participial phrases and absolute phrases. If she wants to produce a powerful argument, she might use balanced phrases or repetition to emphasize certain points. Like basketball players, experienced writers have more options to draw from and are more apt to choose successful strategies than inexperienced writers.

One major aim of this book is to give you the experience to develop a series of useful strategies and to suggest ways of choosing among them in specific writing situations. Using a variety of strategies will help you write papers your audience will consider both interesting and readable.

12 CONSTRUCTING RELATIVE CLAUSES

One useful strategy you can use is called the RELATIVE CLAUSE. You construct a relative clause by replacing a noun or noun phrase with a pronoun like **which, that, who, whom,** and **whose**. For example, if you replace the repeated noun phrase "spear-throwing device" with the relative pronoun **which,** you can make the following two sentences—

> The Cro-Magnons developed a spear-throwing device. ~~The spear-throwing device~~ improved the range of their weapons by thirty yards.

—into a single sentence with a relative clause:

> The Cro-Magnons developed a spear-throwing device **that improved the range of their weapons by thirty yards**.

When you construct a relative clause, you place one sentence into another, as you might place a small box within a larger box. Let's take a second look at how to do it, this time with the following two sentences.

> Kids often start sentences with "If I grow up" rather than "When I grow up."
> The kids live in inner cities.

First, you identify the repeated noun, in this case "the kids." Then you replace the repeated noun phrase with a relative pronoun, "who" this time:

> who
> ~~The kids~~ live in inner cities.

Finally, you place the new relative clause within the sentence, like putting a little box within a bigger box:

> Kids [who live in inner cities] often start sentences with "If I grow up" rather than "When I grow up."

CHOOSING RELATIVE PRONOUNS   **13**

When you create a relative clause, you select a pronoun according to whether the noun it replaces is human or not. If the relative pronoun replaces a noun that refers to things or to animals, like "the sign language" in the following example, you can select either **that** or **which** to introduce the relative clause:

> In dealing with each other, the Native American tribes of the Great Plains used an intricate sign language. ~~The sign language~~ consisted of a series of mutually understood gestures.

> In dealing with each other, the Native American tribes of the Great Plains used an intricate sign language **that consisted of a series of mutually understood gestures**.

OR

> In dealing with each other, the Native American tribes of the Great Plains used an intricate sign language, **which consisted of a series of mutually understood gestures**.

If, on the other hand, the relative pronoun replaces a subject noun that refers to people, then you can select either **who** or **that:**

> The peasant farmers still work in the ancient ways of their ancestors. ~~The peasant farmers~~ till the Nile Delta.

> The peasant farmers **who till the Nile Delta** still work in the ancient ways of their ancestors.

> The peasant farmers **that till the Nile Delta** still work in the ancient ways of their ancestors.

When you replace an object noun phrase that refers to people, you have three choices: **whom, that**, or sometimes no pronoun at all. **Whom** sounds more formal than the other two. So in speaking or writing informally, you generally choose the version with **that** or the version without any relative pronoun:

14 The students had received straight A's for the semester. The college honored ~~the students~~.

$\downarrow$

The students **whom the college honored** had received straight A's for the semester.

OR

The students **that the college honored** had received straight A's for the semester.

OR

The students **the college honored** had received straight A's for the semester.

To replace a possessive noun or a possessive pronoun, as in the next two examples, you use **whose:**

Christopher Columbus did not train as a sailor but as a weaver in his family's wool business. ~~His~~ voyages made him the most famous seafarer in history.

$\downarrow$

Christopher Columbus, **whose voyages made him the most famous seafarer in history**, did not train as a sailor but as a weaver in his family's wool business.

 RELATIVE CLAUSES WITH PREPOSITIONS OR EXPRESSIONS OF QUANTITY

You can sometimes construct a relative clause to follow a preposition like **to, for, of, with, by,** and **in**:

Aesop's fables are famous for the moral lessons they teach. In ~~Aesop's fables~~, animals act like human beings.

$\downarrow$

Aesop's fables, **in which animals act like human beings**, are famous for the moral lessons they teach.

The judge had already escaped two previous attempts on her life. The let- **15**
ter bomb was intended for ~~the judge~~.

The judge **for whom the letter bomb was intended** had already
escaped two previous attempts on her life.

You can also form a relative clause when one of your sentences begins
with a phrase that expresses quantity, like **many of, some of, none of,
several of**, or **all of**:

The Impressionist painters tried to present objects not as they are in fact
but as they appear to the eye. Many of ~~the Impressionist painters~~ lived and
worked in Paris.

The Impressionist painters, **many of whom lived and worked in Paris**,
tried to present objects not as they are in fact but as they appear to the eye.

 PUNCTUATING RELATIVE CLAUSES

Sometimes you have to choose whether to separate a relative clause from
the rest of the sentence with commas. You decide whether to use commas according to how the clause relates to the meaning of the sentence.
The first sentence below, with commas, means something very different
from the identically worded sentence without commas. If you read them
out loud, pausing at the commas, you should be able to hear the difference between them.

Our school's parents and teachers decided against history books, **which
ignore the accomplishments of minorities**.
Our school's parents and teachers decided against history books **which
ignore the accomplishments of minorities**.

The sentence with commas makes two statements: (1) that parents and
teachers decided against history books and (2) that ALL history books
ignore the accomplishments of minorities. The sentence without commas
makes a single statement: that teachers and parents decided against only
those history books which ignore the accomplishments of minorities.

16   When you use a relative clause without commas, you are saying that the information in the clause is true of only some of the things or people you mentioned in the sentence. When you use a relative clause with commas, you are saying that the information in the clause is true for all the things or people mentioned in the sentence. One other important characteristic of a relative clause with commas is that it does not allow you to use **that** as the relative pronoun. You must use **which, who,** or **whom**.

USING RELATIVE CLAUSES FOR ECONOMY, PRECISION, AND EMPHASIS

Relative clauses are fairly simple to construct, and they can help your writing in several ways. To begin with, relative clauses enable you to write more precisely. When two sentences sit next to one another, sometimes it's unclear which is the main idea. For instance, if you wrote the following two sentences, it would be difficult to tell which idea was most important.

> Local alumni groups have been donating more than $300,000 a year to the school's general fund. The university has allowed local alumni groups to contribute the money directly to the sports program.

But if you make the first sentence into a relative clause, the reader will understand that the idea in the relative clause is meant as an interesting additional comment upon the main idea:

> ~~Local alumni groups~~ have been donating more than $300, 000 a year to the school's general fund. The university has allowed local alumni groups to contribute the money directly to the sports program.
>
> ↓
>
> The university has allowed local alumni groups, **which have been donating more than $300,000 a year to the school's general fund**, to contribute money directly to the sports program.

Not only do relative clauses allow you to write precisely, but they also allow you to write more economically. The new sentence with a relative clause is two words shorter than the original, and it eliminates the distracting repetition of the words "local alumni groups."

Because the information in relative clauses normally adds to and comments upon the information in main clauses, relative clauses help you control what you emphasize in your sentences. The most important point a sentence makes is generally stated in a main clause. By deciding which information you will express in a relative clause, you are deciding what to emphasize. The following sentences can be combined in two different ways, depending on whether you convert the first or second sentence into a relative clause. But the resulting sentences differ significantly in emphasis. Read them over and see if you can explain the differences between them.

Chiropractors and naturopathic physicians are generally distrusted by medical doctors. Chiropractors and naturopathic physicians treat illnesses with natural remedies instead of drugs.

Chiropractors and naturopathic physicians—**who treat illnesses with natural remedies instead of drugs**—are distrusted by medical doctors.

OR

Chiropractors and naturopathic physicians—**who are distrusted by medical doctors**—treat illnesses with natural remedies instead of drugs.

The first sentence places the information about chiropractors and naturopaths treating illnesses with natural remedies in a relative clause and in that way tones down this point. The central focus in the first example is the information in the main clause—that practitioners with alternative medical approaches are distrusted by medical doctors. In contrast, the second example places the information about the distrust by medical doctors in the relative clause. So the focus in the second example is that chiropractors and naturopathic physicians treat illnesses with natural remedies instead of drugs.

The focus of a sentence generally determines the content of the sentence that follows it. You would expect the first example to continue in the following manner, making a comment on medical doctors and their view of alternative approaches:

Chiropractors and naturopathic physicians—**who treat illnesses with natural remedies instead of drugs**—are distrusted by medical doctors. Doctors claim that such practitioners of alternative medicine don't substantiate their treatment methods through "scientific" experiments.

18   But you would expect the second example to continue by expanding on the idea that naturopaths and chiropractors treat illnesses with natural remedies, as in the following, which tells why they use natural remedies:

> Chiropractors and naturopathic physicians—**who are distrusted by medical doctors**—treat illnesses with natural remedies instead of drugs. Practitioners of alternative medicine claim to enhance the body's natural healing ability, to treat the cause of disease, not the symptoms.

So it's important to remember that you can affect the focus of your paragraphs when you make relative clauses. The following paragraph, for instance, focuses on the adaptability of the Norway rat; that is the point of the first and last sentence. But the second sentence, because it states how the rat reached North America, shifts the focus from the main point; it disrupts the continuity of the paragraph:

> The Norway rat is regarded by experts as the most destructive mammal on Earth and the most adaptive to changing situations and environments. The Norway rat actually reached this country on the ships of many nations. It abounds in the debris of North American cities, resisting all attempts to control it.

But if you convert the second sentence into a relative clause, you can lessen its importance and keep the paragraph focused on its central point—the rat's adaptability:

> The Norway rat, **which actually reached this country on the ships of many nations**, is regarded by experts as the most destructive mammal on earth and the most adaptive to changing situations and environments. It abounds in the debris of North American cities, resisting all attempts to control it.

 **SUMMARY**

In this unit, you learned how to construct a relative clause by replacing a noun or noun phrase with a pronoun like **which, that, who, whom,** or **whose,** according to whether the noun refers to a human or whether it is possessive. You found out that relative clauses add precision and economy to your writing. You saw how you can often use them to clear up relationships, to make your writing more concise, and to control emphasis in your sentences or paragraphs.

The exercises that follow give you practice both in constructing relative clauses and in using relative clauses to write economically and to focus your sentences and paragraphs. The important point is that relative clauses are useful not simply for completing these exercises but for writing that really counts: essays and research papers as well as letters and job applications. If you do the exercises seriously, the practice they provide should help you make relative clauses one strategy you can use to improve your own writing.

CONSTRUCTING RELATIVE CLAUSES

I. Make each sequence below into a single sentence by converting the marked sentence into a relative clause. Decide whether the clause needs to be separated from the sentence by a comma.

EXAMPLE

1. A weak economy can cloud the job prospects of college graduates.
2. ~~A weak economy~~ discourages older workers from retiring.

A weak economy **that discourages older workers from retiring** can cloud the job prospects of college graduates.

A. 1. Stephen King says the best horror movies appeal to the worst in human nature.
   2. ~~Stephen King's~~ *Misery* portrayed a demented fan trying to keep her favorite author captive.

B. 1. Dogs often pick up some very bad habits.
   2. ~~Dogs~~ copy the behavior of their owners.

C. 1. The diet contains one-third less fat than the American diet.
   2. The Chinese eat ~~the diet~~.

D. 1. Fishermen off the coast of Alaska can now radio the Domino's in Juneau for a pizza delivery to their boats in the Bering Sea.
   2. ~~Fishermen off the coast of Alaska~~ work up an appetite for more than tuna casserole.

E. 1. El Niño can cause droughts in Australia and flooding rains in North America.
   2. ~~El Niño~~ begins with an unusual shift in the southwest Pacific wind.
   3. ~~The shift in the wind~~ changes ocean currents.

II. Make each sequence below into a single sentence by converting **21** one or more of the original sentences into a relative clause. If the sentences allow, write more than one version for each sequence. And decide whether the clause needs to be separated from the sentence by a comma.

1. Huntington, L.I., was once praised by Whitman for its natural beauty.
2. Huntington, L.I., is now the site of a huge megamall.

Huntington, L.I., **which is now the site of a huge megamall**, was once praised by Whitman for its natural beauty.

OR

Huntington, L.I., **which was once praised by Whitman for its natural beauty**, is now the site of a huge megamall.

F. 1. Interactive television gives stubborn couch potatoes new incentives to stay put.
2. Interactive television allows viewers to pay bills and shop for groceries without leaving home.

G. 1. He put sherry on his cornflakes.
2. He wrote jokes on the backs of old envelopes.
3. W.C. Fields was an eccentric but undisputed genius of comedy.

H. 1. Rap music uses aggressive rhythms to express inner-city desperation.
2. Rap music has been dubbed the new poetry of urban America.

I. 1. American children will witness 8,000 television murders by age five.
2. Psychologists claim American children are numb to violence in the media.

J. 1. The trading-card hobby has blossomed into a multi-billion-dollar business.
2. The trading card hobby once dealt only in sports figures.
3. The multi-billion-dollar business swaps cards of such pop culture idols as Batman, Madonna, and Arsenio Hall.

THE MYSTERY OF TEARS

Combine the sentences below into a brief explanatory paragraph that speculates on the causes of emotional tears. Use relative clauses whenever possible. Not every sentence will contain a relative clause; some will contain other structures.

1. Tears are nature's way to keep our eyes wet and cleansed.
2. They are actually drops of saline fluid secreted by a gland.

3. We cry as a reaction to eye irritation.
4. Chopping onions causes irritation.
5. Soap or dust in the eye causes irritation.

6. But why do we shed tears when we are happy?
7. And why do we shed tears when we are sad?
8. We shed tears in pleasure or pain.
9. We shed tears in victory and defeat.

10. Emotional tears have long been a mystery.
11. Such tears are unique to human beings.
12. Some scientists now speculate [this].
13. Through tears our body eliminates certain chemicals.
14. These chemicals build up in response to stress.
15. They create a chemical imbalance in the body.

16. Crying is supposed to make us "feel better."
17. It restores chemical balance to the body.

MAKING RELATIVE CLAUSES IN CONTEXT

Combine the first two sentences of each sequence below into a single sentence with a relative clause. Keep as your main clause the sentence that best relates to the third sentence and leads up to it.

1. Tacos, bagels, and sushi can now be found at fast-food counters everywhere.
2. Tacos, bagels, and sushi were once available only in authentic ethnic restaurants.
3. You had to order such foods at Mexican cantinas, Jewish delicatessens, or Japanese seafood bars.

Tacos, bagels, and sushi, **which can now be found at fast-food counters everywhere**, were once available only in authentic ethnic restaurants. You had to order such foods at Mexican cantinas, Jewish delicatessens, or Japanese seafood bars.

A. 1. Bruce Springsteen's "Long Goodbye" voices one of his favorite themes—feeling trapped.
    2. "Long Goodbye" 's slashing guitar interplay and relentless beat recall songs by the Rolling Stones.
    3. Springsteen seems obsessed with the frustrations felt by a man who wants to get out of his situation but can't keep from staying put.

B. 1. James Dean anticipated the anti-establishment movement of the 1960s.
    2. James Dean starred in the 1950s films *East of Eden* and *Rebel Without a Cause*.
    3. Dean's portrayal of a defiant teen fighting the status quo was a powerful symbol to the generation of youth who protested against the war in Vietnam and racial injustice in America.

C. 1. Our Puritan ancestors convinced generations of Americans that staying in bed to write and think was a sign of moral and physical decay.
    2. Staying in bed to write and think has long been an accepted practice in Europe.
    3. In fact, Winston Churchill did much of the strategic planning for World War II propped up in bed with a brandy glass close at hand.

D. 1. Virtual reality systems may soon compete for thrillseekers' money with theme parks.

2. Virtual reality systems can make you believe you're driving in the Indy 500 or piloting an F-14 Tomcat in combat.

3. You'll be able to take part in such realistic adventures in the comfort of your own living room with a $300 machine the size of your toaster.

E. 1. For a healthy snack, sprinkle cumin, curry powder, or Parmesan cheese on popcorn.

2. Your guests will devour the healthy snack.

3. Then set out big bowls of the treat and watch them gobble it down.

AS AMERICAN AS APPLE PIE

Combine the sentences below to create an explanatory essay that communicates how much American English is a blend of various traditions. Use relative clauses whenever appropriate. Not every sentence will contain a relative clause; some will contain other structures.

1. How American is the American language?

2. It's about as American as jazz.

3. Jazz's European roots reverberate in the reedy whine of the saxophone.

4. Jazz's African roots reverberate in the rhythmic beat of the drums.

5. It's as American as Levi's.

6. Levi Strauss developed the pants for miners in the 1849 goldrush.

7. Levi Strauss was a German immigrant.

8. Of course, the central core of our language comes from England.

9. But we've borrowed words and phrases from languages as diverse as Hebrew and Tahitian.

10. We've borrowed words and phrases from languages as diverse as Chinese and Navaho.

11. Spanish gave us hundreds of words.

12. These include *barbecue, patio,* and *alligator.*

13. Yiddish gave us *bagel, chutzpah,* and *kosher.*

14. Jews spoke Yiddish in Eastern Europe.

15. African-Americans contributed verbal rhythms and rap.

16. As well, African-Americans contributed such distinctly American words as *OK* and *Yankee.*

17. We have to thank Native Americans for most of our place names.

18. Our place names are names like *Mississippi, Ohio,* and *Chicago.*

19. Every ethnic and national group has left evidence of itself in our language.

20. Every ethnic and national group has blended into the fabric of our country.

21. How American is the American language?

22. It is plenty American! [Make this into a fragment to answer the question.]

USING RELATIVE CLAUSES TO CONTROL PARAGRAPH EMPHASIS

Read the following paragraphs in order to decide which sentence in each is out of place. Then strengthen the focus of each paragraph by transforming the out-of-place sentences into relative clauses.

EXAMPLE

We assume that most people who take their own lives are old and sick. But that assumption is incorrect. The truth is that people under 50 are more suicide prone than those over 50. In fact, suicide has become the

26   third leading cause of death among young people between 15 and 25. Suicide is usually the result of severe depression.

We assume that most people who take their own lives are old and sick. But that assumption is incorrect. The truth is that people under 50 are more suicide prone than those over 50. In fact, suicide, **which is usually the result of severe depression**, has become the third leading cause of death among young people between 15 and 25.

A.   Jet lag is apparently worse when you travel eastward, against the sun. Your body seems to adjust more easily to a longer day than to a shorter one. The longer day occurs when you travel westward. Morning light coming six hours early on your way to Europe apparently upsets your body's natural rhythm more than six hours added to a day when you head toward Asia.

B.   If your medicine chest doesn't contain an aloe vera plant, it's not well stocked. The aloe vera contains a sap that Native Americans long used as a treatment for minor burns. The aloe vera looks like a cactus. Squeezed on a burn, the sap cools the skin and prevents blisters.

C.   To save the California condor, the Fish and Wildlife Service spent $25 million on breeding and nurturing a new generation. The California condor's number in the wild had dwindled to one pair by 1987. Naturalists celebrating the release into Los Padres National Forest of the first condors raised in captivity believe the cost was justified. Now there are enough wild condors to re-establish themselves in that protected habitat.

TERM PAPER

Make the following sentences into an entertaining story that makes a point about human nature. Use relative clauses when appropriate. Not every sentence will contain a relative clause; some will contain other structures. To make the story more vivid, you might want to add details of your own.

1.   A trash can sat in the corner of the dorm room.
2.   The trash can was filled with the pages of a term paper.
3.   The pages were crumpled and rejected.

4. The desk was cluttered with 3 × 5 cards and books piled on top of each other.

5. Some of the books were open to pages.

6. The pages were highlighted by yellow marks.

7. Ten typed pages hung down to the floor from the printer of the Macintosh.

8. The Macintosh sat in the middle of the desk.

9. Its fan was making the only sound in the room.

10. Its screen was showing the final paragraph on page 10.

11. Jonathan lay on the bed fully clothed.

12. Jonathan was asleep after a frantic night of writing.

13. Jonathan was asleep after a frantic night of rejecting.

14. Jonathan was asleep after a frantic night of revising.

15. Then the alarm clock sent a shivering ring through the room.

16. The alarm clock had been set for 9:00 A.M.

17. Jonathan stirred.

18. Jonathan was flailing his right arm to shut off the noise.

19. The noise was annoying.

20. He succeeded only in [this].

21. He knocked the clock off the stand.

22. "Damn," he mumbled as he jumped out of bed to pick up the clock.

23. A foul taste was welling up in his mouth.

24. He walked over to the desk and pulled the sheets from the printer.

25. He knocked a box of No-Doz to the floor.

26. Before he could pick up the box, Jonathan heard a rap on the door.

27. And Harry's voice boomed out.

28. "Jon, are you up?"

29. Jonathan opened the door.

30. He didn't want to yell back.

31. Harry asked whether Jonathan had finished the paper for Professor Chabot.

32. Harry was standing in the doorway.

33. Harry was clad only in a towel.

34. "Sure," he answered.

35. "It was easy."

36. "It was just like I said it would be."

UNIT 3

PARTICIPLES

 ## CONSTRUCTING PARTICIPLES

When you first draft a paper, you may write some short, choppy, and repetitive sentences, like these from a description of a boxing match:

> The old heavyweight proved an easy knockout victim. He was dazed. He was reeling.

When you revise, you can eliminate the repetition and choppiness by changing two of the sentences into PARTICIPLES:

> **Dazed and reeling,** the old heavyweight proved an easy knockout victim.

> OR

> The heavyweight, **dazed and reeling,** proved an easy knockout victim.

Dazed is a PAST PARTICIPLE; **reeling** is a PRESENT PARTICIPLE.

When you construct a present participle, you simply add **-ing** to a basic verb form; for example, *read* becomes **reading,** and *shake* becomes **shaking.** When you construct a past participle, you generally use the **-ed** or **-d** form of the verb. For instance, *disturb* becomes **disturbed** and

30   *scare* becomes **scared,** using the familiar **-ed** or **-d** ending. For some irregular verbs, the past participle ends in **-n,** so that *throw* becomes **thrown** and *grow* becomes **grown.** And for a few other irregular verbs, the past participle has individualized forms, so that *sing* becomes **sung,** *go* becomes **gone,** and *stand* becomes **stood.**

 PARTICIPIAL PHRASES

A participle often appears with additional words that add details to it. Together, the participle and the additional words form a PARTICIPIAL PHRASE, such as **obviously bored, noisily burping, circled by the hungry sharks,** or **waving vigorously at the TV camera.** Compare the following two sentences:

> The old heavyweight, **dazed and reeling**, proved an easy knockout victim.

> The old heavyweight, **dazed by a series of hard jabs to his stomach and aimlessly reeling from a powerful punch to his jaw**, proved an easy knockout victim.

After reading the first sentence, you might have asked, "How had the old heavyweight been dazed?" and "Why was he reeling?" Because it answers those questions, the second sentence is more vivid and descriptive.

 THE FUNCTION OF PARTICIPIAL PHRASES

Because participles describe so effectively, they can bring your writing to life. Notice how the sentence below becomes more vivid when you add participial phrases to the main clause:

> In his movies, Arnold Schwarzenegger uses his muscles more readily than his brains.

> In his movies, Arnold Schwarzenegger uses his muscles more readily than his brains, **tossing a futuristic terminator into a vat of molten**

steel in one movie, chopping off barbarians' heads with his gigan-
tic sword in another.

Because participles are created from verb forms, they hold onto some of the sense of movement of verbs and add lively, animated action to your sentences, particularly when you use present participles with their **-ing** endings. In the next example, you can almost feel the nervousness of the job applicant because the sentence uses the present participles **squirming**, **rolling**, **unrolling**, and **reminding**.

The applicant waited alone in the outer office, **squirming on the vinyl chair, rolling and unrolling his resume, and reminding himself to maintain eye contact during the interview**.

USING PARTICIPIAL PHRASES TO SUGGEST RELATIONSHIPS

You can use participial phrases not only to wake up your sentences but also to suggest time or cause-result relationships. Participial phrases suggest such relationships less directly than clauses beginning with terms like "because," "thus," "therefore," and "as a result." Notice how the introductory clause in the first example below *asserts* that Anthony Hopkins made Hannibal the Cannibal frightening "because" he glared at the camera and did not blink, while the participial phrase in the second example simply *suggests* that by glaring and not blinking, the actor created a frightening screen presence:

Because actor Anthony Hopkins glared directly at the camera and did not blink for long periods of time, he made the cannibalistic murderer of *Silence of the Lambs,* Hannibal Lecter, a frightening presence on the screen.

Glaring directly at the camera and not blinking for long periods of time, actor Anthony Hopkins made the cannibalistic murderer of *Silence of the Lambs,* Hannibal Lecter, a frightening presence on the screen.

32   In the next example, the second sentence, because it gives the cause of the vets' problems in the participial phrase "disillusioned by the American public's negative perception of the war," suggests the result, without having to state it directly, as the first example does in the sentence beginning with "therefore":

> Some Vietnam vets were disillusioned by the American public's negative perception of the war. Therefore, they suffered severe mental problems when they returned to civilian life.

> **Disillusioned by the American public's negative perception of the war**, some Vietnam vets suffered severe mental problems when they returned to civilian life.

In the following pair, the time relationship that the first example states directly with the word "then" is only suggested by the participial phrase in the second:

> We pulled off the interstate. Then we descended the exit ramp to fast-food alley, a long block of deep-fry dens and burger joints stamped out of plastic.

> We pulled off the interstate, **descending the exit ramp to fast-food alley**, a long block of deep-fry dens and burger joints stamped out of plastic.

Notice also that the participial phrase in the second sentence almost makes it seem as if the car is still moving, since there is no longer a period to stop the motion of the sentence after the word "interstate."

 ## POSITIONING PARTICIPIAL PHRASES

You can often move participial phrases from one position to another in a sentence—before the main clause, after it, in the middle of it. When you move participial phrases, you can change sentence rhythm, shift emphasis, create sentence variety, even provide links between sentences. Reading your different versions aloud and listening carefully to the differences among them will help you decide just when you can move participial phrases effectively. Consider the following three sentences:

> **Keeping one eye on his professor**, Russ quickly scanned the Batman comic hidden behind his bulky microbiology textbook.
>
> OR
>
> Russ, **keeping one eye on his professor**, quickly scanned the Batman comic hidden behind his bulky microbiology textbook.
>
> OR
>
> Russ quickly scanned the Batman comic hidden behind his bulky microbiology textbook, **keeping one eye on his professor**.

Each version is likely to affect readers differently. In the first, the participial phrase initially captures the readers' attention. It briefly delays the main action of the sentence and perhaps makes readers wonder what will happen, thus heightening the surprise and the humor of the sentence. In the second, the participial phrase interrupts the main action of the sentence, making readers pause twice. These interruptions emphasize "Russ" and "quickly," the words on either side of the commas. The third version places the participial phrase after the main clause, where it becomes a playful commentary on Russ's actions.

Sentences with several participial phrases offer you even more choices: you might keep the phrases together or separate them in various ways. Here are just two variations of a sentence with several phrases:

> Grandma always arrives in the "Blue Bullet," her '58 Olds, **plunging into our driveway, screeching to a halt, tooting her horn, and grinning ear to ear**.
>
> OR
>
> **Tooting her horn**, Grandma always arrives in the "Blue Bullet," her '58 Olds, **plunging into our driveway, screeching to a halt, and grinning from ear to ear**.

While the first sentence opens with Grandma's arrival, the second sentence makes readers wait a bit; in fact, readers "hear" Grandma tooting the horn on her '58 Olds before they even know that she has arrived. If you put participial phrases in different places, you can emphasize different aspects of Grandma's colorful and memorable behavior.

How can you decide where to position a participial phrase? Sometimes the relationship between the phrase and the main action of the sen-

34   tence will tell you the right sequence. If the phrase describes something that happened before the main action of the sentence, the phrase will precede that main action:

> **Introduced twenty years ago as labor-saving devices**, computerized cash registers are now installed in about 85 percent of all chain stores.

If the phrase describes something that happened after the main action of the sentence, the phrase will follow that main action:

> SooMi opened the brightly wrapped package, **discovering a small wooden box held shut by a silver clasp**.
>
> **Temporarily overcome by exhaustion**, the firefighter sat slumped on the curb.

But sometimes you can use present participial phrases to suggest that two actions are occurring simultaneously, whether the phrases come before or after the main clause:

> **Carrying the cumbersome bass drum in front of me**, I jostled my way through the stubborn crowd to the bandstand.
>
> OR
>
> I jostled my way through the stubborn crowd to the bandstand, **carrying the cumbersome bass drum in front of me**.

Sometimes the relationships between sentences will help you figure out where to place a participial phrase. In the next sentence, the phrase **dealing with current technology rather than ghosts or goblins** may occur before or after its subject:

> **Dealing with current technology rather than ghosts or goblins**, contemporary legends preserve the basic structure of classic horror tales.
>
> OR
>
> Contemporary legends, **dealing with current technology rather than ghosts or goblins**, preserve the basic structure of classic horror tales.

But within the context of the following paragraph, you would more likely place the participial phrase at the beginning of its sentence:

Modern life produces its own folktales, called urban legends. **Dealing**   **35**
with current technology rather than ghosts or goblins, contemporary legends preserve the basic structure of classic horror tales. One such
tale concerns an elderly woman who accidentally cooks her dog while trying to dry him in her microwave oven.

When it introduces the second sentence, the participial phrase not
only separates the two occurrences of the word "legends," but—more
important—it also explains the nature of urban legends, connecting the
first sentence and the main action of the second. In that way, it helps to
hold the paragraph together.

 IMPROPERLY ATTACHED PARTICIPLES

You can sometimes make a sentence awkward or even cause confusion
when you begin it with a participle. The following example suggests that
the crowd, not the quarterback, limped away from the huddle:

The injured quarterback limped away from the huddle.
The sympathetic crowd cheered the injured quarterback.

Limping away from the huddle, the sympathetic crowd cheered the
injured quarterback.

The sentence is more clear if you make "the quarterback" the subject of the main clause:

Limping away from the huddle, the quarterback was cheered by the
sympathetic crowd.

Here the participial phrase also suggests a cause-result relationship,
since it is the quarterback's heroic action of playing while hurt that trig-
gers the crowd's sympathetic cheers.

 **SUMMARY**

This unit explains how you can construct two kinds of participles: You make present participles by adding **-ing** to a verb, and you make past participles by using the verb's **-ed** or **-d** form, although irregular verbs have different forms. The chapter shows how participial phrases can add action and life to sentences as well as suggest relationships instead of stating them explicitly. When you position them properly, participial phrases can create emphasis within a paragraph or even help to hold the paragraph together. Remember to use participles in the next paper you write.

CONSTRUCTING
PARTICIPIAL PHRASES

I. Make each sequence of sentences below into a single sentence by converting the marked sentences into participial phrases. Move the phrases to different positions until the sentences sound right to you.

EXAMPLE

1. The new storm swept from North Dakota through Ohio.

2. I̶t̶ sent temperatures below zero.

3. I̶t̶ piled drifts high across roads.

The new storm swept from North Dakota through Ohio, **sending temperatures below zero and piling drifts high across roads**.

OR

Sending temperatures below zero and piling drifts high across roads, the new storm swept from North Dakota through Ohio.

A. 1   A̶d̶a̶m̶ clicked on his calculator with a sigh.

2. Adam sat down heavily at his desk and opened his calculus book.

B. 1. Prosecutor, judge, and jury were convinced of the defendant's guilt.

2. T̶h̶e̶y̶ twisted the facts to support their prejudgment.

C. 1. The mechanic gripped the wrench tightly.

2. T̶h̶e̶ ̶m̶e̶c̶h̶a̶n̶i̶c̶ strained to loosen the frozen bolt.

D. 1. M̶a̶n̶d̶y̶ ̶w̶a̶s̶ mud-covered.

2. M̶a̶n̶d̶y̶ ̶w̶a̶s̶ shivering.

3. Mandy sat hunched over a cup of hot chocolate her father had prepared to drive off the chill.

E. 1. My new roommate burst into our room.

2. S̶h̶e̶ mumbled obscenities.

3.   ~~She~~ flung her purse on the bed.

4.   ~~She~~ glared at my stuffed animal collection.

II. Make each sequence below into a single sentence by converting one or more of the original sentences into a participial phrase. If the sentences allow, write more than one version for each sentence.

EXAMPLE

1.   Roughly 45,000 thunderstorms ravage the Earth every day.

2.   They drench the countryside with torrential rain.

3.   They buffet buildings and trees with howling winds.

Roughly 45,000 thunderstorms ravage the Earth every day, **drenching the countryside with torrential rain and buffeting buildings and trees with howling winds**.

OR

Drenching the countryside with torrential rain and buffeting buildings and trees with howling winds, roughly 45,000 thunderstorms ravage the Earth every day.

F.   1.   Television newspeople are pawns in the ratings game.

   2.   They are often hired and fired on the basis of skin tests given to viewers to measure their emotional reactions.

G.   1.   The locomotive lumbered into Grand Central Station.

   2.   It skidded along the tracks.

   3.   It splashed sparks onto the passenger platform.

   4.   It discharged gray puffs of steam.

   5.   It finally screeched to a halt.

H.   1.   Florence Griffith-Joyner became the most famous American track star of the 1988 Olympics.

   2.   She was called "FloJo" by the press.

   3.   She won gold medals in two races.

   4.   She set Olympic records in both races.

I. 1. The five frigid lakes of Antarctica support only algae and **39**
bacterial growth.

2. They provide scientists with an opportunity to study an
unpolluted, uninhabited environment.

J. 1. The story lines of soap operas show an increased awareness of
social issues.

2. They address homelessness, AIDS, and various addictions.

EAT AND RUN

Using participial phrases whenever appropriate, combine the following sentences into a light-hearted paragraph that makes a connection
between two generations, their dating behavior, and their eating
habits. Not every sentence will contain a participle; you'll be able to
use other structures as well. Add details of your own similar to those
in sentence 2.

1. How different were the teens of the 1950s from today's teens?
2. Teens of the 1950s may have dressed in unfamiliar poodle skirts
and black leather jackets.
3. They had familiar problems.

4. Their problems were these.
5. They didn't know where to go on a date.
6. They didn't have much money to spend on a date.
7. But some teens in Des Plaines, Illinois, found an answer.
8. Their answer solved these teenage dating problems once and
for all.

9. Teens lined up to eat at the new Golden Arches "fast-food"
restaurant.

10. A museum now stands on this hallowed spot.
11. The museum is called "Museum Number 1 Store."
12. The museum commemorates a momentous event in American
teen history.

13. In the parking lot, visitors will find cars from the 1950s.
14. Inside the museum, they will find the original menu.
15. The menu featured only 15-cent burgers, 19-cent cheeseburgers, and 10-cent fries.
16. Museum Number 1 Store was devoted to the concept of "fast" food.
17. It provided no seats for its customers.
18. It was so simple.
19. Guys bought their girls a quick bite.
20. After this, they stood and gobbled their McMeal.
21. They zoomed off to their local sock hop or drag race.
22. Burger meals for under a dollar have become extinct.
23. They have gone the way of the poodle skirt and the sock hop.
24. Today's teens still eat and run at the Golden Arches.
25. But now teens have a new problem.
26. They're not sure who pays.
27. Is it the guy?
28. Is it the girl?

CREATING PARTICIPIAL PHRASES

I. Add details and illustrations to the following sentences by using participial phrases. Add both a past and a present participial phrase to at least two of the sentences.

EXAMPLE

Mom stared at me for a minute.

↓

Horrified at my latest fashion statement, Mom stared at me for a   **41**
minute, **examining the tiny hole in my nose**.

A. The door creaked open.

B. The coach screamed at the referee.

C. The United States depends on oil and gas for most of its energy
    needs.

D. The toddler threw his half-eaten banana at the nearby crowd of
    shoppers.

E. The horsefly buzzed into the kitchen.

II. Choose one of the five sentences below, or write a sentence of your
own. Then, with that sentence as your focus, write a brief paragraph that
includes several details in the form of participles.

EXAMPLE

Rachel wrote her paper on a computer.

Moving her fingers rapidly over the keyboard, Rachel typed her
rough draft into the computer. She edited the paragraph, **using the
mouse to move the cursor**. Sometimes she moved paragraphs on the
screen. She printed the draft and shut down the computer, **deciding not
to revise any further**.

F. Kim rapidly punched the buttons in the elevator.

G. They tentatively reached out their hands toward each other.

H. The pilot managed to pull himself from the wreckage before it
    burst into flame.

I. Ellen quickened her pace to a trot.

J. The driver buckled his seatbelt.

UNDERGROUND RAILROAD

Using participial phrases whenever appropriate, combine the following
sentences into an explanatory essay that reflects on the tragedy of slavery

42   in the pre–Civil War period. Not every sentence will contain a participle; you'll be able to use other structures as well. If you can, add details of your own that will make the essay more vivid.

1. The Underground Railroad was not a railroad made of steam and steel.

2. But it was a secret network of people determined to help fugitive slaves escape from bondage.

3. Its routes led north from the slave states to Canada.

4. Its routes wound their way through the Midwest and New England.

5. The fugitives crossed hundreds of miles of dangerous territory.

6. The fugitives moved from station to station on foot.

7. They slept in barns and churches.

8. They were assisted by brave and dedicated abolitionists.

9. One abolitionist in Elkhart County, Indiana, sympathized with the fugitives.

10. Elkhart County is located south of Lake Erie.

11. He decided to help fugitives.

12. He made his house into a station on the Underground Railroad.

13. He constructed a fireplace in his basement.

14. He kept the fugitives warm during the cold Lake Erie winter.

15. Subsequent owners of the house have converted it into an inn.

16. But they have kept the basement in good condition.

17. They have kept it as a tribute to the Underground Railroad.

18. Cold travelers still stay in the basement.

19. Cold travelers are warmed by the working fireplace.

20. Today, the inn's guests merely defy the wrath of the icy Lake Erie winter.

21. Yesterday, the Underground Railroad's "guests" defied the **43**
wrath of inhuman slavehunters.

MAKING PARTICIPLES IN CONTEXT

Each of the passages below is too wordy and needs a sharper focus.
Reduce the wordiness and sharpen the focus by converting at least one
of the sentences into a participial phrase.

EXAMPLE

Piet Van de Mark, who conducts ocean tours off the coast of Baja California, claims that animals in the wild like people. He notes that grey whales
observe his tour boat from afar, then approach. They touch the craft with
their snouts and refuse to leave until the startled tourists pet them. The
tour guide thinks all this means that nature is not necessarily hostile, that
if you smile at a whale, it might smile back at you.

Piet Van de Mark, who conducts ocean tours off the coast of Baja California,
claims that animals in the wild like people. He notes that grey whales
observe his tour boat from afar, then approach, **touching the craft with
their snouts and refusing to leave until the startled tourists pet
them**. The tour guide thinks all this means that nature is not necessarily hostile, that if you smile at a whale, it might smile back at you.

A. As we entered the main room of the nursing home, I saw my
grandfather sitting bent over in his chair. He rummaged through
the bag on his walker. And he pulled out one item then another
to place on the table before him. These were his remaining pos-
sessions—a few photographs, an alarm clock, a book, and a
pocketknife he'd owned since childhood. I had never realized
until then just how much his life had diminished—from the joy-
ous freedom of childhood to the joyless confinement of old age.

B. Of all the plants on Earth, the poppy has perhaps the most far-
reaching potential for good and ill. When it is processed legally

into codeine and morphine, it provides us with a drug unsurpassed in treating extreme pain. When it is processed illegally into heroin, it brings addiction and misery to hundreds of thousands. It is at once a blessing and a curse.

C. As smoke began to fill the kitchen, the janitor sprinted out of the cafeteria. He coughed painfully and raced for the school's front door. He gasped for air. He strained to hear the fire engines. But all that he could hear were his own rasping efforts to inhale. Would he be able to make it outside, or would he pass out? His chest tightened, but with a final lunge, he burst through the door and gulped down the cold winter air.

HAVE YOU LOST YOUR MARBLES?

Using participial phrases wherever appropriate, combine the following sentences into an essay that explains how marbles, once children's toys, have become expensive collectors' items. Not every sentence will contain a participle; you'll be able to use other structures as well. If you can, add details for vividness, and make whatever other changes you feel will improve the essay.

1. Have you ever knelt around a ten-foot circle?
2. Have you ever flicked a tiny glass ball with your thumb?
3. Have you ever tried to knock one of thirteen marbles out of a ring?

4. Probably not.
5. The reason is that the game of marbles has lost most of its popularity in the last few decades.
6. But it was just about the most popular game for centuries.
7. It was played by Asians.
8. It was played by Europeans.
9. It was even played by Native Americans.

10. The game was especially popular in small-town America.

11. It reached its peak during the Depression.
12. The reason was that marbles were cheap toys.

13. Marbles only cost a nickel.

14. The popularity of the game waned during the 1950s.

15. During the 1950s, TV lured kids away from back-alley activities like marbles and mumbledy-peg.

16. There has been a decline in the popularity of the game.

17. Nonetheless, collectors now take an interest in marbles.

18. Thousands of members attend the Marble Collectors Society of America annual show.

19. At the show, they trade marbles for $75 to $300.

20. Some rare types such as the gold-banded Lutz sell for over $5,000.

21. The Lutz was made in Germany before World War I.

22. No wonder people around the country are looking through attics for their grandparents' toys.

23. And no wonder people around the country are looking through old trunks for their grandparents' toys.

UNIT 4

APPOSITIVES

Sometimes when you're writing, the information you put in one sentence simply identifies or defines something you've said in another:

> Farmers try to control the poinsettia whitefly by digging up entire fields of infested crops. The poinsettia whitefly is a pesticide-resistant superbug.

When this is the case, you may want to make one sentence into a relative clause in order to relate the ideas in the two sentences more closely:

> Farmers try to control the poinsettia whitefly, **which is a pesticide-resistant superbug**, by digging up entire fields of infested crops.

But you can often express information that defines and identifies— information like "a pesticide-resistant superbug"—in fewer words as an APPOSITIVE:

> Farmers try to control the poinsettia whitefly, **a pesticide-resistant superbug**, by digging up entire fields of infested crops.

CONSTRUCTING APPOSITVES

You can construct an appositive from any sentence in which a noun phrase follows the **to be** verb (**is, are, was, were**). Eliminate the subject and the verb, insert commas or dashes, and you've got an appositive. By eliminating the subject, "peanut butter," and the verb, "is," from the second sentence below, you can make the remaining noun phrase, "the favorite food of American children," into an appositive:

In 1904, a Saint Louis doctor introduced peanut butter as a health food for the elderly. ~~Peanut butter is~~ the favorite food of American children.

↓

In 1904, a Saint Louis doctor introduced peanut butter—**the favorite food of American children**—as a health food for the elderly.

Appositive simply means being positioned next to something. Generally, you position an appositive next to the noun that it identifies, whether that noun is at the beginning or end of a sentence.

Deborah Tannen's *You Just Don't Understand,* **a book about the problems of communication between men and women**, suggests that the two genders speak essentially different languages.

Attending college in America made Shizuko homesick for her family, her friends, and even the roadside jinja—**the small shrines that dot the land of Japan**.

 USING APPOSITIVES TO DEFINE
AND SUMMARIZE

Appositives are used principally to expand the meaning of nouns by supplying defining or identifying details about them, as in the poinsettia whitefly example above. Here are some further illustrations. In the first, the appositive **golden leaves and a red barn in Vermont** defines the "ultimate autumn shot." In the second, the appositive **the battleship *Nevada*** identifies the "next target at Pearl Harbor" of the Japanese planes.

Julie won the photo contest with the ultimate autumn shot—**golden leaves and a red barn in Vermont**.

Antiaircraft fire forced the Japanese planes away from their next target at Pearl Harbor, **the battleship *Nevada***.

But appositives can be just as handy for summarizing or generalizing. The appositive in the next example makes a generalization about the fact that "major national airlines are joining forces with successful regional airlines," calling it **a trend that is likely to continue.**

To avoid bankruptcy, some major national airlines are joining forces with successful regional airlines, **a trend that is likely to continue**.

Short summarizing appositives—appositives of one or two words—can produce a striking effect, especially at the end of a sentence, where they bring a reader to a jarring halt:

Half an hour later, the second police diver returned with the same report—**nothing**.

Incorporated into humanistic programs in our schools is one of the most dehumanizing practices in education—**standardized testing**.

Longer summarizing appositives can fill in important background information. Here is a long appositive that sets the current economic status of the South and West into historical perspective:

The "sunbelt" states of the South and West—**states that remained rural and backward during the industrialization of our country**—have come to dominate the U.S. economy during the technological revolution.

When you pack appositives into a series, they summarize by listing characteristics:

Midwesterners will long remember the winter of '77: **the record temperatures and snowfall, the school closings. the impassable streets, the cold homes and offices, the idle factories**.

In Aesop's fables, the animals that overcome great odds represent qualities we want for ourselves: **power, intelligence, thoughtfulness, and honesty**.

USING APPOSITIVES TO SHOW
NEGATIVE QUALITY

Sometimes the best way to explain something is by saying what it is not. You can do just that with negative appositives:

> Less than fifty feet past the intersection, the old Studebaker started making unusual noises, **not the familiar rattles and knocks**.
>
> Bloodhounds are friendly, gentle creatures, **not the vicious beasts their name would lead you to expect**.

You can also make a generalization with a negative appositive:

> On *Married . . . With Children,* Peg Bundy swishes around in skin-tight leggings and strappy high heels—**not the way most moms dress**.

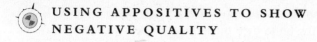

ADJECTIVES AS APPOSITIVES

Whether positive or negative, appositives are normally nouns. But other structures can sometimes function as appositives. Adjectives can be used as appositives, if you move them from their normal position in front of the noun they modify. Here is a sentence with adjectives in their usual position before a noun:

> My blind date turned out to be an honest, fun-loving, affectionate, and wonderful person.

Now here are three of these adjectives—**honest, fun-loving, and affectionate**—shifted to the end of the sentence to function as appositives:

> My blind date turned out to be a wonderful person—**honest, fun-loving, and affectionate**.

If you read the two versions out loud, you'll notice that the sentence with the list of adjectives before the noun "person" sounds almost clut-

50   tered; the one with the list of appositive adjectives more clearly focuses on the fact that "my blind date turned out to be a wonderful person." Appositive adjectives summarize qualities and can help you sharpen the focus of sentences. Like appositive nouns, they can be placed at the beginning, middle, or end of a sentence:

> **Stark, forbidding, awesome, spectacular**—Death Valley is a hauntingly beautiful place to visit, despite its name.
>
> Anne Rice's black Harley-Davidson motorcycle—**beautiful, seductive, and hungry**—glides through the streets of New Orleans like a vampire on the prowl.
>
> Shanghai is different from other Chinese cities—**more European, more cosmopolitan**.

USING APPOSITIVES TO FOCUS AND TO LINK SENTENCES

If you have a choice about which of two sentences to reduce to an appositive, you can usually let focus be your guide. What you keep as a complete sentence will generally be your main focus. For instance, you can make either of the next two sentences into an appositive.

> Avignon is a walled city in southern France. Avignon was the home of the Pope in the fourteenth century.

If the paragraph you're writing is about southern France or about walled cities, you would keep the focus on those topics by making the second full sentence into an appositive and leaving the first as a full sentence:

> Avignon—**the home of the Pope in the fourteenth century**—is a walled city in southern France. It is perhaps the most spectacular of the medieval walled cities in that region.

If, on the other hand, your paragraph is about popes in the fourteenth century, you would focus on that topic by making the second sentence into an appositive:

Avignon, **a walled city in southern France**, was the home of the Pope **51** in the fourteenth century. In fact, the century was a time of confusion in the Church, when one pope was housed in Avignon and another was housed in Rome.

The most common position for an appositive is immediately *after* the noun that it defines. But an appositive can also be placed at the beginning of a sentence *before* the noun. Such an opening appositive can be an especially effective link between sentences. Notice how the appositive **a man who never baked a cake in his life** serves as a bridge between the next two sentences:

High on the list of America's most successful food industrialists stands Duncan Hines. **A man who never baked a cake in his life**, Hines founded a multi-million-dollar food-products company that named its line of premium cake mixes after him.

 USING SPECIAL APPOSITIVES

Certain appositive structures have special forms. Some appositives call for the repetition of the noun, others for an appropriate pronoun, and still others for a connective to link them to a main clause.

Whenever several words separate an appositive from the noun it defines, try repeating the noun:

All of us depend on **services** over which we have no personal control— **services that we accept unthinkingly from dozens of nameless men and women every day**.

With a list, you can repeat the noun several times or simply include it once:

Oprah showed heartwarming stories unfolding in every corner of the nation—**stories of neighbor helping neighbor, stories of cops befriending gang members, stories of teens "adopting" grandparents**.

Oprah showed heartwarming **stories** unfolding in every corner of the nation—**stories of neighbor helping neighbor, of cops befriending gang members, of teens "adopting" grandparents**.

Repeating a noun works well, especially when the appositive includes a long modifier:

Musicologist Peter Schickele (known as P.D.Q. Bach) writes and performs classical music satires—**satires like "Schleptet in E Flat" and the opera "Hansel and Gretel and Ted and Alice."**

But sometimes you may prefer to introduce the appositive with a pro-noun like **one, that, the latter, something,** or **the kind,** rather than repeat the noun:

Musicologist Peter Schickele (known as P.D.Q. Bach) writes and performs classical satires—**ones like "Schleptet in E Flat" and the opera "Hansel and Gretel and Ted and Alice."**

When your appositive provides an example or illustration, you can relate it to the main clause with a connective like **namely, including, especially, particularly, notably, mainly,** or **for example:**

A number of U.S. presidents—**including Lincoln, Roosevelt, and Kennedy**—have died in office.
Some of the world's fastest-growing countries, **notably Pakistan and Bangladesh**, are among the world's poorest.

Of course, you're not limited to using only one appositive at a time. Here's a sentence with three appositives, including one that repeats a noun and one that is negative:

Liz and Jeff Ball wrote *Yardening* for people who just happen to take care of grass and plants, **people like themselves, homeowners, not skilled gardeners**.

PUNCTUATING APPOSITIVES

Appositives are generally set off by commas, dashes, or colons. The different punctuation marks create different effects. Notice how in the first version below, the comma, because it is such a common form of punctuation, hardly calls attention to itself or to the appositive phrase, **a prepaid insurance plan for dogs and cats.** In the second example, the dash—because it creates a longer pause—makes the appositive more emphatic. The colon lends the third version an air of formality:

> Pet owners upset by soaring veterinary costs can now register for Medipet**,** a pre-paid insurance plan for dogs and cats.

> Pet owners upset by soaring veterinary costs can now register for Medipet—a pre-paid insurance plan for dogs and cats.

> Pet owners upset by soaring veterinary costs can now register for Medipet**:** a pre-paid insurance plan for dogs and cats.

When you have a series of appositives separated by commas, it's usually best to set the series off by a dash or colon. In the next example, the single appositive, **an offbeat biologist,** is set off by a comma; the series of appositives—**face mites, body lice, and tooth amoebas**—are separated by commas and set off by two dashes:

> The squiggly creatures that live on people—face mites, body lice, and tooth amoebas—are the subject of a book by Roger Knutson**,** an offbeat biologist.

 **SUMMARY**

This unit explains how to construct an appositive by deleting a subject noun and a "to be" verb from a sentence, usually leaving a noun phrase as an appositive to explain, define, or summarize. Adjectives as well as nouns can sometimes function as appositives. Chosen properly, appositives can help you focus on the central idea of a paragraph; or they can help you link

54 sentences to one another. Some special forms of appositives call for you to repeat nouns or pronouns or to introduce them with connectives. When you punctuate appositives, you typically use commas, dashes, or colons.

Remember to use appositives in the next paper you write.

CONSTRUCTING APPOSITIVES

I. Make each sequence below into a single sentence by converting the marked sentences into appositives. Punctuate the appositives with commas, dashes, or colons, as you see fit.

EXAMPLE

1. In Rwanda, Dian Fossey lived among and studied gorillas.
2. ~~Gorillas are~~ shy, beguiling animals whose numbers have been decimated by poachers.

In Rwanda, Dian Fossey lived among and studied gorillas—**shy, beguiling animals whose numbers have been decimated by poachers**.

A. 1. Rap music offers political commentary on at least two urban problems.
   2. ~~The problems are~~ poverty and despair.

B. 1. Mark Mathabane tells in *Kaffir Boy* of his involvement in the 1976 Soweto Township protests.
   2. ~~Mark Mathabane is~~ a native of South Africa.
   3. ~~The Soweto Township protests were~~ street demonstrations in which hundreds of black South Africans were killed by the police.

C. 1. Disguised as science fiction, *Star Trek*'s plots actually dealt with the cultural problems of the 1960s.
   2. ~~A cultural problem of the 1960s was~~ Vietnam.
   3. ~~A cultural problem of the 1960s was~~ the Cold War.
   4. ~~A cultural problem of the 1960s was~~ civil rights.

D. 1. Early spring is the time of year when your garden emerges from the shadows of winter.

2. ~~Early spring is~~ the time when it shows the first signs of renewal.

E. 1. It's hard to believe now, but the "Beach Blanket" movies of Frankie Avalon and Annette Funicello shocked adults in the 1950s.
    2. ~~These movies include~~ *Beach Blanket Bingo.*
    3. ~~These movies include~~ *Muscle Beach Party.*
    4. ~~These movies include~~ *How to Stuff a Wild Bikini.*

II. Make each sequence below into a single sentence by converting one or more of the original sentences into an appositive. If the sentences allow, write more than one version for each sequence. Punctuate the appositives with commas, dashes, or colons, as you see fit.

EXAMPLE

1. A typical Swiss Army Knife includes a variety of tools.
2. The tools include a watch.
3. The tools include a tiny pen.
4. The tools include a nail file.
5. The tools include a screwdriver.
6. The tools include a metal saw.
7. The tools include pliers.
8. And the tools even include a fish scaler.

A typical Swiss Army Knife includes a variety of tools, **tools like a watch and tiny pen, a nail file and screwdriver, a metal saw and pliers, and even a fish scaler.**

OR

A typical Swiss Army Knife includes a variety of tools: **a watch, a tiny pen, a nail file, a screwdriver, a metal saw, pliers**, and **a fish scaler**.

F. 1. A ten-year study reveals that high school valedictorians do no better in life than their average classmates.
    2. ~~Valedictorians are~~ the "best" students in their graduating classes.

G. 1. The National Safety Council estimates that one out of fifty **57** cars coming at you down the highway has a drunk driver behind the wheel.

2. ~~A drunk driver is~~ a driver with at least a 0.10 percent blood alcohol level.

H. 1. Beatles fans by the thousands trek to Liverpool each year for a magical mystery tour of Fab Four shrines.

2. Strawberry Fields ~~is a Fab Four shrine~~.

3. Abbey Road ~~is a Fab Four shrine~~.

4. The grave of Eleanor Rigby ~~is a Fab Four shrine~~.

5. And the boyhood homes of John, Paul, George, and Ringo ~~are Fab Four shrines~~.

I. 1. The first ready-made clothes were scorned by the American public when they appeared in the early 1800s.

2. ~~The first ready-made clothes were~~ crude.

3. ~~The first ready-made clothes were~~ cheap.

4. ~~The first ready-made clothes were~~ shapeless.

J. 1. Though paleontologists once described them as huge, lumbering creatures, scientists now believe dinosaurs were surprisingly active reptiles.

2. ~~They believe dinosaurs were~~ energetic.

3. ~~They believe dinosaurs were~~ agile.

4. ~~They believe dinosaurs were~~ fast on their feet.

STREET MUSICIAN

Combine the sentences below into a descriptive essay that captures the writer's interest in the blind banjo player. Not every sentence will contain an appositive; you'll be able to make appositives as well as other structures. You might also try to enrich the description with details of your own.

1. I saw street musicians in Boston last summer.

2. The most moving was a blind banjo player.

3. He was a young man about my age.

58

4. He sat in front of Woolworth's.

5. His blank eyes were looking at no one.

6. His damp hair was sticking out from under a red headband.

7. He was an adept musician.

8. He entertained the passersby until his fingers slipped on the strings.

9. His fingers were slick with sweat in the city heat.

10. The slipping made it difficult for him to play.

11. He wiped his hands on a large white handkerchief.

12. He leaned back against Woolworth's front window.

13. The banjo was across his lap.

14. And he sang ballads.

15. They were soft and low intervals of melancholy on a bright Boston day.

CREATING APPOSITIVES

I. Add to each of the following sentences at least one fact or detail in the form of an appositive. For one sentence, add a series of appositives.

EXAMPLE

Some 2000 companies have produced cars in the United States.

Some 2000 companies have produced cars in the United States—**a number that is no longer likely to grow.**

OR

Some 2000 companies have produced cars in the United States, **companies such as Hudson, Nash, Packard, Studebaker, and, of course, General Motors.**

OR

Some 2000 companies—**U.S. and foreign**—have produced cars in the United States.

A.   College life is a series of shocks.

B.   Sean rushed outside with his new double-barreled water gun.

C.   Kelli remembered how thoughts of the dark cellar had filled her with numb excitement.

D.   These are the characteristics of an effective teacher.

E.   Teenagers often wear clothes their parents dislike.

II. Select one of the five sentences below, or write a sentence of your own. Then, with that sentence as your focus, write a brief paragraph that includes several details in the form of appositives.

EXAMPLE

My grandmother hated to exercise.

My grandmother hated to exercise. She used to mock Mom for working out every morning to Jane Fonda tapes. Then Gram injured her back in a car accident—**a rear-end crash on I-75.** She was in a body cast for about three months. At the advice of her physical therapist, she began exercising, doing kneebends and situps, slowly at first, just for a few minutes at a time. After about six months, Gram graduated to aerobics, **the final step in the hospital's rehabilitation program.** She loved it. She dances and stretches to the music with the best of them. Now she's more limber than Mom, almost as good as Jane Fonda.

F.   The old rocking chair reminded Sofia of her grandfather.

G.   The speaker's self-assurance and humor set the tone for the graduation ceremony.

H.   Siblings often have similar interests and talents.

I.   My cousin Vinnie took vitamins by the handful.

J.   *Hamlet* ends in a bloody melee.

BEAM ME UP, COOKIE MONSTER

Combine the sentences below to create an explanatory essay about what the Nabisco symbol on Oreos really means. Not every sentence will contain an appositive; you'll be able to make appositives as well as other structures.

1. Have you ever noticed the circle and cross design on Oreos?
2. Oreos are the world's favorite cookies.

3. Perhaps you should pay attention the next time you peel the chocolate cookie apart.
4. You pull it apart to get to the white stuff in the middle.

5. People who look for secret messages in company logos claim [this].
6. The design is an intergalactic transmission code.

7. Nabisco representatives say [this].
8. The design is actually a Renaissance printer's mark.
9. The company borrowed it for a logo in 1898.
10. It is not an intergalactic signal.

11. Earth kids think Oreos are out of this world.
12. The cookie company never meant to communicate with extraterrestrials. [Make one of these two sentences into a clause beginning with **though.**]

13. Is it any wonder?
14. E.T. preferred Reese's Pieces.

APPOSITIVES IN CONTEXT

Each of the passages below has several sentences that would be more effective as appositives. Reduce the wordiness and sharpen the focus of

the passages by converting those sentences into appositives and placing   **61**
them appropriately.

EXAMPLE

Archaeologists are discovering that family life and relationships may not have changed much since biblical times. As they dig into the ancient cities of the Middle East, scientists find remnants of everyday life. These remnants would have crumbled away long before now in damper climates. One recent archeological expedition found two-thousand-year-old papyrus letters written by a youth away from home. The dig was in Egypt. Roughly translated, the letters read: "Dear Mom and Dad, Please send money."

Archaeologists are discovering that family life and relationships may not have changed much since biblical times. As they dig into the ancient cities of the Middle East, scientists find remnants of everyday life—**remnants that would have crumbled away long before now in damper climates.** One recent archeological expedition, **a dig in Egypt,** found two-thousand-year-old papyrus letters written by a youth away from home. Roughly translated, the letters read: "Dear Mom and Dad, Please send money."

A. Calligraphy is a cinch to learn even when you use a simple, inexpensive kit. Calligraphy is the art of elegant, beautiful hand-writing. Calligraphy is handy for designing party invitations, memorable notes, and attractive posters. It is a valuable skill that can save you money and make you popular with every group on campus.

B. Editors of a leading business magazine set out to write a story about the corporate world's ten toughest bosses. But when they did, they immediately ran into a problem. The problem was fear. Subordinates who managed to overcome their apprehensions enough to grant secret interviews helped the editors to pinpoint one key quality of the "tough ten" right away. It was the bosses' ability to inspire respect tinged with terror.

C. Why are babies twice as likely to be born at midnight as at noon? Why do rejection rates for organ transplant patients jump sharply on the 7th, 14th, 21st, and 28th days after surgery? According to chronobiologists, the reason is that our internal organs move through mysterious but predictable cycles. Chronobiologists are scientists who study the rhythmic motions in plant and animal life. These cycles last minutes, days, months, and even years.

IT'S A BIRD. IT'S A PLANE. IT'S ONLY A MOSQUITO

Make the sentences below into an explanatory essay about how big and bothersome mosquitoes can be. Not every sentence will contain an appositive; you'll be able to make appositives as well as other structures.

1. You are sitting at a backyard barbecue with friends.
2. It's a warm summer evening with the sun just about to set.

3. Suddenly you hear a familiar sound.
4. The sound is the buzz of mosquitoes.

5. Then you feel a sharp bite on your skin.

6. Before you can swat, the offending creature has had a snack.
7. The snack was your blood.

8. Don't feel alone.

9. Throughout human history, mosquitoes have caused more misery than rats and lice combined.
10. The misery has been to people in damp tropical rain forests and dry northern plains.

11. In fact, Ohio records the most cases of mosquito-related diseases every year.
12. Ohio is a cool midwestern state.
13. Mosquitoes can thrive anyplace that water collects.
14. For example, they infest tree boles filled with rain.
15. They infest swamps.
16. They infest even small puddles in the bottoms of abandoned tires.

17. And mosquitoes can grow big.

18. People in Minneapolis–St. Paul refer to giant mosquitoes as their state bird.

19. These giant mosquitoes rule Minnesota's lakes and rivers during the summer.

20. Mosquitoes can become resistant to chemicals, too.

21. Our efforts to kill mosquitoes with DDT and other chemicals have produced generations of mosquitoes.

22. These generations are resistant to pesticides.

23. So the pesky "birds" will likely be at your next backyard barbecue.

24. They will be ready to use you for a snack.

ABSOLUTES

Suppose in a paper describing your friend as she studies late one night, you begin by writing:

> Marie was sitting at her desk. Her head was slightly lowered over a pile of chemistry notes.

When you revise, you may decide you want your reader to see a closer connection between your descriptions of Marie's sitting at her desk and her head lowered over her work, so you join the two sentences with an "and":

> Marie was sitting at her desk, and her head was slightly lowered over a pile of chemistry notes.

But you're still not altogether happy with this version, so you give it another try, and you write the following sentence:

> Marie was sitting at her desk, **her head slightly lowered over a pile of chemistry notes.**

You may like this version best, both because it is concise and because it closely links the details of Marie's sitting at her desk to her head lowered

over her notes. What you've done is to turn the original second sen- **65**
tence into an ABSOLUTE—a phrase that is almost but not quite a complete sentence.

 ## CONSTRUCTING ABSOLUTES

There are two ways to construct absolutes from full sentences. One way
is by removing a form of the verb "be"—such as "is," "are," "was," or
"were." If you remove the word "was" from the sentence "Her head was
slightly lowered over a pile of chemistry notes," you can create the
absolute "her head slightly lowered over a pile of chemistry notes."

A second way to construct an absolute is by changing the main verb
into its **-ing** form. In the following sentences about an ominous evening,
for example, the verbs "gusted" and "gave" can be changed into "gust-
ing" and "giving" to produce a pair of absolutes:

> The evening grew more ominous. The breeze gusted more strongly.
> Whitecaps gave the lake a frothy, sinister appearance.

> The evening grew more ominous, **the breeze gusting more strongly,**
> **whitecaps giving the lake a frothy, sinister appearance.**

You can construct absolutes using either of these two methods—
removing the verb "be" or changing a verb to its **-ing** form. The
method you choose will depend on the sentences you are trying to
revise.

 ## ADDING DETAILS

Like other modifiers—relative clauses, participles, and appositives—
absolutes are useful for adding narrative and descriptive details to your
sentences. When you add details, you make your writing more vivid, and
you give it a richer texture.

Because they have their own subjects, absolutes allow you to shift from a description of a whole to a description of its parts. Remember how the earlier sentence began by describing Marie and then concluded by focusing only on her lowered head? In the next sentence, the absolute shifts the reader's attention from the birch tree as a whole to its branches:

> The sickly birch tree struggled to grow.
>
> ↓
>
> The sickly birch tree struggled to grow, **its scrawny branches stretching up through shadows toward the sunlight.**

In the same way, the series of absolutes in the next example adds details about *Star Trek*'s Captain Picard that help readers see the difficulty of his situation:

> Captain Picard stood alone on the Romulan flagship.
>
> ↓
>
> Captain Picard stood alone on the Romulan flagship, **his phaser set on "stun," his tricorder scanning the area, and his eyes darting into the dark corners of the apparently deserted transporter room.**

 INDICATING CAUSE AND EFFECT

Not only can absolutes add vivid details to your sentences, but they can also suggest cause-result relationships. Suppose, for example, that you wanted to combine the sentences below in order to indicate that the sinking of the battleship was caused by the torpedoes that tore apart its stern:

> The stern of the battleship was torn apart by torpedoes.
>
> The battleship slowly sank into the Pacific.

Your first impulse may be to write:

> Because its stern was torn apart by torpedoes, the battleship slowly sank into the Pacific.

This sentence is perfectly acceptable, but you can suggest the same cause-result relationship more concisely and more subtly with an absolute:

> **Its stern torn apart by torpedoes,** the battleship slowly sank into the Pacific.

Sometimes you can also place the absolute in another position in the sentence. But you must do so carefully. Notice what happens if you rewrite the battleship sentence with the absolute at its conclusion:

> The battleship slowly sank into the Pacific, **its stern torn apart by torpedoes.**

Written this way, the sentence makes it difficult for readers to be sure whether the ship was torn apart at the same time that it sank or before it sank. Generally, if you want to suggest a cause-result relationship, your best choice is to place the absolute at the beginning of the sentence.

 POSITIONING ABSOLUTES

Cause-result or time relationships will often determine whether an absolute can work at the beginning, middle, or end of a sentence. An absolute that refers to an earlier event normally appears before the main clause. (Notice that sometimes absolutes which begin sentences sound better when they are introduced by the preposition "with.")

> Her Melville paper was typed and ready to turn in. Cori walked uptown to meet her friends.

> **Her Melville paper typed and ready to turn in,** Cori walked uptown to meet her friends.

OR

> **With her Melville paper typed and ready to turn in,** Cori walked uptown to meet her friends.

An absolute that refers to an event occurring later than the event in the main clause should generally follow the clause:

68   Gene Kelly began "Singin' in the Rain" softly, **his voice rising to an exuberant crescendo before fading back to echo the familiar opening bars.**

But when an absolute does not suggest cause or a time relationship, you can position it almost anywhere in the sentence, at the beginning, the end, or even in the middle of the sentence:

Their faces lined with exhaustion, the fire fighters trudged back to their truck.

OR

The fire fighters trudged back to their truck, **their faces lined with exhaustion.**

OR

The fire fighters, **their faces lined with exhaustion,** trudged back to their truck.

Sometimes you will want to move an absolute from one sentence position to another for the sake of variety or sound. Other things being equal, though, absolutes work best at the ends of sentences. And that is where writers most often put them:

Dorothy hesitantly took her first steps down the Yellow Brick Road, **Toto clutched in her arms.**

One photograph of Picasso shows the artist at play, **a cowboy hat on his head, a toy gun in his hand, a cigar in his mouth.**

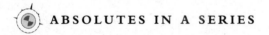 ## ABSOLUTES IN A SERIES

Like other modifiers, absolutes may be used in a series. Using absolutes in a series can be particularly forceful when you want to build the ideas in a sentence toward a climax:

The new pilot brought the crippled aircraft safely down for an emergency landing, **her heartbeat finally slowing, her clenched hands gradually releasing the controls, her relief visible.**

The absolute **her relief visible** has to be the final item in the series **69** because the sentence would not make sense if it appeared elsewhere. To hear the difference, try reading the sentence aloud with **her relief visible** as either the first or second item. Placed at the end, **her relief visible** explains to your readers what it means when the pilot's heartbeat slows and her clenched hands release the controls, an explanation that just doesn't make sense if it appears before the other absolutes.

Knowing that a series of absolutes gains power when its items are placed in order of increasing importance, how would you combine these sentences?

After the prom, the gymnasium was in chaos. A torn banner dangled from the ceiling. The once-beautiful decorations were simply a mess. Burst balloons were scattered all over the floor.

Since the sentence "The once-beautiful decorations were simply a mess" essentially summarizes the chaos in the gym, you should probably place it at the end of the series:

After the prom, the gymnasium was in chaos, **a torn banner dangling from the ceiling, burst balloons scattered all over the floor, the once-beautiful decorations simply a mess.**

 ## USING ABSOLUTES WITH OTHER STRUCTURES

Absolutes are especially useful because they combine with other structures to give your sentences variety and texture. Notice how the next four sentences can be improved by combining them into a single one that includes an appositive and a participial phrase and that ends with an absolute:

Chagall's "Bella au Col Blanc" is a sensitive portrait of his first wife. Her name was Bella. She is dressed in a low-cut dark dress. A wide, white collar sets off her graceful features and black hair.

↓

70   Chagall's "Bella au Col Blanc" is a sensitive portrait of his first wife, Bella, dressed in a low-cut dark dress, **her graceful features and black hair set off by a wide, white collar.**

Because such combinations of structures are compact and rhythmically interesting, they provide you with useful stylistic options.

 ## PUNCTUATING ABSOLUTES

You generally separate an absolute from other sentence parts with a comma:

> The defendant rose and faced the judge, **a mixture of anger and resentment blazing in her eyes.**

But if you want to emphasize the details in the absolute, you may use a dash:

> The defendant rose and faced the judge—**a mixture of anger and resentment blazing in her eyes.**

A dash can be especially effective when you have to separate a series of modifiers from a main clause. Here is the sentence about Picasso, with a dash replacing the first comma:

> One photograph of Picasso shows the artist at play—**a cowboy hat on his head, a toy gun in his hand, a cigar in his mouth.**

Notice how the dash helps to emphasize the series by making the reader pause just a bit longer before reaching the vivid descriptive details that follow.

 ## SUMMARY

In this unit, you learned that an absolute is a phrase that is almost but not quite a full sentence. An absolute includes a full subject but lacks a complete verb. You learned different ways to construct absolutes: by remov-

ing forms of the verb "be" and by changing a verb into its **-ing** form.
Absolutes add details to sentences, just as other modifiers do, but they can
also suggest cause-result and time relationships. When you use absolutes,
you should be careful both to place them in the most effective position
in your sentence and to punctuate them effectively, with either a comma
or a dash. Absolutes are an economical way to add real power and subtle
insight to your writing; keep absolutes in mind as you work on your next
draft.

CONSTRUCTING ABSOLUTES

I. Make each group of sentences below into a single sentence by converting the marked sentences into absolutes. Move the absolutes to different positions until the sentences sound right to you.

EXAMPLE

The combine cut its way steadily through the winter wheat.

Its blade ~~was~~ churning.

Its blade churning, the huge combine cut its way steadily through the winter wheat.

OR

The huge combine—**its blade churning**—cut its way steadily through the winter wheat.

OR

The huge combine cut its way steadily through the winter wheat, **its blade churning.**

A. 1. The dragon kite soared across the afternoon sky.
   2. Its long green tail ~~whipped~~ in the wind.
B. 1. Carlos walked up to the arena's front entrance.
   2. The concert ticket ~~was~~ in his hand.

C. 1. It was a perfect morning for a hike.
   2. The air ~~was~~ crisp.
   3. The sky ~~was~~ steel blue.
   4. Fleecy clouds studded the sky.

D. 1. The Harley sped away.
   2. Its tail light disappeared into the distance.

E. 1. Houdini was locked in the casket.

2.   His arms ~~were~~ confined in a straitjacket.

3.   His legs ~~were~~ manacled with chains.

II. Make each sequence below into a single sentence by converting one or more of the original sentences into an absolute.

EXAMPLE

When I walked in, Grandpa was sitting at the kitchen table.

The newspaper was spread before him.

His morning cup of coffee steamed in his mug.

When I walked in, Grandpa was sitting at the kitchen table, **the newspaper spread before him, his morning cup of coffee steaming in his mug.**

F. 1.   The maneuvers of the U.S. Air Force Thunderbirds are an awesome sight.

    2.   The F-16s zoom toward one another at a wicked speed.

G. 1.   The zoology lab was decorated with Gary Larson's "Far Side" cartoons of weird animals.

    2.   The walls were plastered with martini-swilling beetles.

    3.   The bulletin boards were festooned with cigarette-smoking dinosaurs.

H. 1.   Hummingbirds seem to defy the laws of gravity.

    2.   Their tiny bodies hover in one spot like miniature helicopters.

I. 1.   At the closing bell, the signs of the market crash were everywhere on Wall Street.

    2.   One trader in stock-index options sobbed, "It's the end of the world!"

J. 1.   The grueling race was finally over.

    2.   The distance runner collapsed onto the cinders.

    3.   She was gasping for breath.

    4.   Her chest was heaving.

    5.   Her face was a splotchy red and gray.

RED HOT CHILI PEPPERS

Make the following sentences into an essay that explains some of the distinctive features of the red hot chili pepper. Not every sentence will contain an absolute; you'll be able to make other structures as well. Feel free to add details to make your essay more vivid.

1. The chili pepper has been called the world's most popular spice.
2. The chili pepper is used by cooks from Central America to Asia.

3. But most people associate chilis with Mexican food for good reason.
4. Over 200 varieties of chili peppers grow in Mexico.

5. The heat in chilis comes from capsaicin.
6. Capsaicin is a potent oil found in the interior ribs near the seeds of the pepper.

7. Cooking with chilis can be like playing with fire.
8. For this reason, cooks should wear rubber gloves for protection.

9. Many careless cooks have been scorched by the fiery power of capsaicin.
10. I accidentally hurt myself one time using chilis in a bean dip.
11. My skin was burned.
12. My eyes were stung.

13. You can douse a tongue on fire and neutralize the oil's heat.
14. You suck a lime wedge.

15. But just how hot can a chili pepper be?

16. Experts use a scale of 0–120 to rate the heat level.
17. One hundred and twenty represents the hottest.

18. Many people find the pickled jalapeño peppers on ballpark nachos rather hot.

19. But they only reach a heat score of 20.

20. The champion hot peppers are unquestionably habaneros.
21. Habaneras hit 120 on the scale.

22. You would find me fully prepared to deal with habaneros.
23. Rubber gloves would protect my hands.
24. An entire bushel of limes would be sliced into wedges.

25. I've learned the hard way about red hot chili peppers.

CREATING ABSOLUTES

I. To each of the following sentences add at least one fact or detail in the form of an absolute. Add a series of absolutes to any two sentences. Try to make the sentences vivid and lively.

EXAMPLE

Diane stood motionless at the end of the diving board.

Diane stood motionless at the end of the diving board, **tears streaming down her cheeks.**

Diane stood motionless at the end of the diving board, **hands at her sides, heels slightly raised, every muscle anticipating action.**

A. Zach's mother finally arrived.
B. The party turned out to be a lot of fun.
C. A growing percentage of undergraduates hold full-time jobs.
D. The election turned into a landslide.
E. I walked into the pouring rain.

76   **II.** Choose one of the next five sentences, or create a sentence of your own, and write a paragraph with it as the controlling idea. Add illustrations and details in the form of absolutes and other modifiers.

EXAMPLE

Her dad had never seen Jenny so happy.

Her dad had never seen Jenny so happy. Her jeans, smeared with mud, were torn at the knees. Her sweatshirt, which had been so bright and yellow that morning, looked like a filthy brown rag. Her untied wet sneakers barely clung to her feet, **their soggy laces dragging on the ground.** Her hair was wild, sticking together in sweaty clumps. But a smile creased her dirt-stained face. "I found a big puddle, Daddy!" she exclaimed.

F.   It was just the kind of book I wanted to read.

G.   From across the street, the house looked deserted.

H.   My computer began to act up.

I.   Here I am, writing to you.

J.   College students have become more politically active in the 1990s.

AMUSEMENT PARKS

Make the following sentences into an essay that suggests how amusement parks appeal to kids of all ages. Not every sentence will contain an absolute; you'll be able to make other structures as well. Feel free to add details in order to make your essay more vivid.

1.   Amusement parks aren't just for kids any more.

2.   Today's amusement parks are resort areas.

3.   They are complete with hotels and nightclubs.

4.   They are complete with restaurants and variety shows.

5.   Children enjoy the rides.

6. Their cries of delight echo across the park.

7. Parents and grandparents tour flower gardens or watch from shaded benches.

8. Young adults also enjoy the rides.

9. You can see them on the water rides.

10. Their clothes are drenched.

11. Their faces are flushed with laughter.

12. Their arms are linked in friendship.

13. Amusement parks can even be places of romance.

14. Couples walk arm in arm among the flowers.

15. Couples use the rides as an excuse.

16. They cling to one another in public.

17. The couples have their pictures taken together.

18. They pose in outrageous costumes.

19. They have their half-eaten candied apples in hand.

20. Their sunglasses are casually shoved up into their hair.

21. The amusement park is a fun place.

22. It is for kids of all ages.

MAKING ABSOLUTES IN CONTEXT

Reduce the wordiness and tighten the connections in each passage below by converting at least one of the sentences into an absolute. Revise in other ways as well to improve each passage.

EXAMPLE

Situated on an island in San Francisco Bay, Alcatraz was the most notorious prison in U.S. history. For three decades, Alcatraz housed America's

78

most famous criminals. Its cellblocks were filled with legendary convicts such as Al Capone, Machine Gun Kelly, and Robert Stroud, the "Birdman of Alcatraz." "The Rock," as Alcatraz was called by the prisoners, had the reputation of being escape proof. And there were but fourteen escape attempts in twenty-nine years. San Francisco Bay's frigid waters and treacherous currents scared would-be escapees. San Francisco Bay discouraged all but the most desperate escape artists. Just one prisoner ever reached the mainland, only to be captured immediately and returned to his cell. Abandoned since 1963, Alcatraz remains an ominous and foreboding landmark off the California coast.

Situated on an island in San Francisco Bay, Alcatraz was the most notorious prison in U.S. history. For three decades, Alcatraz housed America's most famous criminals, **its cellblocks filled with legendary convicts such as Al Capone, Machine Gun Kelly, and Robert Stroud, the "Birdman of Alcatraz."** "The Rock," as Alcatraz was called by the prisoners, had the reputation of being escape proof. And there were but fourteen escape attempts in twenty-nine years. **Its frigid waters and treacherous currents scaring would-be escapees,** San Francisco Bay discouraged all but the most desperate escape artists. Just one prisoner ever reached the mainland, only to be captured immediately and returned to his cell. Abandoned since 1963, Alcatraz remains an ominous and foreboding landmark off the California coast.

A. The two boys leaned against the willow tree beside the stream. Their fishing poles were resting on sticks. Their eyes were gazing at the bobbers floating on the ripples. The fish didn't take the lines but periodically teased the boys, nibbling at the bait and jumping within arm's reach of the bank. The boys tried changing bait and rods and places. Nothing worked. One tiny bluegill did strike late in the afternoon but fell off just as it was drawn near the bank. Because their stomachs were crying for food, because their backs were burning from too much sun, and because their legs were stiff from sitting, both boys gathered their gear and headed for home.

B. Part of a comic strip's appeal is its exploitation of human relationships. Since the early 1900s, comic strips have made fun of some of the most complex of human emotions. Their characters have envy, jealousy, and greed. In one of the first comic strips, Krazy Kat skidded across the page. His feline eyes were filled with adoration for Ignatz Mouse. Ignatz, however spent his days throwing bricks at Krazy. Today Garfield the Cat bedevils his friend Odie. But deep down we know that Garfield really loves the simple-minded dog. The characters in comic strips have changed, but the Sunday "funnies" still reflect our attitudes about one another and help us laugh at ourselves.

C. If you are experiencing too much stress and looking for a fun way to relieve it, try juggling. Once a skill mastered only by circus performers, juggling is now taught in stress-management workshops for doctors, nurses, managers, and others in need of stress relief. With some practice, you might find yourself stepping up close to the wall and juggling some balls on the rebound. Your hands will be drumming the air, and your mind will be freed from the thought of your declining grade point average or your crucial exam tomorrow. Or if you are a fitness enthusiast, for the ultimate in recreation, try "joggling"—juggling balls or beanbags while running around the track.

PADDLE WHEEL FESTIVAL

Make the following sentences into a letter that captures a young woman's joy at witnessing a small river-town celebration. Not every sentence will contain an absolute; you'll be able to make other structures as well. Feel free to add details in order to make your essay more vivid.

Dear Sarah,

1. Do you remember my friend Amy from Titusville?
2. Titusville is that little river town downriver.

3. Well, the girls in the dorm warned me [about this].
4. There isn't much to do in Titusville.
5. All you can do is sit on the bank.
6. And you can watch the coal barges float by.

7. So Amy invited me down to the annual Riverboat Festival last week.
8. I said yes, but only to be polite.

9. I expected the trip would be a dull experience.

10. I couldn't have been more wrong.

11. The sternwheel riverboat is a magnificent old boat built in the nineteenth century.

12. Its whitewashed decks gleam beside the bright red paddle wheels.

13. Its tall smokestacks stand like coal-black sentinels above the deck.

14. The townspeople held a ball on the riverboat.

15. They dressed in nineteenth-century splendor.

16. The women were in white gowns.

17. The men were in black tuxedos and tall hats.

18. The dance was held in a huge ballroom on the boat.

19. The ballroom was lined with gilded mirrors.

20. The whole event was like stepping back in time.

21. It was an elegant ballroom scene from *Gone with the Wind*.

22. It was with Rhett Butler and Scarlett O'Hara.

23. On the next day, the blaring music of a steam calliope announced [this].

24. A second boat had arrived.

25. So the race could begin.

26. The two boats were beautiful as they slowly moved upriver.

27. Smoke was belching from their stacks.

28. Sternwheels were churning.

29. That night the sky was lit by fireworks.

30. And local bands paraded through the streets.

31. They played songs like "My Old Kentucky Home" and "Swannee River."

32. Sarah, I never thought I'd be moved by old-time songs like those.

33. But I was.

34. Wow! Were those other girls in the dorm wrong.

35. Titusville may be dull most of the year.
36. But during the festival, it's great.
37. It's so colorful.
38. And it's so exciting.

39. I'm glad Amy asked me to come.

Your friend,
Kate

UNIT 6

COORDINATION AND SUBORDINATION

When you connect thoughts of equal importance, the strategy you are using is called COORDINATION; when you single out one thought as more important, the strategy you are using is called SUBORDINATION.

 SIMPLE COORDINATION

In everyday talking and writing, we use coordination more frequently than any other composing strategy. It's so simple and so basic that all of us were coordinating almost as soon as we began to talk. We often put together words, phrases, and clauses into simple coordination patterns like **students and teachers; happy with her achievement but tired from the struggle;** and **when the Clintons travel to Washington or when they return to Little Rock.** Simple coordination uses familiar COORDINATORS like **and, but,** and **or.**

Using these familiar coordinators, you can even connect full sentences:

Some species of whales are nearing extinction.

Many countries refuse to accept even a partial ban on whale hunting.

Some species of whales are nearing extinction, **but** many countries refuse to accept even a partial ban on whale hunting.

There are over 3,000 baseball players in the minor leagues.
Only about 700 of them will ever reach the majors.

There are over 3,000 baseball players in the minor leagues, **and** only about 700 of them will ever reach the majors.

A second and more formal way of coordinating full sentences is by replacing the comma, and usually the coordinator as well, with a semi-colon:

There are over 3,000 baseball players in the minor leagues; only about 700 of them will ever reach the majors.

A third strategy, if you want to make the second sentence clearly command attention, is to separate the two sentences with a period and begin the second with a conjunction:

Some species of whales are nearing extinction. **But** many countries refuse to accept even a partial ban on whale hunting.

You can vary the effects of simple coordination by interrupting the coordination with a modifier. You put the modifier right after the coordinator and set it off from the rest of the sentence by commas or dashes:

Some species of whales are nearing extinction. **But, because of the large sums of money at stake,** many countries refuse to accept even a partial ban on whale hunting.

 PAIRED COORDINATION

To show a stronger relationship between two words, two phrases, or two clauses, you can use PAIRED COORDINATORS. There are five paired coordinators:

1. both . . . and
2. either . . . or
3. neither . . . nor
4. whether . . . or
5. not only . . . but (also)

Because their connecting power is greater than that of single coordinators, paired coordinators help to emphasize the connection between the elements they join:

Neither the rain **nor** the sleet

Whether to study for the exam **or** party with her friends

Both when you exercise **and** how you exercise

Not only is Mexican food growing in popularity in the United States, **but** Americans now buy more salsa than ketchup.

Like those with single coordinators, sentences with paired coordinators may be interrupted by modifiers that add details or that help define the writer's attitude. The interruption usually occurs just after the second coordinator of the pair:

Not only is Mexican food growing in popularity in the United States, **but— amazing as it may seem**—Americans now buy more salsa than ketchup.

 SERIES COORDINATION

Another coordination pattern involves the SERIES, a list of three or more words, phrases, clauses, or sentences combined with commas and with a coordinator before the final item:

Many Americans find Hillary Clinton an impressive First Lady.

She is a caring mother and wife.

She is an accomplished attorney.

She speaks intelligently and articulately about important issues.

Many Americans find Hillary Clinton an impressive First Lady. **She is a** **85** **caring mother and wife, she is an accomplished attorney, and she speaks intelligently and articulately about important issues.**

More than likely, however, you will use series coordination with parts of sentences rather than full sentences:

Many female moviegoers think Dracula is **sexy, dangerous, and irresistible.**

The inexperienced bobsledders hurtled **down the icy track, over the high-banked curve, and into a snowbank.**

Sherlock Holmes scrutinized the dead man's mud-caked boots and deduced **where he had lived, how he had been murdered, and when the murder had occurred.**

Like other patterns, the series offers a number of options. You can make the series move slowly and seem lengthy and drawn out and perhaps even tired by omitting commas and repeating the coordinator:

A trip to the supermarket can be a terrible ordeal—**a crowded parking lot and noisy kids and carts that don't go straight and long checkout lines.**

To make the series more rapid, to suggest urgency, excitement, anger, fear, you can eliminate all the coordinators:

Vietnam differed from all earlier American wars in **the elusiveness of the enemy, the widespread drug use among our troops, the American soldiers' sense of outrage.**

Just as two coordinated structures may be interrupted by a modifier, so may the three or more items of a series:

The special effects scenes in *Jurassic Park* required the expertise of stunt coordinators, makeup technicians, and—**most especially**—computer graphic artists.

A series with more than three coordinated words or phrases offers especially interesting opportunities. Instead of lumping items together in a series, as in the following sentence—

African-American writers like Frederick Douglass, W.E.B. DuBois, Zora Neale Hurston, and Malcolm X have written important autobiographies.

—you can group them into pairs:

African-American writers like Frederick Douglass **and** W.E.B. DuBois, Zora Neale Hurston **and** Malcolm X have written important autobiographies.

Rather than simply placing the pairs next to one another, you can use prepositions to designate specific relationships between them:

African-American writers **from** Frederick Douglass and W.E.B. DuBois **to** Zora Neale Hurston and Malcolm X have written important autobiographies.

The series, the paired series, and the series with prepositions, all create different rhythms in sentences. Read each of the sample sentences aloud to see how the different series coordination strategies change the sounds and shift emphasis and sense in these sentences. However the series is arranged, try to order it so that the most important item, if there is one, comes last. Notice that in the sentences above, the most recent and prominent African-American writers, Zora Neale Hurston and Malcolm X, appear at the end of the series.

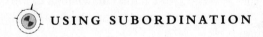 **USING SUBORDINATION**

Let's go back to the two sentences about whales:

Some species of whales are nearing extinction.
Many countries refuse to accept even a partial ban on whale hunting.

Simple coordination indicated that these two sentences were equally important:

Some species of whale are nearing extinction, **but** many countries refuse to accept even a partial ban on whale hunting.

If you want to suggest that one of the sentences is more important than **87** the other, you can combine them in different ways:

Although some species of whales are nearing extinction, many countries refuse to accept even a partial ban on whale hunting.

OR

Because many countries refuse to accept even a partial ban on whale hunting, some species of whales are nearing extinction.

By using words such as **although** or **because,** you make the less important sentence into a SUBORDINATE CLAUSE and keep the other as a main clause.

 SUBORDINATORS

A subordinate clause is introduced by a SUBORDINATOR, an adverb, or adverb phrase that relates the meaning of the subordinate clause to the meaning of the main clause. Here is a list of subordinators which can help you specify contrast, time, place, condition, and degree:

Contrast:
Although
Even though
While

Cause:
Because
Since
As

Time:
When
Whenever
While
Once
Before
After
Since
Until
As long as

88   **As soon as**

Place: **Where**
                               Wherever

Condition: **If**
                               When
                               Provided that
                               In case
                               Assuming that

Negative condition: **Unless**

Alternative condition: **Whether or not**

Degree: **Inasmuch as**
                               Insofar as
                               To the extent that

As this partial list suggests, you often have a choice among several subordinators. To indicate a time relationship between these two clauses—

> The Mongol invaders threatened to conquer all Europe.
> Then Genghis Khan's death forced them to return to Asia.

—you may choose among the subordinators **until, before,** and **just when:**

> **Just when** the Mongol invaders threatened to conquer all Europe, Genghis Khan's death forced them to return to Asia.
>
> OR
>
> The Mongol invaders threatened to conquer all Europe **until** Genghis Khan's death forced them to return to Asia.

Even when the meaning commits you to subordinating one sentence and not the other, you may still have a choice among subordinators:

> Michelangelo's *Pietà* was damaged by a madman.
> Museum officials display it behind a protective glass shield.

Because ⎫
Since ⎬ **Michelangelo's Pietà was damaged by a madman,**
After ⎭ museum officials display(ed) it behind a glass shield.

Any one of these subordinators is appropriate in this sentence because each logically links the step taken by the museum officials to protect the sculpture (the result) to the madman's act (the cause). But there is a difference between the subordinators. **Because** emphasizes the cause, **after** emphasizes the time sequence (first the damage, then the protection), and **since** gives roughly equal emphasis to cause and time sequence.

 POSITIONING SUBORDINATE CLAUSES

In the sentences about Michelangelo's *Pietà*, the subordinate clauses come before the main clause. But subordinate clauses occur either at the end or in the middle of sentences. You can control the emphasis and meaning of your sentences by varying the placement of subordinate clauses. Look at these two sentences:

If local residents are to put up with them, nuclear plants are a clean and economical way of producing vast amounts of much-needed energy.

OR,

Nuclear plants are a clean and economical way of producing vast amounts of much-needed energy, **if local residents are willing to put up with them.**

Despite the suggestion that residents may have reason to be uneasy, the first sentence implies that nuclear plants are desirable, but the second version implies a grimmer view, directing attention less to the plants' economic advantages than to the residents' concern for safety. A sentence tends to impress on the reader what it says toward the end, where the stress naturally falls. A dash, instead of a comma, lengthens the pause and places greater emphasis on **if,** adding to the reader's uneasiness:

Nuclear plants are a clean and economical way of producing vast amounts of much-needed energy—**if local residents are willing to put up with them.**

Where you position a subordinate clause within your sentence also depends in part on the surrounding sentences. In principle, you can make a subordinate clause out of any simple sentence, as long as you can link its meaning in some logical way to the meaning of another sentence. Either one of the two given sentences can be subordinated. But you have to remember that main points normally go into main clauses and less important, or subordinate, points into subordinate clauses. It is also true that the sentence you choose for your main clause and the one you choose for your subordinate clause will affect the sentences that come before and after them.

Let's look at those sentences about the whales one last time to illustrate how sentences affect one another:

Some species of whales are nearing extinction.

Many countries refuse to accept even a partial ban on whale hunting.

Although some species of whales are nearing extinction, many countries refuse to accept even a partial ban on whale hunting.

OR

Because many countries refuse to accept even a partial ban on whale hunting, some species of whales are nearing extinction.

In the first combined sentence, the main clause focuses on the refusal of many countries to ban whale hunting, so the reader expects that the next few sentences will continue that discussion. They might mention some of the countries, perhaps, or discuss their reasons for refusing to change their laws.

In the second combined sentence, the main clause focuses on the near extinction of some whale species. Here the reader expects the next few sentences to discuss the plight of the whales, maybe by naming some of the endangered species or even by giving statistics regarding the dwindling numbers of a particular species of whale.

The choice of which sentence to subordinate is a pretty important one, as you can see, because it can determine the direction of the rest of a paragraph or essay.

 ## SIMPLIFYING SUBORDINATE CLAUSES

Subordination is a helpful way to indicate how your ideas are related, but you'll need to be careful when you use subordination to avoid becoming wordy. A subordinate clause with the same subject as the main clause can sometimes be simplified to a more concise phrase. When you spot a word like "is," "are," "was," or "were" in a subordinate clause, take it as an invitation to eliminate unnecessary words:

> Although they ~~were~~ common a hundred years ago, red wolves no longer populate our woods in significant numbers.

> **Although common a hundred years ago,** red wolves no longer populate our woods in significant numbers.

 ## SUMMARY

When you coordinate structures, you imply that they are weighted equally. You can put them together with simple coordinators, paired coordinators, or series coordinators. Another way to put structures together is to use subordination. Subordinating one clause to another usually indicates that the material you've placed in the subordinate clause is not as important as the material placed in the main clause. When you use subordination to make two sentences into one, you can begin to shape entire paragraphs as well as strengthen your sentence structure.

USING PATTERNS OF COORDINATION
AND SUBORDINATION

I. Make each of the following groups of sentences into a single sentence by using one or more of the patterns of coordination: simple coordination, paired coordinators, series coordinators.

EXAMPLE

1. New Hampshire does not have a general sales tax.
2. New Hampshire does not have an income tax.
3. New Hampshire is the only state that doesn't have at least one of the two taxes.

New Hampshire is the only state without **either** a general sales tax **or** an income tax.

OR

New Hampshire is the only state that has **neither** a general sales tax **nor** an income tax.

A. 1. Lawyers should be committed to their clients.
    2. Lawyers should also be committed to the judicial process.
    3. Lawyers should be committed to the operation of justice.

B. 1. You can usually recognize the villains of cartoon adventure programs in two ways.
    2. The villains laugh fiendishly.
    3. The villains speak with foreign accents.

C. 1. Cave diving is incredibly complex.
    2. It is risky.
    3. It is exhilarating.

D. 1. The viewers of pantomime are aided by the supple mind of the actor.

2. The viewers of pantomime are aided by the supple body of the actor.

3. The viewers of pantomime can see what is not there.

4. The viewers of pantomime can hear what is not said.

5. The viewers of pantomime can believe the impossible.

E. 1. The specific fruits that Wrigley uses to make Juicy Fruit gum remain a closely guarded secret.

2. The fruit flavorings probably include lemon.

3. The fruit flavorings probably include orange.

4. The fruit flavorings probably include pineapple.

5. The fruit flavorings most definitely include banana.

II. Make each sequence of sentences below into a single sentence by converting one or more of the original sentences into a subordinate clause. For several of the sequences, do more than one version. You may want to review the list of subordinators in this chapter.

EXAMPLE

Many Americans use their microwaves to make popcorn.

The Iroquois Indians used heated sand to pop theirs.

Although many Americans use their microwaves to make popcorn, the Iroquois Indians used heated sand to pop theirs.

OR

While many Americans use their microwaves to make popcorn, the Iroquois Indians used heated sand to pop theirs.

F. 1. Giant Amazon water lilies range up to seven feet across.

2. Giant Amazon water lilies are large enough to provide living space for insects, birds, and lizards.

G. 1. The United States spends more money on medical care than any country on earth.

2. The United States has more spectacular medical technology than any country on earth.

3. The United States has one of the highest ratios of doctors and hospitals to people.

4. Nevertheless, the United States lags behind several European countries in reducing infant mortality rates and extending life expectancy.

H. 1. The Western world continues to regard acupuncture with suspicion.

2. Perhaps the reason is that acupuncture is so alien to our own concept of medical treatment.

I. 1. Ben Nighthorse Campbell won election to the U.S. Senate in 1992.

2. At that time he became the first Native American to be elected Senator.

J. 1. The Soviet Union was a U.S. ally during World War II.

2. The Soviet Union was our arch-enemy during the fifty years of the Cold War despite that.

GIMME A BREAK

Use coordination and subordination to combine the sentences below into a letter that might persuade the young man's parents to fund his trip to Florida. Not every sentence will contain either coordination or subordination; you'll be able to use other strategies as well. Add details for vividness, and change whatever you feel will improve the letter and make it more convincing.

Dear Mom and Dad,

1. How are you?

2. I miss everyone.

3. I want to see you soon.

4. But something has come up that I need to ask you about.

5. I have a chance to go to Florida.
6. I have a chance to enjoy the beaches.
7. I have a chance to enjoy Disney World.
8. I have a chance to enjoy golf.

9. Matt and Chris are driving down to St. Petersburg for spring break.
10. They are two guys in my dorm.

11. Both are good students.
12. Both are very mature.
13. I'll be quite safe traveling with them.

14. Anyway, they're leaving Friday of exam week.
15. They're driving down to the Sandy Shores Motel.
16. The motel is right on the beach in St. Pete.

17. They're going to enjoy the beach.
18. They're going to make day trips to Disney World and Busch Gardens and the St. Pete Country Club for golf, too.

19. Sounds like fun, right?

20. But here's the tough part.
21. The cost is about $350 more than I have.

22. The cost will include gas.
23. The cost will include food.
24. And of course, the cost will include the motel.
25. You lend me the money.
26. I won't have enough to go.

27. So would you lend me the $350?

28. I want to repay you as soon as possible.
29. For this reason, I will work overtime at the pool this summer.

30. I know you want me to come home for spring break.

31. This is a great chance for me.
32. So please lend me the money.

33. And let me go.

34. I promise I won't disappoint you by getting into trouble.

35. I promise I won't let you down by getting into trouble.

With love,
Sam

REVISING PATTERNS OF COORDINATION AND SUBORDINATION

I. Make each of the following sentences more effective by changing the patterns of coordination.

EXAMPLE

For decades, FBI agents wiretapped the phones of U.S. citizens with the attorney general's approval, and they didn't have warrants.

For decades, FBI agents wiretapped the phones of U.S. citizens **with** the attorney general's approval and **without** warrants.

A. More people live by themselves, and more women work, and more money is available, and for these reasons, one of every three U.S. food dollars now goes to restaurants or fast-food places.

B. James Bond is a refined gentleman; James Bond is a witty conversationalist; James Bond is a ruthless killer; and James Bond is a charming companion.

C. *Ren and Stimpy* may have been the most unusual TV cartoon series ever shown because it employed crudely exaggerated

drawings of dogs and cats and it lovingly depicted bodily func-   **97**
tions in graphic detail. Not only that, it also delivered memorably
sophisticated satire of American culture.

D. New York City may be the art capital of the world. New York
City may not be the art capital of the world. It is definitely home
to some of the most important art museums in the United States.

E. Spike Lee's film *Do the Right Thing* offered genuine insight into
the rage behind the Los Angeles riots of 1992, and John Single-
ton's film *Boyz N the Hood* offered genuine insight into the rage
behind the Los Angeles riots of 1992.

II. Make each pair of sentences below into a single sentence by converting one of the original sentences into a subordinate clause; then reduce
the clause to a phrase.

EXAMPLE

1. You are traveling in Scotland.
2. Then you surely want to visit the city of St. Andrews and its famous
golf course.

When you are traveling in Scotland, you surely want to visit the city of
St. Andrews and its famous golf course.

When traveling in Scotland, you surely want to visit the city of St.
Andrews and its famous golf course.

F. 1. You are denied credit.
2. Then you are entitled to an explanation.

G. 1. They were just a handful of men and women.
2. Still, American transcendentalists (like Ralph Emerson and
Margaret Fuller) exerted a powerful influence in the nineteenth century.

H. 1. Shakespeare's King Lear was unable to tell the difference
between true love and false love.

 2. For this reason, he lost his kingdom and eventually his life.

I. 1. They were once deserted during the summer months.

 2. Ski resorts have now created popular warm-weather attractions like the Alpine Slide.

J. 1. You are in doubt about deductions on your tax return.

 2. Then call the IRS collect.

NO MORE BURGERS

Use coordination and subordination to combine the sentences below into an essay that persuades the reader of the need for shifting to a vegetarian diet. Use reasons and examples of your own whenever you choose. Add details for vividness, and change whatever you feel will improve the paragraph and make it more convincing. Not every sentence will contain either coordination or subordination; you'll be able to use other strategies as well.

1. Meat eaters have usually regarded vegetarians as emaciated fanatics.
2. The fanatics pick at a few leaves, nuts, and berries.
3. These fastidious leaf lovers may know something that most steak lovers don't want to know.

4. Populations continue to grow.
5. Available land dwindles rapidly.
6. As these occur, there will be less and less food for the world's hungry mouths.

7. Vegetarian diets encourage wiser use of our animal resources.
8. Vegetarian diets encourage wiser use of our land.
9. For these reasons, we should shift to basically vegetarian diets.

10. We must make this shift.
11. Without that, we face hunger.
12. The hunger is massive.
13. The hunger is global.

14. Here is a startling example. **99**

15. A steer weighs 1,100 pounds.
16. A steer devours almost three tons of nutrients during its life.
17. The steer yields only 460 pounds of edible meat.
18. This means that the steer must gobble up over twelve pounds of food for every pound of its own edible meat.

19. This becomes clear, then.
20. We can feed more people with corn than with sirloins.
21. We can feed more people with lentils than with T-bones.
22. We can feed more people with soybeans than with ribeyes.

23. In addition to the points above, we don't need all that meat for nutrition.
24. Even the World Health Organization acknowledges [this].
25. Properly combined, meatless meals supply all the nutrients essential to the human diet.

26. A fresh fruit salad is a meatless meal.
27. A catch-of-the-day rainbow trout is a meatless meal.
28. Hot vegetable soup is a meatless meal.
29. Swiss cheese fondue is a meatless meal.
30. They are also nutritious meals.

31. All indications suggest that meatless meals provide plenty of nutrition.
32. They do so at lower cost.
33. They do so with more economic use of the land.

34. It may be some time before famines force us to do something.

35. Nonetheless, we may have to sacrifice burgers for broccoli.
36. We may have to serve spaghetti without meatballs.

37. While this is true, it is not too soon to start retraining our taste buds right now.

38. Anyone for eggplant casserole?

USING PATTERNS OF COORDINATION AND SUBORDINATION IN CONTEXT

Strengthen each paragraph below by using coordination where appropriate or by converting one or more of the original sentences into a subordinate clause. Try to make the paragraph more concise and more sharply focused.

EXAMPLE

Hershey's once called its candy bar the "Great American Chocolate Bar." And Hershey, Pennsylvania, may just be the Great American Small Town. It has clean, tree-lined streets, and it has magnificent gardens. You can also find museums and a 76-acre amusement park, not to mention a school for underprivileged children. The aroma from the chocolate factory is pervasive. For this reason, there is no pollution to smell. Founded by candy magnate Milton Snavely Hershey, the little paradise reportedly has no jail. It does not have poverty. It has a definite surplus of chocolate. For sure.

Hershey's once called its candy bar the "Great American Chocolate Bar." And Hershey, Pennsylvania, may just be the Great American Small Town. It **not only** has clean, tree-lined streets, **but** it **also** has magnificent gardens. You can also find museums and a 76-acre amusement park, not to mention a school for underprivileged children. **Because the aroma from the chocolate factory is pervasive,** there is no pollution to smell. Founded by candy magnate Milton Snavely Hershey, the little paradise reportedly has no jail **and no poverty, but** it has a definite surplus of chocolate. For sure.

A.   More and more teachers moonlight because they cannot make **101**
it on their regular income. They are victims of declining pay
scales and the lack of public support for their efforts. According
to one expert, teachers have only two choices. One choice is
that they can leave teaching. The other is that they can find second jobs to supplement their income. Many teachers have found
their other jobs to be lucrative and enjoyable. For this reason,
they are taking the first alternative and resigning. And those who
leave the teaching profession are often the best. They are the
type it can least afford to lose.

B.   The Chinese are taking desperate measures to curb their population explosion. Women in China may have babies. To have
babies, they must get permission from their local planning com-
mittee. Such committees take their authority seriously. Parents
of unapproved babies face rough treatment—in one recent case,
a $200 fine. The parents also received a public scolding. They
were also denied a grain ration for the child.

C.   Modern advertising agencies perpetuate a medieval concep-
tion of romance. Poets no longer sing about "courtly love";
they did that in the Middle Ages, in the days of the trouba-
dours. But the male is still the active suitor, and the woman is
the passive object of his worship. She is portrayed as decora-
tive. She is portrayed as precious. She is portrayed as innocent,
waiting for her knight to return on his "white horse"—a
Corvette. Such ads exclude anyone who does not fit the rich,
beautiful, white, heterosexual stereotype. Thus, they are
almost pernicious. They exploit women and limit them to passive roles.

LAST CALL

Use coordination and subordination to combine the sentences below
into an essay that persuades its readers that drinking by the young has
become a serious social problem. Not every sentence will contain either
coordination or subordination; you'll be able to make other structures as
well. Add details for vividness, and change whatever you feel will
improve the paragraph and make it more convincing.

1.   A 9-year-old arrested for drunken driving in a stolen BMW?

2. It sounds incredible.

3. In one recent year, nearly 200 children under 11 were arrested for drunken driving in one part of the country alone.

4. Police files record thousands of other crimes.

5. Vandalism is one of those crimes.

6. Theft is one of those crimes.

7. Even rape is one of those crimes.

8. These crimes were committed by children who were drunk.

9. Arrests are made.

10. Nonetheless, drunkenness among teens and preteens continues to spread.

11. And alcoholism among teens and preteens continues to spread.

12. Young drunks crash local dances.

13. Teenage gangs clash in Burger King parking lots.

14. Students gather at Friday night drinking blasts.

15. These are high school students.

16. And these are junior high school students.

17. Even respected students gather.

18. But it's not always party time.

19. Teenage drinking has increased so much.

20. There are now over one million alcoholics under age 21.

21. In addition, there are now over twenty-five special Alcoholics Anonymous chapters.

22. Their activities are geared solely to teens and preteens.

23. Alcohol abuse accounts for the majority of young suicides.

24. Not only that, at least 15,000 traffic deaths are attributed to teenage drinking each year.

25. And 75,000 serious injuries are attributed to teenage drinking each year.

26. Too many parents condone drinking at home.

27. Too many parents condone drinking at social gatherings.

28. This is despite these sobering facts.

29. Booze is the same drug the parents themselves enjoy.

30. For this reason, many parents are thankful that their kids are trying only booze, not marijuana, heroin, or cocaine.

31. Young people are coaxed by their peers.

32. Young people are encouraged by their parents.

33. Young people often resort to drinking like adults.

34. Young people often resort to committing crimes like adults.

35. Young people often resort to dying like adults.

36. Dying like adults is saddest of all.

UNIT 7

PREPOSITIONAL PHRASES AND INFINITIVE PHRASES

 CONSTRUCTING PREPOSITIONAL PHRASES

You probably can't speak or write more than a few sentences without using a PREPOSITION. When you tell **about** your job **at** the Taco Bell **near** the mall **outside of** town, argue **for** or **against** prayer **in** public school, brag that your new computer can play chess **like** a master, or explain how scientists turn saltwater **into** fuel **by** a new chemical process—you're using prepositions. By using prepositions, you can make relationships more specific between and among sentence parts, and you can establish points of reference for readers, like road signs on a highway.

The most common prepositions are **at, by, for, from, like, of, on, to,** and **with;** others include **after, before, between, despite, during, over, through, under, until,** and **without.** Some prepositions consist of more than one word, such as **according to, as far back as, because of, contrary to, except for, in addition to, in compliance with, in the absence of, rather than,** and **thanks to.**

A preposition never occurs by itself. As its name suggests, it is a *pre-position:* it is positioned before a noun or noun phrase, which serves as its object. A preposition together with its object forms a PREPOSITIONAL

PHRASE, such as **with us, under the broiling desert sun, because of**   **105**
her previous success in political campaigns, and **according to the**
National Weather Service forecast.

 THE ROLE OF PREPOSITIONAL PHRASES

Because prepositional phrases occur so frequently, it's easy to forget how
much they can help you write clear, expressive prose. Prepositional
phrases function in two important ways: they help you clarify statements
by indicating such concepts as manner, reason, likeness, cause, and condition, or they provide the context for statements by indicating such concepts as place and time. In other words, you can use prepositional phrases
to develop ideas and direct readers through your writing. Notice that
prepositional phrases in the next sentence indicate place:

> I crossed the U.S. 36 bridge and drove **past Elwood, Kansas, across
> the Missouri's rich farmland, through bustling Troy,** and **up wood-
> ed valleys to the West's high rolling plain.**

But the prepositional phrases do more than indicate place. They encourage us to feel the movement **past, across, through,** and **up,** until—
along with the writer—we get **to** the West's high, rolling plains.

In the next example, the prepositional phrase **After the *Challenger***
disaster indicates time; it tells when Americans began to realize the dangers of space exploration:

> **After the *Challenger* disaster**, Americans realized that space explo-
> ration had tremendous risks.

Besides place and time, prepositional phrases can also indicate such
adverbial concepts as manner, reason, likeness, and condition, as in the
following sentences:

> *Manner:* **With a brush strapped to his hand,** the French Impressionist
> Renoir continued to paint despite his arthritis.

> *Reason:* **Because of her ability to speak Spanish,** Lisa received sev-
> eral teaching offers from Texas elementary schools.

106   *Likeness:* **Like Swiss army knives,** some Stone Age tools served multiple purposes—scraping, cutting, and drilling.

Condition: Vegetarians get plenty of protein from nuts and dairy products, whole grains, and beans, **despite the common belief that only meat provides adequate amounts of protein.**

REDUCING CLAUSES TO PREPOSITIONAL PHRASES

Sometimes you will be able to substitute a prepositional phrase for an entire clause, allowing you to be more concise. You may also find that when a full clause doesn't quite convey the precise relationship you intended between two ideas, you can use a prepositional phrase to clarify your ideas. In the next example, the clause **although they have a menacing appearance** becomes the prepositional phrase **despite their menacing appearance:**

~~Although they have a~~ menacing appearance, most reptiles aren't really vicious if you leave them alone.

Despite their menacing appearance, most reptiles aren't really vicious if you leave them alone.

As you revise your early drafts, you might look closely to see where you can reduce clauses to more concise prepositional phrases.

BALANCED PHRASES

You can use prepositions to create balanced phrases, either in pairs or by repetition in a series. When you use paired prepositions such as **from . . . to, with . . . without,** or **for . . . against,** you imply that you've balanced opposites or even suggest that you've completely covered a subject:

Historians have blamed the mad dancing epidemics of southern Europe **107** in the Middle Ages on just about everything, for example, on mildew in the rye meal and on religious fanaticism.

↓

Historians have blamed the mad dancing epidemics of southern Europe in the Middle Ages on everything **from** mildew in the rye meal **to** religious fanaticism.

A series, on the other hand, lists parallel points and links them in a tight chain, strengthening their relationship:

The Chinese have built a society **with** an educational system radically different from ours, **with** aspirations challenging some of our most cherished values, and **with** a strong sense of mission at times enviable, at times frightening.

Just as they can heighten relationships between phrases, paired prepositions can heighten relationships between sentences. From the two sentences below, it's clear that the Pony Express made mail delivery from one coast to another much faster:

Mail to California from Massachusetts took up to six long weeks by ship. But then the Pony Express was started, and the same mail took only ten days.

But when you open the first sentence with **before,** you make the reader anticipate what comes after:

Before the Pony Express, mail to California from Massachusetts took up to six long weeks by ship. **After** the Pony Express, the same mail took only ten days.

In fact, linking sentences either with a pair or series of prepositions is one way you can achieve coherence and emphasis between sentences. Notice that by repeating the preposition **under** in the next pair of sentences, you not only link the sentences tightly but also emphasize how much worse things became in Eastern Europe under communism:

While the Czar ruled, only the single nation of Russia was oppressed. But during the rule of the Communist Party, many Eastern European nations such as Lithuania and Estonia were also enslaved.

108   **Under** the rule of the Czar, only the single nation of Russia was oppressed. **Under** the rule of the Communist Party, many Eastern European nations such as Lithuania and Estonia were also enslaved.

Prepositional phrases are simple, easy to use, and functional. They can help you orient your readers and clarify your sentences.

 ## CONSTRUCTING INFINITIVE PHRASES

Similar in appearance to prepositional phrases are phrases made with adverbial INFINITIVES. Such infinitive phrases are always introduced by the word **to** or the phrase **in order to** followed by either a simple verb form as in **to see, in order to write,** or **to daydream** or a verb phrase as in **to earn money for college** or **in order to recycle newspaper.** Adverbial infinitives generally imply something that a person might want to do:

My friends and I wanted to create the sound of a motorcycle on our bikes.

My friends and I would clip a baseball card onto the spokes with a clothespin.

To create the sound of a motorcycle on our bikes, my friends and I would clip a baseball card onto the spokes with a clothespin.

 ## POSITIONING INFINITIVE PHRASES

While the sentence about the bicycles has the infinitive at the beginning, you may also use adverbial infinitive phrases at the end of a sentence:

Medical students serve an internship **in order to gain firsthand experience in treating patients.**

The desperate accountant embezzled thousands from his company **to pay his gambling debts.**

When you use an infinitive phrase in the middle of a sentence, it creates an interesting variation in the rhythm of the sentence by separating the subject from its predicate. In the example, the infinitive phrase interrupts the sentence, creating just a bit of suspense for readers who may wonder what the EPA researchers have done: **109**

> EPA researchers, **in order to measure the damage done to forests by air pollution,** are exposing trees to auto emissions, then spraying them with "homemade" acid rain.

You can use either commas or dashes to separate infinitive phrases from main clauses. Because dashes create longer pauses than commas, they give added emphasis to the phrases, especially in the middle or at the end of a sentence:

> The desperate accountant embezzled thousands from his company—**to pay his gambling debts.**

> EPA researchers—**in order to measure the damage done to forests by air pollution**—are exposing trees to auto emissions, then spraying them with "homemade" acid rain.

Infinitive phrases, like prepositional phrases and other modifiers, can occur in a series, either before or after a main clause:

> **To meet our energy needs, to compete with foreign industry, to clean up our environment, and to maintain our standard of living,** we need staggering amounts of new capital.

For variation, you may omit the word **to** after the first infinitive in a series:

> **To meet our energy needs, compete with foreign industry, clean up our environment, and maintain our standard of living,** we need staggering amounts of new capital.

Like other phrase-length modifiers, those with adverbial infinitives can often replace whole clauses:

> Because she wants to erase the traditional image of God as a man, our minister refers to God as a woman.

110   **To erase the traditional image of God as a man,** our minister refers to
God as a woman.

 ## MISUSED INFINITIVE PHRASES

Sometimes you have to be careful when you use infinitive phrases, especially when you begin a sentence with one. Readers will expect that an infinitive phrase at the beginning of a sentence is going to say something about the subject of the main clause that immediately follows it. In the following example, readers will anticipate that the person showing delight over the cheese will be the next person mentioned in the main clause.

> **To show his delight with his first taste of Camembert cheese,** Napoleon kissed the waitress who served it to him.

But notice what happens if the main clause begins with the waitress rather than Napoleon:

> **To show his delight with his first taste of Camembert cheese,** the waitress who served it to him was kissed by Napoleon.

In this sentence, readers will be confused about who is delighted—the waitress or Napoleon. Be careful when you place infinitives in sentences that you do not confuse your readers.

 ## SUMMARY

You can use both prepositional phrases and infinitive phrases to convey details and to guide readers through your writing. Because they express such adverbial relationships as place, time, manner, and reason, prepositional phrases give readers the background information and orientation necessary to understand the other ideas in your sentences. With infinitive phrases you can suggest intention or purpose. You can move both prepositional phrases and infinitive phrases from one sentence position to another and use them to replace long clauses in order to make your writing more concise, more varied, and more interesting.

CONSTRUCTING PREPOSITIONAL PHRASES AND INFINITIVE PHRASES

Make each set of sentences below into a single sentence using one or more prepositional phrases (Example I) or infinitive phrases (Example II).

EXAMPLE I: PREPOSITIONAL PHRASES

1. There are an increased number of women in the work force.
2. Women still earn less than men. [Combine these sentences by starting the first sentence with the preposition "in spite of."]

In spite of an increased number of women in the work force, women still earn less than men.

A. 1. There are short movie stars like Mickey Rooney, Michael J. Fox, and Danny DeVito.
   2. The myth that movie heroes have to be tall has been dispelled. [Combine these sentences by starting the first sentence with the preposition "because of."]

B. 1. The U.S. entertainment industry produces the second largest trade surplus of any American industry.
   2. The reason is the extensive export of motion pictures and of music and videocassette recordings. [Combine these sentences by starting the second sentence with the preposition "thanks to."]

C. 1. There is overwhelming evidence that seat belts save lives.
   2. Several states still do not have mandatory seat belt laws. [Combine these sentences by starting the first sentence with the preposition "despite."]

D. 1. There were layers of dirt and dust covering the old desk.
   2. The rolltop turned out to be a handcrafted colonial antique. [Combine these sentences by starting the first sentence with the preposition "under."]

E. 1. There are wheelchair athletes racing in the Special Olympics.

2. Wheelchair athletes also raced in the 1992 Olympic Games in Barcelona. [Combine these sentences by starting the first sentence with the preposition "in addition to."]

EXAMPLE II: INFINITIVE PHRASES

1. Whitney wanted to graduate with honors in sociology.

2. So she wrote a senior thesis on urban gangs.

Whitney, **in order to graduate with honors in sociology,** wrote a senior thesis on urban gangs.

F. 1. The auditorium management wanted to prevent crowd-control problems.

2. The auditorium management initiated reserved seating for rock concerts.

G. 1. The aim of the school was helping students understand death as the natural end of a life cycle.

2. The school introduced a noncredit course entitled "Death."

H. 1. Some rock musicians now wear earplugs on stage.

2. They hope to avoid going deaf from their own loud music.

I. 1. Many Americans want to protect themselves from muggers and rapists.

2. Many Americans take instruction in the martial arts.

J. 1. Early Puritans wanted to prevent adultery.

2. They employed such deterrents as whipping, branding, and imprisonment.

ODD COUPLES

Using prepositional phrases and infinitive phrases whenever appropriate, make the following sentences into a brief essay explaining how neatness and sloppiness may be determined by the brain. Not every sentence will **113** contain a prepositional phrase or an infinitive phrase; you'll be able to make other structures as well. As you do this exercise, feel free to add details from your own experience that might make it more informative.

1. Suppose your roommate dusts and vacuums.

2. He does this because he wants to be happy.

3. And suppose you are an incorrigible slob.

4. Then the two of you are a classic example of an "odd couple."

5. Many odd couples simply cannot get along.

6. But even though they have their differences

7. Others apparently manage to live together successfully. [Combine with item 6 by using the preposition "despite."]

8. This often happens because opposites attract.

9. Some experts say [this].

10. Neat people can't help being neat.

11. Sloppy people can't help being sloppy.

12. The habits of neat people and sloppy people are determined by their brains.

13. This was in a recent study.

14. Researchers found that 80 percent of people identified as left-brain individuals claimed [this].

15. They were neat.

16. Researchers found that 75 percent of those identified as right-brain people admitted [this].

17. They were sloppy. [Combine these five sentences by beginning with a prepositional phrase that starts with the preposition "in."]

18. The left side of the brain controls rational and analytic thinking.

19. The right brain is the center of creativity and intuitive thinking.

20. The left brain wants you to be organized and tidy.

21. The right brain wants you to be spontaneous and unpredictable.

22. Suppose you want to avoid conflict the next time your room-mate yells at you to pick up your mess.

23. Remember each of you may be innocently driven.

24. You may be driven by the preferences of your dominant brain hemisphere.

REDUCING CLAUSES

I. Make each of the following sentences more concise by reducing one or more of the full clauses to a prepositional phrase. Rearrange parts of the sentence when necessary.

EXAMPLE I

If you want to avoid damaging your eyes, look into the sun only through a special filter, a dark glass, or a film negative.

To avoid damaging your eyes, look into the sun only through a special filter, a dark glass, or a film negative.

A. An Elvis record collection is incomplete if it doesn't include a copy of "Viva Las Vegas." [Make this sentence more concise by reducing the **if** clause to a prepositional phrase beginning with the preposition "without."]

B. You see sunlight passing through a glass prism, and sunlight shows up as a spectrum of colors: red, orange, yellow, green, blue, and, finally, violet. [Make this sentence more concise by reducing the opening clause to a prepositional phrase beginning with the preposition "after."]

C. The Bermuda Triangle mystery has not been reinforced by eyewitness reports, but similar mysteries, like UFOs, Bigfoot, the Loch Ness Monster, and the Abominable Snowman, have been reinforced by eyewitness reports. [Make this sentence more concise by reducing the opening clause to a prepositional phrase **115** beginning with the preposition "unlike."]

D. Dinosaurs used to be fascinating and scary, but then came Barney, and now little kids love to sing along with the huge creatures. [Make this sentence more concise by reducing the clause beginning with "but" to a prepositional phrase beginning with the preposition "after."]

E. The late nineteenth century saw the advent of the railroad and the telegraph, and, as a result of this, our world shrank more in a single generation than in the preceding 5,000 years. [Make this sentence more concise by reducing the opening clause to a prepositional phrase beginning with the preposition "because of."]

II. Make each of the following sentences more concise by reducing one or more of the full clauses to an infinitive phrase. Rearrange parts of the sentence when necessary.

EXAMPLE II

The Nigerian writer Chinua Achebe wrote his powerful novel *Things Fall Apart* because he wanted to educate his people about their own history.

The Nigerian writer Chinua Achebe wrote his powerful novel *Things Fall Apart* **in order to educate** his people about their own history.

F. If they wish to make their bread dough rise properly, bakers must dissolve yeast in water that is just the right temperature: 105–115°F.

G. If you hope to make the best possible first impression, your résumé should be free of all spelling and typographical errors.

H. My cousin took up skydiving because he hoped to overcome his fear of heights.

I. If you want to join the Polar Bear Club, you must willingly swim in an icy river in mid-December.

116   J.   Officer Suarez, who wanted to hit the bullseye consistently, steadied her revolver with both hands.

INCA EXPRESS

Using prepositional phrases and infinitive phrases whenever appropriate, make the following sentences into an essay that explains how an ancient people solved the problem of long-distance communication. Not every sentence will contain a prepositional phrase or an infinitive phrase; you'll be able to make other structures as well.

1. The Incas wanted to rule their vast empire effectively.
2. For this reason, the Incas needed an efficient system of long-distance communication.

3. They lacked both telegraphs and horses.
4. They had to develop a highly organized express message system.
5. They used messengers called *chasquis*.

6. The first *chasqui* would memorize a message for the Lord-Inca.

7. He would carry a conch shell, a mace, and a slingshot in his sack.
8. The messenger would start the long journey to Cuzco, the Inca capital. [Combine these sentences by making a prepositional phrase that begins with the preposition "with."]

9. The messenger carried the weapons for a reason.
10. The reason was to protect himself from enemies.

11. He would blow on the conch shell as he neared the next chasquis station.
12. The next *chasquis* station was 1½ miles away.

13. A fresh messenger would be waiting at the station.
14. A fresh messenger would memorize the message.
15. Then a fresh messenger would carry it to the next station.

16. The message would travel from one station.

17. The message would travel to the next station.

18. The message would eventually reach the Lord-Inca.

19. The *chasqui* messenger service could cover 1,250 miles in five days.

20. The *chasqui* messenger service could average more than ten miles per hour.

21. It was a true Inca express.

MAKING PREPOSITIONAL PHRASES AND INFINITIVE PHRASES IN CONTEXT

The paragraphs below lack focus and coherence because some sentences are wordy and others are not clearly related to one another. Strengthen each paragraph by using prepositional phrases and infinitive phrases to revise those weak sentences. Make whatever other changes you think might strengthen the paragraph. Be sure to write out the complete paragraph.

EXAMPLE

Bach's life differs little from the lives of other musicians in the eighteenth century unless you consider the fact that he wrote better musical compositions. When he was alive, Bach was an obscure musician, trudging from court to court for jobs as choirmaster or organist. He remained obscure for over a hundred years. But his music was "discovered" in the nineteenth century. Our own century considers Bach's work impervious to time and the composer himself a living presence to whom almost everyone in music is somehow indebted. We consider the Beatles indebted to him and Beethoven as well.

118   **Except for the quality of his musical compositions,** Bach's life differs little from the lives of other musicians in the eighteenth century. **During his lifetime,** Bach was an obscure court musician, trudging from court to court for jobs as choirmaster or organist. He remained obscure for over a hundred years, until his music was "discovered" in the nineteenth century. Music lovers of our own century consider Bach's work impervious to time and the composer himself a living presence to whom almost everyone in music, **from Beethoven to the Beatles,** is somehow indebted.

A.   There are obvious differences in size and appearance between elephants and humans. Elephants and humans still share similar characteristics. Elephants live to the same age as humans, at times reaching the age of 70. You can compare them to humans also in that elephants can live almost anywhere, whether in dry savannas or dense rain forests. When they need to change their environment, they use their strength to tear down trees, thus creating grasslands. Elephants are also among the most intelligent of mammals, and they have been known to recognize human friends a decade after their last encounter. They have one fatal weakness—their ivory tusks can be made into beautiful human jewelry.

B.   Choosing a hat to wear isn't always as simple as it sounds. In Turkey, the fez, which is made from red felt, was popular as long ago as the eleventh century. But early in the twentieth century, Turkey's rulers wanted to westernize their nation. Turkey's rulers abolished fezes as part of that country's national dress. Tradition-conscious Turks who insisted on wearing the fez changed their minds. They changed their minds because government executions of several fez wearers took place. Sometimes the choice of a simple hat, it seems, has had deadly consequences.

C.   The popular film *A League of Their Own* was based on actual events. With the military draft calling the ballplayers to war, Chicago Cubs owner Phillip K. Wrigley feared the collapse of the major leagues. He hoped to prevent the demise of professional baseball. He formed the All-American Girls Professional Baseball League. The league had a patronizing name, but the teams successfully drew many fans to the ballpark for over a decade. This was attributable to the women's great skill and athletic ability. It took thirty-six years of waiting, but finally, in 1988, "The Girls of Summer" were honored by a display at the Baseball Hall of Fame.

DRESSED TO KILL   **119**

Using prepositional phrases and infinitive phrases whenever appropriate, make the following sentences into an explanatory essay that supports the old adage about clothes making the person. Not every sentence will contain a prepositional phrase or an infinitive phrase; you'll be able to make other structures as well.

1. It was easy.
2. You could tell the good guys from the bad in the old cowboy movies.

3. The good guys looked good.
4. The bad guys looked bad.
5. The good guys never lost their hats in fights.
6. And the good guys wore light-colored clothing.
7. The good guys were like Roy Rogers and Gene Autry.

8. On the other hand, the bad guys lost their hats frequently and always wore black.
9. The bad guys were like the crooked sheriff and the nasty rustler. [Combine these sentences by starting with the prepositional phrase "like the crooked sheriff and the nasty rustler."]

10. You might laugh at Hollywood stereotypes.
11. But some psychologists agree [about this].
12. People do reveal their personalities with their clothing.

13. The clothes we wear every day tell others who we are.

14. Some people wear loud clothes.
15. Those people have loud personalities.

16. Optimists tend toward bright clothes.
17. Pessimists prefer gray neutral clothing.

18. The 80s generation wanted to signal their rebellion against their parents' values.

19.   To do so, the 80s generation adopted a new form of dress.

20.   The new form of dress was highlighted by torn jeans and unlaced high top sneakers.

21.   But not only is clothing revealing of your personality.

22.   The clothing you wear can also identify your authority. [Combine these sentences by beginning with a prepositional phrase that starts with the preposition "in addition to."]

23.   One study of clothes reported [this.]

24.   Students apparently react to symbols of authority.

25.   Students work harder for teachers who dress in suits.

26.   Students don't work as hard for teachers in shirtsleeves.

27.   And do you want to move up the corporate ladder?

28.   Then be prepared for this.

29.   Dress properly in dark, pinstriped suits.

30.   And never wear green.

31.   For some reason, people who wear green are judged to be less honest and less likeable.

32.   So it seems that this is the case.

33.   Roy Rogers and Gene Autry had the right idea.

34.   The good guys do look good.

35.   The bad guys do look bad.

UNIT 8

NOUN SUBSTITUTES

 TYPES OF NOUN SUBSTITUTES

When you're writing quickly to produce an early draft, you sometimes state an observation in a single clause or sentence and then comment on it with the next. To relate the two clauses, you might refer to one of them with a pronoun like **this, that,** or **it:**

1. You could deposit nuclear waste in outer space. **This** would be one way to solve a difficult dilemma.

2. Some people blame all social problems on moral decay. **That** is a gross oversimplification.

3. Laura was late for her trial, and **it** really made the judge furious.

4. Why don't more Americans listen to classical music? **This** is a mystery to Europeans.

Pronouns that refer to whole clauses are generally vague. To make relationships between statements more clear and specific, you can replace words like **this, that,** and **it** by combining the two sentences, converting one of them into a NOUN SUBSTITUTE.

In example 1, you can change the first sentence into a GERUND phrase:

~~You could~~ deposit nuclear waste in outer space. **This** would be one way to solve a difficult dilemma.

↓

Depositing nuclear waste in outer space would be one way to solve a difficult dilemma.

In example 2, you can make the first clause into an INFINITIVE phrase:

~~Some people~~ blame all social problems on moral decay. **That** is a gross oversimplification.

↓

To blame all social problems on moral decay is a gross oversimplification.

In example 3, you can convert the first sentence into a **THAT** CLAUSE:

Laura was late for her trial, and **it** really made the judge furious.

↓

That Laura was late for her trial really made the judge furious.

In example 4, you can transform the question into a **WH**-CLAUSE:

Why don't more Americans listen to classical music? **This** is a mystery to Europeans.

↓

Why more Americans don't listen to classical music is a mystery to Europeans.

An infinitive, a gerund, a **that** clause, or a **wh**-clause retains the meaning it had as a full sentence. When you combine it with another sentence, you clearly specify the relationship between the two.

CONSTRUCTING INFINITIVES AND GERUNDS

You make a gerund phrase by changing the verb in a clause to an **–ing** form. For instance, in the following example you can make the verbs "smoke" and "cooks" into **smoking** and **cooking:**

~~You~~ smoke cigarettes.

This is dangerous to your health.

Smoking cigarettes is dangerous to your health.

~~Philip~~ cooks with tofu.

Philip loves **this**.

Philip loves **cooking with tofu.**

Sometimes when you make a gerund phrase, you turn the original subject into a possessive form, like **dog's** in the next example:

The neighbors complained about **this.**

The dog howled and whined.

The neighbors complained about **the dog's howling and whining.**

In much the same way that you convert a clause into a gerund phrase, you can convert a clause into an infinitive phrase, by changing the verb form. To make a verb into an infinitive, you usually add the word "to." In the following example, the verb "play" becomes the infinitive **to play:**

~~Women players can~~ play in a European volleyball league.

It is the only way for women players to turn pro after college.

To play in a European volleyball league is the only way for women players to turn pro after college.

When you change a clause into an infinitive phrase, you can sometimes keep the subject of the verb by placing it after the word "for," as in the next example:

A restaurant earns five stars.

This means it has superior food and service.

For a restaurant to earn five stars means it has superior food and service.

124 You sometimes have the option of changing a clause into either a gerund phrase or an infinitive phrase, according to which sounds best to you:

> Michael Keaton likes this.
> ~~He~~ plays Batman.

> Michael Keaton likes **playing Batman.**
>
> OR
>
> Michael Keaton likes **to play Batman.**

 ## USING INFINITIVES AND GERUNDS TO MAKE YOUR SENTENCES FORCEFUL

Because they are verbs which you convert into nouns, infinitives and gerunds retain the force of verbs, their movement and vitality. So when you have a choice between an infinitive, a gerund, or a noun, you might opt to use an infinitive or gerund for its verbal force. Notice how the gerund **protesting** gives the second sentence more oomph:

> *Protests* against apartheid have won South African blacks more freedoms.
>
> **Protesting** against apartheid has won South African blacks more freedoms.

The second example is more vigorous because the gerund **protesting** suggests movement, while the noun "protests" seems not to move. Nouns tend to be impersonal and static. Verbs made into nouns tend to keep their verbal punch. In the next set of sentences, the infinitive **to deliver** and the gerund **delivering** both give more sense of the activity than the noun "delivery":

> The Chinese restaurant began the delivery of dinners in the local area.
>
> The Chinese restaurant began **to deliver** dinners in the local area.
>
> The Chinese restaurant began **delivering** dinners in the local area.

CONSTRUCTING NOUN CLAUSES **125**

To turn a sentence into a **that** clause, You put the word "that" in front of it:

E.T. said **this.**
He really needed to phone home.

E.T. said **that he really needed to phone home.**

Personal computers did not exist until 1978.
This is hard to believe.

That personal computers did not exist until 1978 is hard to believe.

You make **wh**-clauses from questions. The two kinds of **wh**-clauses correspond to the two kinds of questions in English. The first kind of question can be answered with "yes" or "no." For example:

Did the Red Sox win yesterday?

To make a yes-no question into a **wh**-clause, you first convert the question into a statement and then add **whether** or **whether or not** in front:

The reporter asked the President **this.**
Would taxes be raised again this year?

Taxes would be raised again this year.

The reporter asked the President **whether taxes would be raised again this year.**

The second kind of question is introduced by a word such as **when** or **what** or **how,** as in:

When is payday?

This kind of **wh**-question demands that you answer with more than yes or no. You must say where or what or how, as the question demands.

126 To make the second kind of question into a **wh**-clause, you use one of
the following words:

what	**where, wherever**
who, whoever	**when, whenever**
whom, whomever	**why**
whose	**how, how much, however**
which, whichever	

Here are some examples of **wh**-clauses:

Many Kansans know this.

What is it like to live through a tornado?

Many Kansans know **what it is like to live through a tornado.**

The Gulf War made the public realize this.

How dependent are we on Middle Eastern nations for oil?

The Gulf War made the public realize **how dependent we are on Middle
Eastern nations for oil.**

What began as the tinkering of two hackers in a suburban garage?

It became the Apple Computer Company.

What began as the tinkering of two hackers in a suburban garage
became the Apple Computer Company.

 REARRANGING NOUN SUBSTITUTES

Sometimes putting a **that** clause into a subject position makes a sentence
front-heavy and awkward, as in the next example:

That personal computers did not exist until 1978 is hard to believe.

When that happens, you can move the clause to the end of the sentence **127** and place an "it" in the subject position:

It is hard to believe **that personal computers did not exist until 1978.**

You can move infinitive phrases from the subject position in the same way, by adding an "it" in the subject position:

To marry in June is traditional.

It is traditional **to marry in June.**

For an old athlete to attempt a comeback defies common sense.

It defies common sense **for an old athlete to attempt a comeback.**

USING NOUN SUBSTITUTES FOR BALANCE AND PARALLELISM

Balanced noun substitutes can make your writing appear thoughtfully constructed. Notice how much stronger the following sentences are with balanced phrases:

To vote Republican means that you will be endorsing big business.

To vote Republican means **to endorse big business.**

You support the labor movement by voting Democratic.

Voting Democratic means **supporting the labor movement.**

When you balance structures, you generally say that one thing is like another. But balancing can sometimes imply a comparison, as in the next sentence, which suggests how great a singer Barbra Streisand is by comparing her to the greatest English poet:

128   **To say that Barbra Streisand sings** is **to say that Shakespeare scribbled.**

Just as you can strengthen a sentence by balancing noun substitutes, you can often strengthen longer stretches of writing with noun substitutes in a series. The following draft is loosely constructed because sentence structures don't emphasize how closely related their ideas are:

> The new law would require the Justice Department to inform U.S. citizens if they are victims of eavesdropping by foreign agents. Then the foreign agents must be required to stop the eavesdropping. And they are ordered out of the country.

But the revision, which turns the loosely connected sentences into the balanced infinitive phrases **to inform U.S. citizens** . . . , **to request foreign agents to stop the eavesdropping**, and **to order them out of the country** . . . , shows how closely related the separate ideas are. The revision drives home the point clearly and forcefully by building on the rhythm of the infinitive series:

> The new law would require the Justice Department **to inform U.S. citizens who are victims of eavesdropping by foreign agents, to request the agents stop the eavesdropping,** and **to order the agents out of the country if they persist.**

You can achieve similar results with a series of **that** clauses.

> The new law would require **that the Justice Department inform U.S. citizens who are victims of eavesdropping by foreign agents, that it request the agents stop the eavesdropping,** and **that it order the agents out of the country if they persist.**

 SUMMARY

This unit introduces you to four types of noun substitutes: infinitives, gerunds, **that** clauses, and **wh**-clauses. You create infinitives and gerunds by changing verb forms. You generally add "to" in order to make a verb

into an infinitive and an "-ing" to make it into a gerund. Infinitives, **129**
gerunds, and noun clauses can help you tie loosely related sentences
together more tightly. And when you balance them or put them in a
series, noun substitutes add both oomph and structure to your writing.
Try using noun substitutes in your own writing, especially when you
spot a vague "this," "which," or "it" or when you notice loosely connected sentences.

CONSTRUCTING NOUN SUBSTITUTES

Make each set of sentences below into a single sentence using the type of noun substitute specified in the example. You can make more than one version for some of the sequences.

EXAMPLE I: GERUNDS OR INFINITIVES

1. Millions of people have begun [this].
2. They garden for relaxation and exercise.

Millions of people have begun **to garden for relaxation and exercise.**

OR

Millions of people have begun **gardening for relaxation and exercise.**

A. 1. You can bury a dead cat at midnight.
   2. Or you can rub the spot with grasshopper spit.
   3. [This] might cure warts as effectively as medical treatment.

B. 1. Someone says [this].
   2. History is a record of dates and battles.
   3. [This] ignores most of history's significance.

C. 1. Because it's a fruit not a vegetable, [this] can be tricky.
   2. You classify the tomato.

D. 1. You reduce your weight.
   2. [It] is not just a matter of [this].
   3. You clip a diet from a magazine.

E. 1. Swindlers love [this].
   2. They find suckers.
   3. Suckers dream of quick profits.

EXAMPLE II: THAT CLAUSES OR WH-CLAUSES   **131**

THAT CLAUSE.

1. The Earth's climate may be changing rapidly because of industrial pollution.
2. Scientists and environmentalists recognize [this].

Scientists and environmentalists recognize **that the Earth's climate may be changing rapidly because of industrial pollution.**

WH-CLAUSE.

1. Too many children know [this].
2. What is it like to grow up with parents who hate each other?

Too many children know **what it is like to grow up with parents who hate each other.**

F. 1. Health spas nationwide are betting [this].
    2. Boxing aerobics—a blend of boxing moves and aerobic dance steps—will attract men into aerobics classes.

G. 1. What does the Olympics boil down to?
    2. [It] is world-class events for athletes.
    3. And it is world-class business for commercial sponsors.

H. 1. Should prisoners be used for medical experiments?
    2. [This] is not only a legal question.
    3. But it is a moral question as well.

I. 1. What makes *Mad* magazine work?
    2. [It] is its cunningly chaotic art.
    3: And it is its spoofs of modern life.

J. 1. Television still considers men more competent.
    2. If you want to prove [this], just count how few news anchor teams contain two women.

SAVING THE FORESTS, SAVING OURSELVES

Using noun substitutes—gerunds, infinitives, and **that** clauses—whenever appropriate, make the following sentences into an essay that explains why we must save the rain forests. Not every sentence will contain a noun substitute; you'll be able to make other structures as well.

1. Nowhere is life more abundant than in the tropical rain forests.
2. Or nowhere is life more threatened than in tropical rain forests.

3. Rain forests supply material resources for developed nations.
4. And rain forests supply agricultural land for undeveloped nations.

5. So we burn the forests down at a feverish pace.
6. And we hack the forests down at a feverish pace.

7. In the past, [this] was easy.
8. We considered the loss of forest land as the price for progress.

9. But now scientists, government officials, and common people recognize [this].
10. Rain forests are fragile environments.

11. [This] and [this] destroy animals and plants.
12. You cut rain forests.
13. You burn rain forests.
14. Animals and plants can't be renewed.
15. Suppose we continue [it].
16. We destroy forests at the present pace.
17. Then we will damage the atmosphere.
18. And we will wipe out sources for new medicines to cure AIDS, cancer, and diabetes.

19. We have finally learned [this].
20. The welfare of our planet is clearly linked to the welfare of the rain forests.

CREATING NOUN SUBSTITUTES

In each of the following sentences, replace the pronoun in boldface with a noun substitute—a gerund, an infinitive, a **that** clause, or a **wh-** clause. In sentences where the pronoun is "it," you have the additional option of keeping "it" and inserting the noun substitute elsewhere in the sentence. Try experimenting with different kinds of noun substitutes.

EXAMPLE

It proved to be a terrible marketing error.

It proved to be a terrible marketing error **for Coca Cola to change Coke's original formula.**

OR

Changing Coke's original formula proved to be a terrible marketing error.

OR

What Coca Cola did when it abandoned its original formula proved to be a terrible marketing error.

A. **This** is a good example of the American preoccupation with sports.
B. It threatened to endanger our relationship.
C. What none of us could understand was **this.**
D. You should have decided **that** before you mailed the letter.
E. **This** can be a difficult task for some people.

I SCREAM FOR ICE CREAM

Using noun substitutes—gerunds, infinitives, and **that** clauses—whenever appropriate, make the following sentences into an essay that explains ice cream isn't as American as we generally think. Not every sentence will contain a noun substitute; you'll be able to make other structures as well.

134

1. We like [this].
2. We think of ice cream as an all-American treat.

3. But ice cream had [this].
4. Its beginnings were in the frozen desserts of fifteenth-century Europe.

5. The Europeans mixed snow or ice with fruit juices.
6. They did it to make frozen desserts.

7. Then they began [this].
8. They experimented with other frozen liquids to mix with the juices.
9. Sometimes the liquid was milk or cream.

10. It took costly equipment in order to do [this].
11. They mixed and preserved the creamy concoctions.
12. Therefore only the wealthy could indulge in these primitive iced creams.

13. Ice cream became more affordable and more popular.
14. It happened in both Europe and the United States.
15. It happened with the advent of insulated ice houses and hand-cranked freezers.

16. Maybe we can't lay claim to ice cream.

17. But we can rejoice [this].
18. We invented the cone.

REVISING WITH NOUN SUBSTITUTES

Revise each of the following sentences to make the most effective use of noun substitutes—gerunds, infinitives, **that** clauses, and **wh**-clauses. Rearrange the parts of your sentence when necessary.

Spain, which has seventeen distinctive cooking regions, is loved by culinary experts for that reason.

What culinary experts love about Spain is that it has seventeen different cooking regions.

A. Solar power is all about one thing; it converts the sun's energy into electricity.

B. If you use the lap-shoulder belt, studies show that this will reduce the chance that you will be killed by a car accident by 60 percent.

C. You can contribute to the Conscience Fund of the U.S. Treasury Department, which is one way that citizens who suffer second thoughts about cheating on their tax returns can soothe their consciences.

D. Getting their children into college used to be the goal of millions of Americans; nowadays, with the spiraling costs of higher education, it has become the bigger challenge to pay for college.

E. People doze at the wheel, and this is the major reason that motorists run off the road and hit parked vehicles, according to a recent study involving 2000 accidents.

SMILING BABIES

Make the following sentences into an essay which argues that LeBoyer's delivery room procedures are better than traditional methods. Not every sentence will contain a noun substitute; you'll be able to make other structures as well. If you can, add details for vividness.

1. "That's simply beautiful."
2. This was all the new orderly could say.

3. The new baby lay in her mother's arms.
4. She lay quietly and contentedly.
5. Her eyes were bright and alert.

6. This smiling baby seemed almost too happy.

7. She was not like newborns delivered in hospitals several years ago.

8. Then, newborns seemed to be on guard.

9. Their bodies were tense.

10. They were like boxers about to defend themselves.

11. The smiling babies are delivered by special procedures.

12. The procedures were developed by a French obstetrician.

13. The obstetrician is Frederick Leboyer.

14. Leboyer says [this]

15. Traditional hospital deliveries inflicted needless pain and trauma on infants.

16. He claims [this].

17. The pain and trauma scar children psychologically.

18. The pain and trauma make them aggressive and violent adults.

19. So he turned traditional delivery practices topsy turvy by [doing this].

20. He replaced blazing lights.

21. He replaced grating noises.

22. He replaced nerve-jangling procedures.

23. He introduced comforting darkness.

24. He introduced soothing music.

25. He introduced gentle handling.

26. He reduced the jolt of [this].

27. Babies are transferred from a warm womb to a cold world.

28. Leboyer carefully rests the newborn on the mother's stomach for a few minutes.

29. Then he cuts the umbilical cord.

30. Afterwards, he treats the baby to a comforting bath in luke-warm water.

31. At first, traditional physicians expressed doubts about [this].   **137**

32. Did Leboyer's methods work?

33. But all results indicate [this].

34. Leboyer's patients bear happier babies.

35. And happier babies stand a better chance of [this].

36. They stay happier throughout their lives.

37. After all, who can deny [this]?

38. A loving, caring entry into life is better than a harsh, grating one.

39. And what mother wouldn't rather have a smiling baby than a crying one?

PART TWO

PARAGRAPH STRATEGIES

**PART TWO
AT A GLANCE**

UNIT 9

COHERENCE

Writing is a little like guiding a group on a tour. When you lead a tour, you need to relate individual sites to one another, or you'll yank your group from one landmark to the next in a herky-jerky fashion rather than take them on a smooth journey between landmarks. When you write, you need to relate individual sentences and paragraphs to one another, or you'll yank your readers from one structure to the next in a herky-jerky fashion rather than take them on a smooth journey between ideas. Look at the three sentences below, for example:

Many people exercise every day and never lose weight. Exercising is important. The only sure way to lose weight is to eat less.

They seem to contrast the relationship between exercise, eating less, and losing weight. But they don't make the contrast clear. That's because they lack a connective word or phrase that would smooth the transition from one sentence to the other and clarify the precise relationship between exercising, losing weight, and eating less. The two versions below include those connectives:

Many people exercise every day and never lose weight. Exercising is important. **Still,** the only sure way to lose weight is to eat less.

OR

141

142   Many people exercise every day and never lose weight. **No doubt** exercising is important, **but** the only sure way to lose weight is to eat less.

The connectives **still** and **no doubt . . . but** in these two versions link
the three ideas by making explicit the contrast between the two
approaches to losing weight. By linking the ideas, they move readers
from sentence to sentence without disruption. When the ideas in sentences and paragraphs are clearly linked to one another, a passage has
COHERENCE.

This chapter will explore three major strategies you can use to link
sentences to one another within paragraphs and across paragraph boundaries. These STRATEGIES OF COHERENCE are (1) using connective words
and phrases; (2) referring to earlier words and phrases (by repetition,
through synonyms, and through pronouns); and (3) arranging sentences
into structural patterns, including the proper ordering of old and new
information.

 **USING CONNECTIVES**

CONNECTIVE WORDS

Sometimes the logical connection between sentences is so obvious
that you don't need to signal it with a connective. The relationship
between the next two sentences is straightforward. The second sentence clearly gives three examples to illustrate the generalization in the
first sentence:

> Most people can learn the basics of even a complex craft quickly. In just
> weeks, they can learn to carve, weave, or embroider.

Adding a connective like **for example** to such a passage in order to
directly state the relationship is probably unnecessary.

But whenever the connection between two sentences is not obvious,
you can provide a link between them with an appropriate connective.
The specific relationship between sentences will determine which connective works best. Here are some common connectives for indicating
specific types of relationships:

1. The second sentence gives an illustration or example: **first, for example, for instance, for one thing, to illustrate.**
2. The second sentence adds another point: **and, also, too, then, second, equally, for another thing, furthermore, moreover, in addition, similarly, next, again, above all, finally.**
3. The second sentence restates, summarizes, or shows a result: **in fact, so, thus, therefore, as a result, accordingly, in other words.**
4. The second sentence expresses a contrast: **but, still, yet, however, even so, by contrast, on the contrary, nevertheless, on the other hand.**

In the next passage, the connective **but** indicates the contrast between what prisons should be and what they really are:

A prison should serve as a correctional institution where a criminal is taught to deal with the outside world. **But** our prisons often harbor more crime within their walls than criminals find on the street.

The next paragraph contains a list of sentences following the topic sentence. The connectives **first, second,** and **third** clearly indicate their relationship to one another, making them into a coherent passage. **For one thing, for another thing,** and **finally** would have worked as well:

What explains the growing trend for couples to put off having children until they've been married for several years? **First,** the high divorce rate is making newlyweds think twice about starting families right away. **Second,** many young couples want to be more financially secure before having children. **Third,** more married women prefer to devote time to their careers before having babies.

CONNECTIVE PHRASES AND CLAUSES

When you revise a paragraph, you sometimes need more than a common connective to fill a gap between two sentences. You may need a longer phrase or clause or even a full sentence. In the next paragraph, for instance, a clause beginning with a connective—**but when the rain does come**—sharpens the contrast and bridges the gap between the tor-

144 rential downpours and the typical dry weather in certain arid regions of
the world:

> Some arid regions of the world receive an average of only two- or three-
> hundredths of an inch of rain annually and may go for years without get-
> ting a drop. It usually comes in torrential downpours.

↓

> Some arid regions of the world receive an average of only two- or three-
> hundredths of an inch of rain annually and may go for years without get-
> ting a drop. **But when the rain does come,** it usually comes in torrential
> downpours.

USING REFERENCES

Besides using connectives, you can link sentences with references to earlier words and phrases, by repeating words, by creating synonyms, and by
using pronouns.

WORD REPETITION

The simplest way to use references for coherence within a paragraph is
to repeat an important word or phrase. Repetition is especially effective
when it emphasizes the topic of the paragraph. The topic in the next
paragraph, Agatha Christie's mysterious disappearance, is established in
the first two sentences by the words **mystery, mysterious,** and **disappearance.** But notice how the last sentence trails off because the writer
doesn't pick up on those words:

> Agatha Christie earned world renown as the author of numerous **mystery**
> tales. But none of the tales is more **mysterious** than that of her own **dis-
> appearance** in December of 1926. Waves of shock rumbled throughout
> the British public when the newspapers proclaimed that Christie had van-
> ished. Not until several months later was she discovered, supposedly
> afflicted with amnesia, working as a nanny in a Yorkshire manor house. To
> this day, her fans are intrigued because she was gone for so long without
> being discovered.

In the next version, the writer revised the last sentence to repeat the words **mystery** and **disappearance:**

> Agatha Christie earned world renown as the author of numerous **mystery** tales. But none of the tales is more **mysterious** than that of her own **disappearance** in December of 1926. Waves of shock rumbled throughout the British public when the newspapers proclaimed that Christie had vanished. Not until several months later was she discovered, supposedly afflicted with amnesia, working as a nanny in a Yorkshire manor house. To this day, her fans are intrigued by the **mystery** of her **disappearance.**

The repetition of key words links the last sentence to the first, establishing coherence and reinforcing the topic as well. By repeating key words or phrases, you can often make an entire paper as well as a paragraph more coherent.

SYNONYMS

Another effective reference strategy is the use of synonyms. With synonyms, instead of repeating a word directly, you repeat indirectly with a word that has the same or a similar meaning. In the next paragraph, the writer chose to use the synonyms **bikes, them, a way, biking,** and **pedaling** rather than repeat **bicycling** or **bicycles** in each sentence.

> **Bicycling** in America has grown at an explosive rate. **Bicycles** used to be sold to parents for their children. Now those same parents buy **bikes** for themselves as well. Executives ride **them** to work in order to stay out of traffic jams. Suburbanites have found **a way** to do their shopping without competing for a parking place at the mall. High school and college students find **biking** an economical alternative to cars and buses. And even grandma and grandpa enjoy **pedaling** for exercise.

Like repeated words and phrases, synonyms can drive home the meaning of a passage. Throughout the next paragraph, for example, the various synonyms for **endangered** not only link the sentences but also restate and reinforce the topic—that the red wolf is an endangered species:

> The red wolf is an **endangered** species. Its numbers have **declined perilously,** both because of willful **slaughter** subsidized by government bounty and because of the wolf's **susceptibility** to the **deadly destruc-**

tiveness of intestinal parasites. And now the species may face total **extinction** because of its ability to breed with a closely related but far more numerous cousin, the coyote. Thus, having survived the worst that humans and worms can do, the red wolf is now **endangered** by the **loss** of its own distinguishing genes.

Remember that you can overuse synonyms as well as any other strategy of coherence; so you'll often want to mix strategies in your own writing. Notice that the example paragraph not only includes several synonyms for **endangered** but also repeats the word in the final sentence. In this case, the writer repeats **endangered** both to bring the paragraph full circle and to avoid using too many synonyms.

Sometimes a synonym with a broader meaning summarizes one or more preceding statements. In the following passage, **such migrations** is used as a summarizing synonym.

Eels, whales, salmon, turtles, and birds—and even bees and butterflies—travel long distances, sometimes thousands of miles annually over unmarked terrain, to reach specific spawning grounds or to find food or living space. While **such migrations** have been observed and recorded since ancient times, science offers no clear explanation of how animals navigate.

The summarizing synonym **such migrations** establishes coherence by linking the second sentence to the first. Summarizing synonyms are commonly accompanied by words like **such, this, these,** and **of this sort.**

PRONOUNS

A third kind of reference is through pronouns like **she, he, it, they, this, that, his, her, their, some,** or **another.** A pronoun is, in effect, a synonym which gets its meaning by referring to an earlier word or group of words. In the next example, the pronouns **they** and **their** keep the focus of the paragraph on people born under the astrological sign Virgo:

Virgos are simple and gentle people, with a need to serve humanity. Careful and precise by nature, **they** make excellent secretaries and nurses. **Their** warm, shining eyes and **their** bright appearances conceal **their** burning desire for love.

In the next passage, not only does the pronoun **he,** in reference to
Ben Franklin, ensure coherence, but its recurrence also links the succes-
sive sentences into a forceful pattern, with four sentences in a row beginning with **he.** Then, to emphasize the almanac writer's major theme, the
last sentence shifts from the pronoun **he** to the synonym **the advocate
of the spartan life.**

> In *Poor Richard's Almanack,* **Benjamin Franklin** advises colonial Ameri-
> cans against leisure activities, noting that "sloth" brings illness and short-
> ens life. **He** claims that only labor is truly satisfying. **He** warns that to be in
> debt is to fear the day when repayment must be made. **He** also says that
> the more you spend, the more you want. If **he** were around today, **the
> advocate of the spartan life** would surely advise contemporary Ameri-
> cans to increase their eight-hour work day, stop their credit-card buying
> sprees, and break their addiction to computer games and TV movies.

 ## ARRANGING SENTENCES

As a third major strategy of coherence, you can arrange sentences into
structural patterns; this usually includes placing parallel ideas into parallel
structures or organizing old and new information into proper sequences.

STRUCTURAL PATTERNS

Look for the possibility of arranging sentences into structural patterns
whenever you make parallel points. If, for instance, you have done some
research and concluded that in the 1960s pop music was shaped by radically different geographic and cultural influences, you might write a
paragraph like this:

> The 1960s brought to American pop music a fusion of radically different
> geographic and cultural influences. The influence of religion and mysticism
> which came from the East made popular such instruments as the tabla
> and sitar. A Caribbean influence was southern in origin, branching into
> such forms as reggae and calypso, with their steel drums and marimbas.
> But folk music, perhaps the most important influence on pop music at the

time, with its simple melodies and melodramatic lyrics, came from the
West, particularly from Britain and the American Midwest.

The paragraph has a clear topic sentence and contains interesting details,
but it also has ideas that lend themselves to a parallel structural arrangement. Since the separate influences all "came from" somewhere—the
East, the South, or the West—you could sharpen the relationship of the
details to the topic sentence if you organized the paragraph according to
geographic sources:

> The 1960s brought to American pop music a fusion of radically different
> geographic and cultural influences. **From the East came** the influence of
> religion and mysticism, which made popular such instruments as the tabla
> and sitar. **From the South came** the Caribbean influence, branching into
> such forms as reggae and calypso, with their steel drums and marimbas.
> **And from the West,** particularly from Britain and the American Midwest,
> **came** folk music, with its simple melodies and melodramatic lyrics, result-
> ing in perhaps the most important influence on pop music at the time.

If you read the paragraph out loud, you'll see that such patterning does
more than sharpen relationships. It moves a reader from sentence to sentence, guiding the journey from one idea to the next. Note that patterning does not mean mechanical repetition. The last phrase in this series
does not repeat the pattern exactly. It begins with **and** and is separated
from the verb **came** by the prepositional phrase **particularly from
Britain and the American Midwest.** Repeating the words **from the
. . . came** organizes the paragraph into a smooth flow of sentences.
Breaking the pattern in the last sentence helps to add interest and variety.
If you become pattern conscious, you are in a better position both to recognize the lack of coherence in your first drafts and to make effective
revisions.

OLD AND NEW INFORMATION

Readers expect a sentence in a sequence of prose to start where the previous one left off. That is, a sentence generally begins with "old" information, some reference to what has already been said. And then it moves
to "new" information, an idea that carries the thought further. So you
can create coherence by arranging information into the order a reader
expects: first old information (in the subject) then new information (in

the predicate). Read through the next paragraph to see what happens **149**
when you violate this principle:

> *Naked Came the Stranger* was probably the most interesting literary hoax
> of this century. Staff members of the newspaper *Newsday* wrote the
> chapters of the book independently, without knowledge of each other's
> work. It was intended as an incoherent pornographic novel, to be pub-
> lished under the pseudonym Penelope Ashe.

What happens when you violate this principle about old and new information is that you create a moment of uncertainty for the reader. The
first sentence presents *Naked Came the Stranger* as a literary hoax. The
reader expects that the second sentence will begin with either a reference
to the book or a reference to literary hoaxes. But the second sentence
does neither; it opens with a new topic, **staff members of the newspaper *Newsday*.** If you arrange the second sentence so that it begins with
old information, like **the chapters of the book,** you satisfy the reader's
expectations. In this paragraph, that arrangement of old and new information also creates a structural pattern of coherence with ***Naked
Came the Stranger* was. . . . The chapters of the book were. . . . It
was. . . .**

> ***Naked Came the Stranger* was** probably the most interesting literary
> hoax of this century. **The chapters of the book were** written indepen-
> dently by staff members of the newspaper *Newsday,* without knowledge
> of each other's work. **It was** intended as an incoherent pornographic
> novel, to be published under the pseudonym Penelope Ashe.

 ## CONNECTING PARAGRAPHS

To link one paragraph to another within a story or essay, you can use the
same strategies that link sentences within a paragraph. Just remember that
the indentation which marks a new paragraph has a tendency to create a
greater gap between paragraphs than exists between sentences within a
single paragraph. So you have to pay special attention in order to smooth
the transition from one paragraph to another.

For example, the second paragraph in the next passage originally
lacked a bridge to connect it to the first paragraph. Because it cites an

150   additional argument against capital punishment, the second paragraph
can begin with a connective like **furthermore:**

> Capital punishment complicates the administration of justice. It leads to
> lengthy trials and unjustified verdicts, and it places a burden on courts of
> appeal. It also forces taxpayers to support all those waiting their turn for
> execution on death row.
>
> **Furthermore,** the Eighth Amendment to the Constitution bars "cruel and
> unusual" punishment, and execution is surely both cruel and unusual.
> There is simply no humane way to kill people. Nor are gas chambers,
> electric chairs, or lethal injections "usual" causes of death.

In this case, the connective **furthermore** doesn't provide a strong enough
link between the paragraphs. The word implies that the second paragraph
will simply add some new evidence to the argument against capital punishment, probably on the same level of seriousness as the argument in the
first paragraph. In fact, what the second paragraph does is introduce a
much more complicated argument against capital punishment than the
fact that it inconveniences courts and taxpayers. The second paragraph
argues that capital punishment denies Americans their constitutional right
not to be punished in a cruel and unusual manner. Capital punishment
kills—unusually as well as cruelly—it notes. To move the reader from the
lighter to the weightier topic, you should probably try a more elaborate
transition that points out the difference between the topics in the two
paragraphs and that builds a stronger bridge between them as well:

> Capital punishment complicates the administration of justice. It leads to
> lengthy trials and unjustified verdicts, and it places a burden on courts of
> appeal. It also forces taxpayers to support all those waiting their turn for
> execution on death row.
>
> **But when a person's life is at stake, such inconveniences seem
> trivial. A far more fundamental objection to capital punishment is a
> constitutional one:** the Eighth Amendment to the Constitution bars
> "cruel and unusual" punishment, and execution is surely both cruel and
> unusual. There is simply no humane way to kill people. Nor are gas cham-
> bers, electric chairs, or lethal injections "usual" causes of death.

It took two sentences to bridge the gap here. The first notes how
trivial the inconveniences mentioned in the earlier paragraph are; the
second explicitly states that the topic of the new paragraph is **a far more**

fundamental objection. The two-sentence transition carefully guides   **151**
the reader across the large gap from one idea to the next.

 SUMMARY

The main point of this unit is that you have to pay attention to your writing in order to guide your readers from one sentence to the next and from one paragraph to another. When you provide the links between such structures, your writing has coherence. Strategies that can help you achieve coherence include the use of connectives and connective phrases; reference to a previously stated word or phase by repetition, synonyms, or pronouns; and the arrangement of sentences into patterns, including the proper ordering of old and new information. You can use these same strategies to help connect your paragraphs.

USING CONNECTIVES

Improve the coherence of each paragraph below either by inserting a common connective between sentences that lack bridges between them or by creating your own transitional phrase to bridge the gap. As an alternate assignment, revise a paragraph in a paper of your own to improve its coherence.

EXAMPLE

To ease the legal problems faced by couples involved in divorce, more than one half the states have passed laws accepting simple incompatibility as legitimate grounds for dissolving a marriage. No-fault divorce is proving to have unexpected disadvantages. It may be doing as much harm as good.

To ease the legal problems faced by couples involved in divorce, more than one half the states have passed laws accepting simple incompatibility as legitimate grounds for dissolving a marriage. **Yet** no-fault divorce is proving to have unexpected disadvantages. **In fact,** it may be doing as much harm as good.

OR

To ease the legal problems faced by couples involved in divorce, more than one half the states have passed laws accepting simple incompatibility as legitimate grounds for dissolving a marriage. **Like some other well-meant reforms,** no-fault divorce is proving to have unexpected disadvantages. **In some situations** it may be doing as much harm as good.

A. Rape clinics teach women various methods of self-defense. Panic-stricken women cannot always use this training in a real situation.

B. Most supermarkets are laid out in a manner designed to entice you to spend money on food and other items you didn't plan to buy. Smart shoppers can guard against the lure of the displays and spend their money wisely.

C. The clang, clang, clang of the trolley could be heard in every major city of the nation before World War II. After the war, people moved to the suburbs and built superhighways; electri-

cally powered vehicles were replaced by cars and buses. City **153**
planners are looking into the possibility of building new trolley
systems, because they are cheaper and cleaner than other forms
of mass transportation.

D.   The dolphin is an especially appealing animal—intelligent, playful, and altogether winsome. No one but a brute would desire
its extinction. Every time a large tuna boat makes its catch, hundreds of dolphins are killed. The U.S. government enforces strict
regulations against tuna fishermen. Many fishermen threaten to
join the fishing fleets of other nations less concerned about the
well-being of dolphins. Many have already gone. With every
fisherman's departure, the plight of the dolphin becomes more
desperate. If the American fleet is disbanded, U.S. regulations
will have no protective force, and the dolphin is doomed.

E.   If you've ever seen the giant panda, you know how closely it
resembles a bear. It is shaped like a bear—with massive body,
large head, and short, stubby legs. It is built like one—sometimes as long as 6 feet and as heavy as 300 pounds. It can stand
on its hind legs and use its sharp claws to climb trees. It walks on
the soles of its feet, just as bears do. Its harlequin outfit—the
basically creamy white body with black bursts on the ears, over
the eyes, around the chest and back, down the forelegs, and
along the hind legs—is the only trademark that recalls the panda's true relative, the raccoon.

WITH A DODO HERE AND A TURKEY THERE

Combine the following sentences into an explanatory essay about how scientists plan to use turkeys to help germinate the seeds of the nearly extinct
calvaria tree. Then, where necessary, improve the coherence between sentences by using the strategies of coherence discussed in this chapter.

1.   Scientists have long known [this].
2.   There are close interrelationships in nature.

3.   Scientists have only recently learned [this].
4.   The extinction of an animal may cause the death of a species of
plant.

5. Thirteen calvaria trees grow on the island of Mauritius.

6. The trees are beautiful and rare.

7. Mauritius is best known as the last refuge of the dodo bird.

8. The dodo bird was bulky and flightless.

9. Each of the over 300-year old trees is dying.

10. Not a single calvaria has sprouted in the last three centuries.

11. The dodo became extinct three centuries ago.

12. The calvaria seeds have thick shells.

13. Apparently no calvaria has sprouted [for this reason].

14. The calvaria seeds must be worn down in the digestive tract of the dodo.

15. Help for the calvaria may be on its way.

16. The help may be in the form of the domestic turkey.

17. Turkey gizzards contain stones for crushing food.

18. These stones are much like the stones in the gizzards of the dodo.

19. Scientists are now experimenting to see [this].

20. Can the tree survive with the help of the turkey?

USING REFERENCE

Improve the coherence of each paragraph below by using pronouns or synonyms for reference. Be sure to write out each paragraph. As an alternate assignment, revise a paragraph in a paper of your own to improve its coherence.

EXAMPLE

Dancing is a cultural universal. In many cultures, dancing helps define group identity and enhance morale. Dancing has a central place in festive or religious events, and dancing may be an important factor in **155** courtship.

↓

Dancing is a cultural universal. In many cultures, **it** helps define group identity and enhance morale. **It** also has a central place in festive or religious events and may be an important factor in courtship.

A. Chicago, at the southern tip of Lake Michigan, has spent a half century and billions of dollars developing a good water system. Chicago draws a billion gallons a day from the lake, to serve over five million people. But now that Chicago's lake water has become almost too dirty for treatment, Chicago may be forced to get water elsewhere—and pay more for it.

B. Patchwork quilts today are among the antiques increasing steadily in worth. Once common in every household, the quilts were treasured, too, by the pioneers who made the quilts. The quilts provided color and gaiety for the crude, drab pioneer cabins. The quilts' combination of small, various-shaped pieces in geometric designs made use of otherwise useless scraps of fabric. And, since many patchwork pieces were cut from old clothing, the quilts even provided a sense of continuity with the past.

C. An American company under government contract is often faced with the choice of buying American-made goods, which are expensive, or foreign-made goods, which are cheaper. If the American company buys American goods, the company may anger taxpayers by failing to keep prices low. But if the company buys foreign goods, the company may endanger the jobs of American workers. Confronting the issue, Congress passed a law compelling American companies with government contracts to give preference to American goods and services.

TOMBSTONES

Combine the following sentences into a brief essay that explains how tombstones tell us as much about the living as they do about the dead. Then, where necessary, improve the coherence between sentences by using the strategies of coherence discussed in this chapter.

1. Tombstones would seem to record only remembrances of the dead.

2. Tombstones are actually interpreters of the culture of the living.

3. The interpreters are highly eloquent.

4. Tombstones change over the centuries.

5. These changes clearly reflect changes in the values of the civilizations that created the tombstones.

6. The stones of colonial New England give solemn witness to the piety of our Puritan ancestors.

7. The stones are frequently adorned with a winged head.

8. The head depicts death.

9. Biographical facts are engraved on the stones.

10. These facts are often augmented with a warning to the passer-by of the inevitability of death.

11. The willow and urn motif testifies to the romanticism of the early nineteenth century.

12. The romanticism was more hopeful.

13. The romanticism came a few generations after the Puritans.

14. The romanticism showed a symbolic rendering of life out of death.

15. The Victorian preoccupation with material goods of this world is demonstrated.

16. The Victorian preoccupation is demonstrated by the tombstones and mausoleums of that period.

17. The tombstones and mausoleums are massive and ornate.

18. You can only wonder [this].

19. How will future generations interpret our own civilization?

20. They will interpret it when they consider the anonymity of grave markers that grace our modern "Memorial Parks."

21. The anonymity is flat and uniform.

22. The grave markers are row upon row.

23. The grave markers are mechanically perfect.

USING STRUCTURAL PATTERNS

Improve the coherence of each paragraph below by arranging sentences into structural patterns and/or by ordering old and new information. Be sure to write out each paragraph. As an alternate assignment, revise a paragraph in a paper of your own to improve its coherence.

EXAMPLE

> To become finalists in the competition for scholarships, the semifinalists must supply biographical information, maintain high academic standing, and perform well on a second examination. In addition, their high school principal must endorse them.

> To become finalists in the competition for scholarships, the semifinalists must supply biographical information, maintain high academic standing, perform well on a second examination. In addition, **they must earn the endorsement of their high school principal**.

A. For Northerners, Lincoln was a hero because he ended slavery and saved the Union. But because he destroyed one of the staples of the economy, Lincoln was regarded as a villain by Southerners.

B. Because they are produced when conscious controls are lowered, doodles reveal personality in much the same way dreams do. Psychologists at Michigan State University found that students who draw houses on their class notes yearn for security, while aggressive personalities draw sharp objects. Spiders, bugs, and mice are drawn by deeply troubled people. And if you have a "normal" personality, you are likely to draw pictures of domestic animals—dogs, cats, and horses.

C. The weather forecaster on the evening news may have all the latest information from radar and satellites to give an accurate forecast. Old-timers claim you can be accurate just by watching natural signs. For an indication of fair skies ahead, look for gnats swarming in the setting sun. Noisy woodpeckers signal rain on the way. When bubbles collect in the middle of your morning coffee, fair weather is coming. But it's time to look for an umbrella when the bubbles ring around the edge.

158   **GENE BLUES**

Read the following twenty-one sentences to get a sense of their meaning. Then, by (1) reordering sections A–D and (2) rearranging the sentences within each section, construct a coherent essay that explains why
the creation of new forms of life through gene transplants is frightening.

A. 1. Because the transplanted genes are accepted readily by the
        bacteria and are able to reproduce themselves in succeeding
        generations, the result of the transplant is a permanent new
        life form.

    2. No one knows how it would react to the environment out-
        side the laboratory or to humans and animals.

    3. These creations are a part of recombinant DNA research,
        which involves transplanting one or more foreign genes
        into loops of DNA in a bacteria.

    4. Its observable physical characteristics are all that is known
        about this new life.

B. 5. Perhaps scientists, who usually oppose public control of
        their research, have agreed so readily to those guidelines
        because they, too, fear the consequences of a mistake.

    6. But so little is known about the newly created organisms,
        how can the scientists know that the safeguards are adequate?

    7. And the safeguards do not apply to commercial companies
        like Eli Lilly and General Electric, which are also conduct-
        ing research in the field.

    8. In response to these fears, the National Institute of Health
        has offered a set of guidelines to ensure the safety of recom-
        binant DNA research.

    9. They cannot know whether the safeguards are accurate.

   10. One safeguard was a complete ban on transplanting cancer
        viruses.

   11. No such mistakes have been made yet, though perhaps one
        is the limit.

   12. Another safeguard required that only weakened *E. coli* bac-
        teria be used, so that they could not survive for long away
        from the lab.

C. 13.   Perhaps these creations could wreck the environment, eat-   **159**
         ing up chemicals or destroying the soil.

   14.   Some people are afraid that cancer viruses transplanted into
         bacteria could spread cancer.

   15.   And, since most of the experiments use the bacteria *E. coli,*
         which live in humans, a new combination could turn out
         to be highly infectious to humans.

   16.   They are afraid that a transplant between two completely
         different species, such as frogs and bacteria, could create
         new diseases to which humans would be susceptible.

   17.   Because of this uncertainty, fears have flared up.

D. 18.   No one knows what would happen if some of these organ-
         isms were to escape from the laboratory, but doubtless there
         is a risk of disease or death in humans.

   19.   Scientists are creating new forms of life, and these new
         creatures do not have spikes through their necks, like
         Frankenstein monsters.

   20.   These forms of life involve gene transplants and are locked
         away in research laboratories, hopefully in safekeeping.

   21.   Yet they may be more dangerous than any Frankenstein
         monster could ever be.

UNIT 10

REARRANGEMENT AND REPETITION FOR EMPHASIS

A skilled orator uses a variety of techniques to keep her audience interested and to emphasize her main ideas. She changes rhythms. She speaks louder or whispers. She pounds the lectern or stands motionless. She repeats key phrases and sentences. But writers can't pound the lectern or turn up the volume. What they can do is rearrange words and phrases and repeat structures in order to EMPHASIZE ideas as well as make their writing appealing and forceful.

 **REARRANGING**

When you REARRANGE for emphasis, you need to remember two important facts about word order in English. The first is that our word order is relatively fixed, with most sentences following a subject-verb-object (or complement) pattern. When you depart from this pattern, you change the meaning or emphasis within a sentence and can even change the **161** function of a sentence within a paragraph. The second basic fact is that the beginning and ending positions in a sentence play different roles. The beginning, which is the second most emphatic position, usually tells the reader what the sentence is about and in some way connects the sentence to what has been said before, to ensure continuity. The end of the sentence is the most emphatic position; this is where you usually place the most important word or phrase.

TAKING ADVANTAGE OF BEGINNINGS AND ENDINGS

In the sentence below, "Who's Whoooooo," the title of the tourist guide, occurs in the middle, where it receives little attention.

> The U.S. Travel Service now makes available to tourists **"Who's Whoooooo,"** a guide to haunted houses.

If you choose to emphasize the title of the guide, simply shift that phrase to the beginning or end of the sentence:

> **"Who's Whoooooo"**—it's a guide to haunted houses that the U.S.Travel Service now makes available to tourists.

OR

> The U.S. Travel Service now makes available to tourists a guide to haunted houses—**"Who's Whoooooo."**

What is true of the order of words within sentences is also true of the position of sentences within paragraphs. You can guide the reader's attention to your major points by placing the most important sentences in either the first or last positions. The next paragraph emphasizes that skateboarding is dangerous; notice how it underscores that point.

> Skateboarding may be the most exhilarating of all sports, but it's also the most dangerous. Apparently, the thrill comes from the speed—some champs do sixty-five miles per hour—and from the challenge posed by the unlimited possibilities for new stunts. Although few have tried stunts

162   like "pipe riding" or the "gorilla grip," in one recent year skateboarders suf-
fered over 130,000 injuries—twenty of them fatal. Enthusiasts insist that
what you do with skateboards has no limit. At least twenty of them
learned otherwise.

In the opening sentence, the word **dangerous** appears in the
emphatic end position as the climax of parallel phrases: **the most exhilarating . . . the most dangerous**. The danger is emphasized by the
short, crisp closing sentence. The final word—**otherwise**—acknowledges that death does set limits on skateboarding. The paragraph below
contains the same information but arranges the sentences to emphasize
that the dangers of skateboarding are less important than its exhilaration.
See if you can tell how it emphasizes the exhilaration rather than the
danger of skateboarding.

Although it may be the most dangerous sport, skateboarding is also the
most exhilarating. Injuries do occur—over 130, 000 in one recent year,
twenty of them fatal. But consider the thrill that comes from the speed—
some champs do sixty-five miles per hour—and from the challenge posed
by the unlimited possibilities for new stunts, like "pipe riding" and the
"gorilla grip." While some practitioners may inevitably perish in trying new
tricks, enthusiasts insist that what skateboards can do has no limit.

The paragraph begins to signal its emphasis in the first sentence,
which ends with the word **exhilarating.** Though the second sentence
acknowledges that injuries may occur, the connective **But** at the start
of the third sentence indicates that the thrills of skateboarding outweigh its dangers. Finally, the key statement **what skateboards can
do has no limit** occupies the paragraph's most emphatic position—its
end. When you control emphasis, you control meaning in sentences or
paragraphs.

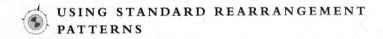

USING STANDARD REARRANGEMENT PATTERNS

Sometimes, standard rearrangement patterns can help you emphasize
your ideas. The first of these is the INTRODUCTORY WHAT pattern; by
inserting **what** and a form of **be**—either **is, was, are,** or **were**—into a

sentence along with rearranging some words, you can highlight the con-   **163**
trast between two sentences:

> After the last bunch of guys left the party, the house seemed unnaturally
> quiet. The argument when our parents came home was not so quiet.
>
> ↓
>
> After the last bunch of guys left the party, the house seemed unnaturally
> quiet. **What** was not so quiet **was** the argument when our parents came
> home.

Like the pattern with **what,** the INTRODUCTORY IT pattern, which
inserts **it** and a form of **be,** along with **who** or **that,** also highlights contrasts. Writing about a senator who had received more applause than the
President, you might say:

> The President was applauded enthusiastically, but the senator from Ten-
> nessee received the largest ovation.

But by using **it was . . . who,** you can suggest an even stronger contrast between the two ovations:

> The President was applauded enthusiastically, but **it was** the senator from
> Tennessee **who** received the largest ovation.

The PASSIVE is the most commonly used and probably the most commonly abused rearrangement pattern. To construct a passive from an
active sentence, move the object noun to the front, add a form of **be,** and
move the subject noun into a phrase with **by.** When you place the subject noun in a "by phrase," you emphasize its agency—its role in carrying
out the action of the verb:

> Congress approved the new federal budget.
>
>
>
> The new federal budget **was** approved **by Congress.**

Because it shifts the object noun phrase to the front of the sentence,
the passive can help you to control the flow of sentences in a paragraph as
well as to emphasize the agent in a sentence. Remember that the first
part of a sentence usually contains information linked to earlier sentences. The second sentence in the next example should have **the blast**

164 in the initial position, to link it with the subject of the first sentence, **a nasty explosion:**

> A nasty explosion rocked Lab B in the Science Building yesterday. A small jar of putric acid caused the blast.

You can correct the problem by making the second sentence into a passive:

> **A nasty explosion** rocked Lab B in the Science Building yesterday. **The blast** was caused by a small jar of putric acid.

You can sometimes omit the "by phrase" of a passive—especially when the "by phrase" contains information repeated elsewhere in your paper or commonly known by your readers. For instance, if your readers know that most people think of Einstein as the greatest mind of the twentieth century, you can eliminate that phrase and save three words, as in the next example:

> Most people call Einstein the greatest mind of the twentieth century.

> Einstein is called the greatest mind of the twentieth century **by most people.**

OR

> Einstein is called the greatest mind of the twentieth century.

Omitting the "by phrase" can help you tighten your sentences, but it can also lead to a common misuse of the passive—to hide the person who is responsible for actions. In the next example, the memo writer does not want to admit that her office is firing ten employees, so she couches the act in a passive and omits the agent:

> As of July 30, ten members of the design staff will be terminated **by the personnel office.**

> As of July 30, ten members of the design staff will be terminated.

Readers often feel cheated or manipulated when writers do not reveal the agent of an action. So be careful that you don't omit the "by phrase" unless your readers already know the information in it or unless leaving it out will not in any way "cheat" your readers.

BREAKING ESTABLISHED PATTERNS

As you write, you establish patterns that your readers come to expect. If you occasionally break these patterns, you can create emphasis in paragraphs and sentences. For example, following several long sentences, you can provide a striking and emphatic contrast by writing a short sentence or even a deliberate fragment:

> Legend has it that Robin Hood was a noble criminal leading a band of "Merry Men" who robbed from the rich and gave to the poor—loyal servants of King Richard unfairly pursued by the evil Sheriff of Nottingham. The historical Robin was a small-time mugger leading a band of crooks and drunks who robbed, raped, and swindled rich and poor alike. **Real criminals aren't noble!** (or **So much for legends!**)

You can achieve emphasis not only by disrupting your own writing patterns but also by departing from the basic sentence patterns of the language. In English, the subject-verb-object pattern is so common that readers tend to notice any departure from it. You can create emphasis either by changing the order of the words or by interrupting the normal movement of the sentence. One uncommon but effective option is placing a critical word or phrase at the beginning of a sentence. Notice how, by moving **Barcelona** to the front of the next example, you can make that word nearly shout at the reader.

> The very word "Barcelona" evokes images of a vibrant, tumultuous, exotic city.

> **"Barcelona"**—the very word evokes images of a vibrant, tumultuous, exotic city.

The fronted word may be set off with a dash—as above—or with punctuation marks like ellipses, exclamation points, and colons. Sometimes you can front a verb, along with an adverb like **only** and **first,** or a negative like **nowhere, not until,** or **never:**

> The governor came first, then her economic advisors.

> **First came** the governor, then her economic advisors.

166   When you interrupt a sentence with a word, phrase or clause, you emphasize the interrupting element and what immediately follows it.

> Amnesty International—**now more than 200,000 strong**—uses the force of public opinion to combat the violation of human rights worldwide.

Interrupting one sentence with another sentence can be especially striking:

> A number of major corporations encourage their employees to exercise at lunchtime. Exxon, AT&T, and Johnson & Johnson are a few of these corporations.

> A number of major corporations—**Exxon, AT&T, and Johnson & Johnson are a few**—encourage their employees to exercise at lunchtime.

Rearrangement will work best if you don't overuse it. Your use of rearrangement should be justified by a need for proper emphasis or to control the movement from one sentence to another.

 REPETITION

Advertisers deliberately repeat words and phrases in order to drive home a message to potential customers. *Mademoiselle* calls itself "the magazine more **select** women **select**." Jif peanut butter asserts that "**choosy** mothers **choose** Jif." Lexus emphasizes that its interior is designed for drivers who can afford luxury when it states, "To those who have taken **the opportunity to** advance, we offer **the opportunity to** retreat." Sometimes the words and phrases are not repeated exactly but only balanced to correspond in rhythm and structure. So a record company claims that "Gospel music is **good news** in **bad times**" and Parker Brothers touts Othello as a board game that "takes only **a minute to learn** but a **lifetime to master**." The strategies of REPETITION that work in advertising copy can work just as well in order to help you achieve emphasis and produce pleasing, dynamic writing.

You can use repetition to emphasize key terms in sentences. The next sentence states matter-of-factly grandfather's condition before he died:

My grandfather had nothing left except memories before he died.

Repeating the word **nothing** makes grandfather's condition much more poignant:

My grandfather had **nothing** left before he died, **nothing** except memories.

Repetition can emphasize, and it can direct the reader's attention to important contrasts. In the next sentence, you can strengthen the contrast between Sally's loafing **in the sun** and her friends' working **on the job** by repeating **spent long hot days:**

While all Sally's friends spent **long hot days on the job,** she **spent long hot days in the sun,** soaking up a tan.

Sometimes you can omit words and phrases in repeated constructions in order to produce more concise, harder hitting statements:

Some lawyers are arrogant, **and** some **lawyers are** simply reserved.

Some lawyers are arrogant, some simply reserved.

When you revise, look for places where you can use repetition and balance to achieve emphasis or to reinforce a contrast. The following two sentences can be made into a far stronger and more concise single sentence by changing **other students drink beer** into **for others** in order to contrast that phrase with **for some students:**

Beer drinking has become a way of life for some students. And other students drink beer in order to escape.

Beer drinking has become a way of life **for some students** and a means of escape **for others.**

In the next pair of sentences, the writer missed the opportunity to produce a contrasting pair of infinitive phrases that would have reinforced her point:

Do you believe that children are immune to constantly repeated violence? If you do, you are ignoring the most basic principles of developmental psychology.

To believe that children are immune to constantly repeated violence is **to ignore** the most basic principles of developmental psychology.

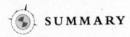 SUMMARY

This unit teaches you how to use rearrangement and repetition in order to make your writing appealing as well as forceful. You can emphasize words and phrases if you move them to the beginnings or endings of sentences or if you use them to interrupt normal sentence order. The same is true of sentences within paragraphs. You can sometimes achieve emphasis through standard rearrangement patterns like the introductory **it,** the introductory **what,** or the passive. Besides taking advantage of emphatic positions and standard patterns, you can highlight ideas through repetition and balance. Experiment with rearrangement and repetition to make your papers more compelling and dynamic.

REARRANGEMENT AND REPETITION WITHIN SENTENCES

A word or phrase in each of the sentences below can be made more emphatic if you rearrange the sentences to take advantage of sentence positions or repetition. Rearrange the sentences as indicated by the suggestions in parentheses.

EXAMPLE

International economics since World War II has become too complex for any single theory to explain or for any single government to control. [Emphasize the phrase "since World War II" by rearrangement.]

Since World War II, international economics has become too complex for any single theory to explain or for any single government to control.

A. Gourmet cooks and health-food nuts ignore Shakespeare's warning that onions and garlic destroy "sweet breath." [Emphasize the agency of "gourmet cooks and health-food nuts" with a passive sentence.]

B. Cincinnati is blessed with more than its share of good restaurants, and it is blessed with less than its share of smut. [Emphasize the contrast between "good restaurants" and "smut" with a balanced construction.]

C. Alfred Nobel hoped to be remembered for his peace prize, not his invention of dynamite. [Emphasize Nobel's hope with an introductory "what" pattern.]

D. Alan Shephard, Jr. was the first American in space, and he also was the one to hit a golf ball on the moon for the first time. [Emphasize the contrast between hitting a golf ball and being the first in space with a balanced structure.]

E. Many readers enjoy the misadventures of the disreputable Bill the Cat. The beguiling penguin Opus functions as the central character in the comic strip *Outland*. [Emphasize "the beguiling penguin" as the "central character" with an introductory "it" pattern in the second sentence.]

F. Freud would have remained in Vienna had not the Nazis forced him to leave, much against his desires. [By interrupting the sentence with the final phrase, emphasize how much leaving was against Freud's desires.]

G. There doesn't seem to be enough fresh air around anymore. [Highlight "fresh air" by shifting that phrase to the front of the sentence.]

H. A vampire bat's digestive system is so specialized that it can't consume anything but blood. They have superefficient kidneys, for instance. [Interrupt the first sentence with the second in order to emphasize the specialization of the vampire bat's digestive system.]

I. In the 1920s, entering a beauty pageant was considered a risqué break with social conventions. In the 1990s, many women consider entering a beauty pageant to be a demeaning experience. [By making the second sentence passive, to balance the first sentence, emphasize how demeaning some women feel beauty pageants to be.]

J. First-year psychology students were given a choice between writing a term paper and participating in experiments that involved electric-shock machines. That was some choice they were given. [Highlight the dilemma of the students' "choice" by making the last sentence an emphatic fragment.]

BLIND DATE

Make the following sentences into a humorous essay. Rearrange sentences and paragraphs, whenever appropriate, in order to emphasize that the young man judges too easily on appearances. Not every sentence can be rearranged; you'll be able to make some sentences into structures you've studied in other chapters. Add details of your own to highlight important points.

1. The well-dressed young man held his finger on the front door bell for ten seconds or more.

2. He stopped only when he heard steps.

3. They were clop, clop, clopping down stairs.

4. The door opened.

5. The open door revealed a hippopotamus of a woman in a terry cloth bathrobe.

6. Her hair was in a towel.

7. There was a small puddle of water beneath her, where she had dripped.

8. The surprised young man brushed his jacket with his hand.

9. Then he said,

10. "I'm Larry Baldwin. I'm here to pick up Rose Ann."

11. The woman mumbled something and turned her huge frame.

12. She pointed toward a couch in the living room.

13. Larry made a place for himself.

14. He picked up sections of the morning paper that lay strewn across the couch.

15. He folded the paper neatly.

16. Then he placed it atop a pile of magazines on the floor next to the coffee table.

17. The woman stared while Larry straightened the pile.

18. He was oblivious to her.

19. He stopped when this happened.

20. He heard the clop, clop, clop of wooden clogs on the stairs.

21. He thought, "Good grief, what did I get myself into?"

22. "Would Rose Ann be fat like her mother?"

23. "And would she be untidy like this house?"

24. But the click of heels descending the stairs startled him into awareness.

25. He turned quickly to see a slender young woman.

26. She had bright, dancing eyes.

27. She was beautiful.

28. She was in a yellow sundress.

29. Larry nearly jumped from the couch.

30. He hit his knee on the coffee table.

31. And he stuttered.

32. "Hi, I'm L- L- L-"

33. He was unable to finish his name.

34. Rose Ann replied.

35. "Yes, I know. You're Larry."

36. "Susan told me about you."

37. She reached over to pick some lint from his jacket.

REVISING SENTENCES FOR EMPHASIS AND FOCUS

In each of the following paragraphs, rearrange the sentence in brackets in order to emphasize an important point, to sharpen paragraph focus, or to establish sentence flow.

EXAMPLE

At the beginning of the twentieth century, the United States yearned to be a global power, which in those days meant having a large navy. But the U.S. Navy was divided into two fleets, one on the East Coast, one on the West. [The completion of the Panama Canal allowed the nation to fulfill its dream.] By linking the two oceans, the canal made the separate fleets into one great navy.

At the beginning of the twentieth century, the United States yearned to be a global power, which in those days meant having a large navy. But the U.S. Navy was divided into two fleets, one on the East Coast, one on the

West. **It was** the completion of the Panama Canal **that** allowed the nation   **173**
to fulfill its dream. By linking the two oceans, the canal made the separate
fleets into one great navy.

A.   [Even the word "hiccup" is funny.] It imitates the silly sound
     you make when air bounces up and down inside you as if it's on
     a trampoline. But hiccups are funniest when someone else has
     them—right?

B.   Elias Howe is given credit for inventing the sewing machine.
     [But Isaac Singer made it the most popular machine in histo-
     ry.] With his partner, Edward Clark, Singer developed the
     marketing techniques of buying on installment and trade-ins.
     He also overcame the nineteenth century prejudice that
     allowing women to operate machines violated the laws of
     nature.

C.   The gondolas of hot-air racing balloons are equipped with con-
     trols that allow balloonists to change the altitude and direction
     of their craft—but not the speed, which is determined by air
     currents. [Accuracy counts in balloon racing. Speed does not
     count.] Victory belongs to the balloonist who lands closest to
     the target.

MARILYN

Using rearrangement wherever appropriate, combine the sentences
below into an essay that explains why Marilyn Monroe was a tragic figure who still fascinates the public. Not every sentence can be rearranged;
you'll be able to make some sentences into structures you've studied in
other chapters.

1.   The name "Marilyn" still evokes magic for moviegoers.

2.   Marilyn Monroe has lost none of her power to move us.

3.   Marilyn Monroe has lost none of her power to intrigue us.

4.   Marilyn Monroe has lost none of her power to disturb us.

5.   She does this more than thirty years after her death.

6.   Her biography might have been written by Dickens.

7. As a child, she was abandoned by her parents.

8. And she grew up in an orphanage and foster care.

9. She rose to meteoric success as an actress.

10. She became the symbol of the blonde movie goddess of the 1950s.

11. She was innocent, yet she was seductive.

12. But fame and fortune never made her happy.

13. She wanted to be known for her talent and intelligence.

14. She did not want to be known for her body.

15. She went through two disastrous marriages.

16. One was with ballplayer Joe DiMaggio.

17. One was with playwright Arthur Miller.

18. And she supposedly had a romance with John Kennedy.

19. And she supposedly had a romance with Robert Kennedy.

20. She died in her apartment.

21. Apparently, she was a suicide.

22. Some fans and friends still claim [this].

23. She was killed by the CIA in order to erase her connections to the Kennedys.

REVISING FOR PARAGRAPH EMPHASIS

Revise each of the three paragraphs below to make the material printed in boldface more emphatic.

EXAMPLE

It wasn't supposed to happen. But while everyone turned the other way, thousands of small towns across the country **stopped dying,** and thus quietly turned around what was supposed to be an "irreversible" population trend. What's more, the "boondocks" are growing twice as fast as metropolitan areas and, for the first time since frontier days, beginning to wield political and economic influence.

↓

The "boondocks" stopped dying. It wasn't supposed to happen. But while everyone turned the other way, an **"irreversible"** population trend **reversed.** Small towns across the country are growing twice as fast as metropolitan areas and, for the first time since frontier days, beginning to wield political and economic influence.

A. For a long time, **but not anymore,** Japanese corporations used Southeast Asia merely as a cheap resource for raw materials and as a training ground for junior executives who needed minor-league experience. Now Japan has moved significant manufacturing facilities to countries like Thailand and Malaysia. Japan has learned that Western countries that have turned their backs on merchandise labeled "Made in Japan" will willingly accept goods from underdeveloped countries in Southeast Asia.

B. We are so used to blaming modern industrial growth for the destruction of the natural environment that we sometimes overlook the damage done by less sophisticated means. **Unchecked industrial growth may pollute the air, but the land is being ravaged by herd management that is unscientific.** Every year, cattle and sheep farmers in nonindustrial societies turn nearly seventeen million acres of land into desert by overgrazing. This process of "desertification" has destroyed three-fourths of the forest land in Argentina in fifty years, and in western India in a single decade one-third of the arable land has been destroyed.

C. According to comedian George Carlin, **football is a ruthless, warlike game, but baseball is a warm and pastoral game.** Football, for example, is played on the gridiron, but baseball is a game that is played on a field. A defensive football player tackles his opponent, but in baseball, an opponent is only tagged by a defensive player. A violation in football draws a penalty, but a mistake is merely an error in baseball. A football team can score on a bomb, but on a sacrifice a baseball team can score. And, of course, the object of football is to break through to the end zone, while in baseball to run safely home is the idea.

WORDS AND THINGS

Using rearrangement wherever appropriate, combine the sentences below into an essay that explains how words may originate. Not every sentence can be rearranged; you'll be able to make some sentences into structures you've studied in other chapters.

1. A language is like a biological system.
2. Its various parts are constantly adapting to new situations.

3. Words are the part of the system to study.
4. Words are the most interesting part.

5. Words are the cells of language.
6. They are forming.
7. They are dying.
8. They are splitting up into parts.

9. Words originate in all sorts of ways.
10. Some seem to have been made up purely for the way they sound.
11. Some words were originally the names of people or even towns.
12. These are like *sandwich* and *hamburger.*

13. The Earl of Sandwich didn't like to interrupt his gambling with meals.
14. So he had his servants slap some meat between two slices of bread.
15. It was a handy snack at the gaming table.

16. Thus the earl became immortal.
17. He gave his name to our favorite food.

18. *Hamburger* took its name from the city that originally made it famous.
19. The city was Hamburg, Germany.
20. The hamburger is the world's most famous sandwich.

21.   It is never called a sandwich anymore.   **177**

22.   The *burger* part of the word now means any kind of ground meat in a bun.

23.   So we are inundated with various kinds of burgers.

24.   We are inundated with *beefburgers.*

25.   We are inundated with *venisonburgers.*

26.   We are inundated with *steakburgers.*

27.   We are inundated with *doubleburgers.*

28.   We are inundated with *cheeseburgers.*

29.   And we are even inundated with *pizzaburgers.*

30.   As long as the language is alive, its cells will continue to change.

31.   The cells of the language are its words.

32.   The cells will form.

33.   The cells will die.

34.   The cells will break up into parts to start the process again.

U N I T   1 1

TONE

Let's suppose you witnessed some students cheating during an exam. Afterward, you write a letter to your best friend, who is at school in a different state. You start the letter by saying, "These jerks are going to ruin the curve, and my grade will go right into the john. They had crib sheets up their sleeves, if you can believe that stupidity." Then your professor calls you and asks you to write her a report about what you saw. Your report begins, "During the final examination on December 11, I observed two students apparently consulting handwritten notes concealed in their shirt sleeves."

We could say your "tone" in each of these pieces of writing is different. Tone is the aspect of the writer that readers can hear as they read. You generally change your tone according to whom you're writing for, what you hope to accomplish in the writing, and how you feel about what you're writing.

In the letter to your friend, your tone is informal and angry. With such a familiar audience, you're comfortable using slang and letting your emotions out. You're probably interested in making your friend understand your anger and evoking sympathy for your situation. After all, you're irate about the topic. In your report to the professor, however, your tone is more formal, since you don't know the professor very well, and you recognize that she is a powerful person. Your objective is to provide her with the information she has requested, so you control the

anger, provide concrete details, and choose longer words. The two situations are quite different—and so is your tone in each.

TONE IN SENTENCES

Writing effectively requires you to control your tone by carefully selecting words, structuring sentences, and choosing details to make them
consistent with one another and with the purpose of your writing. Suppose, for example, you are writing a paragraph or brief essay on the
increased sales of vitamin E. In your opening sentence, you intend to
include these two facts:

> The sales of vitamin E have doubled in the past eight years.
>
> The increase in sales has been helped by statements from health-food
> enthusiasts and doctors.

You might put these facts together into a sentence like this:

> The sales of vitamin E, thanks to statements from health-food enthusiasts
> and doctors, have doubled in the past eight years.

This sentence sounds impartial and doesn't reveal your attitude
toward the increased sales of the vitamin E. If you began with such a sentence, you reader would not know, at least at first, whether you thought
the American public was wise or foolish in doubling its consumption of
the vitamin. Of course, there's nothing wrong with sounding impartial. If
your purpose is simply to inform your readers, it might be appropriate to
write an impartial-sounding sentence.

CONTROLLING TONE

But let's suppose you have decided to write an essay for your health class
critical of the American public's gullibility in flocking to "miracle cures."

180   Because it sounds neutral, the sentence above really wouldn't help you achieve that objective.

If you know your purpose (to criticize certain behavior) and know who your readers will be (members of your health class), you can probably find the tone you need in a piece of writing; you can adjust your tone in the sentence to make it negative:

> The sales of vitamin E, thanks to the claims of health-food enthusiasts **promoting "miracle" cures** and doctors **pushing "alternative" treatments,** have doubled in the past eight years.

Or you can make the sentence even more negative. In the next example, the phrases **deceptions and lies**, **health-food faddists**, and **medical quacks** let your readers know exactly where you stand and give your sentence a harsh, negative tone:

> The sales of vitamin E, thanks to the **deceptions and lies** of health-food **faddists** and **medical quacks,** have doubled in the past eight years.

The harsh tone in the sentence would be especially appropriate for readers who share your negative attitudes toward vitamin E. But for readers who don't start out on your side—and perhaps there are some in your health class—the sentence may sound too strong, too opinionated, perhaps even biased. If so, you may try to *suggest* your feelings instead of stating them harshly. You can create a strongly negative tone without sounding as harsh by changing the diction:

> The sales of vitamin E, thanks to the **claims** of **a few health-food enthusiasts** and **well-meaning doctors,** have doubled in the past eight years.

Let's suppose, however, that the more you research this topic, the more convinced you become that vitamin E deserves its wondrous reputation, leading you to change your mind about the purpose of the essay. So you now wish to praise vitamin E. With such changes in your attitude and purpose for writing, your tone will certainly change as well.

By choosing words and details with more positive associations, you can rewrite the sentence about increased vitamin E sales to sound very different:

> The sales of vitamin E, thanks to statements from health-food **experts** and doctors, have doubled in the past eight years.

OR

The sales of vitamin E, thanks to **reports** from health-food experts and doctors, have doubled in the past eight years.

OR

The sales of vitamin E, thanks to the **testimony** of health-food experts and doctors, have doubled in the past eight years.

Because **experts** seem more trustworthy than simple **enthusiasts,** and because both **reports** and **testimony** carry more weight than mere **statements,** the three sentences above have a more positive tone than the original, more neutral version. But you can go even further in creating an approving tone by making the doctors who support vitamin E seem more prestigious:

The sales of vitamin E, helped by the testimony of health-food experts and leading **medical authorities,** have doubled in the past eight years.

This is an even more powerful endorsement of vitamin E because **medical authorities** sound as if they are more knowledgeable and important than **doctors.**

 SENTENCE STRUCTURE

So far in every example the basic sentence structure has been the same ("The sales of vitamin E . . . have doubled in the past eight years"), and the tone has been changed by replacing some important words. But you can also control your tone by changing the structure of your sentences, moving important ideas to more prominent positions. Let's take one more look at the bluntly worded sentence above:

The sales of vitamin E, thanks to the **deceptions and lies** of health-food **faddists** and **medical quacks,** have doubled in the past eight years.

You can make the tone seem more negative by moving the phrase about the deceptive behavior of health-food faddists and medical quacks to the end of the sentence, where it becomes more emphatic:

182   In the past eight years, the sales of vitamin E have doubled, thanks to **the deception and lies of health-food faddists and medical quacks.**

Or you can also emphasize the deceptive behavior of health-food faddists by placing the phrase at the beginning of the sentence and setting if off with a dash to call more attention to the deception and lies:

The deception and lies of health-food faddists and medical quacks—that's what has helped double the sales of vitamin E in the past eight years.

The tone in both of these sentences sounds angrier because of the careful use of sentence structure.

 FORMAL AND INFORMAL TONE

The tone in the previous sentences about vitamin E ranges from negative to positive, but the sentences are alike in that each is formal, serious, and relatively impersonal. Sometimes the writing situation calls for a more informal, more personal tone. If you want to make the sentence less formal and more personal, you have a number of options. The simplest way to personalize your tone is to introduce yourself into the sentence as **I:**

I find it hard to believe, but the sales of vitamin E, spurred on by the claims of health-food faddists **and medical quacks,** have doubled in the past eight years.

You can also make the sentence informal if you establish a relationship between yourself and the reader. One way of relating to your reader is to ask a question:

Why have the sales of vitamin E doubled in the past eight years? Largely because of the claims of health-food faddists **and medical quacks.**

OR

Who is responsible for the skyrocketing sales of vitamin E over the past eight years? Mainly health-food faddists and medical quacks.

An even more direct way of relating to readers is by addressing them as **183**
you:

> **You** may be surprised to learn that over the past eight years the sales of
> vitamin E have doubled, in large part because of the claims of health-food
> faddists and medical quacks.

> OR

> Did **you** know that, thanks to the claims of health-food faddists and med-
> ical quacks, the sales of vitamin E have doubled in the past eight years?

The informality of your writing will usually be increased by contrac-
tions, slang, and short, simple words instead of longer, more complex
ones. Informal writing often includes exclamations, deliberate sentence
fragments, and short rather than long sentences:

> **It's** hard to believe, but **it's** true. In just eight short years, the sales of vit-
> amin E have doubled! Why? Because-health food **buffs and quack doc-
> tors** have been telling people that **it's** good for their health.

> OR

> This may surprise you, but twice as much vitamin E is sold today as eight
> years ago. **Twice as much!** And **I'll** tell you why. It's because people have
> **swallowed** what some natural-food **fans and quack doctors** have told
> them.

The more informal your writing becomes, the more your tone will
sound as if you're speaking. Whether you want to give your writing an
informal or a more formal tone depends on who your readers are, what
your purpose is in writing to them, and how you feel about your subject.

 TONE IN PARAGRAPHS

Paragraphs provide even more options for creating tone than sentences.
Here's an impartial-sounding paragraph about recent events in astronomy:

> Several astronomers feel that it is time for the U. S. government to create
> an outer space early warning system to detect large asteroids before they
> collide with Earth. Astronomers estimate a 1-in-10,000 chance that an

asteroid large enough to end civilization will strike during the next fifty years. A 2.5-mile-wide asteroid named Toutatis orbited within 2.2 million miles of the planet in 1992. Another space rock large enough to be seen on earthbound telescopes passed by later that same year. The smaller of the two was still big enough to destroy a major city, while the larger one could have easily put an end to human life on Earth in much the same way a collision with an asteroid may have led to the dinosaurs' extinction. The purpose of the early detection system would be to alert the government in time to launch rockets with atomic devices to destroy or at least deflect the invading asteroid. It is not certain, however, if any system could have sufficient accuracy to detect a potential collision early enough to allow time for a rocket launch; both near-misses in 1992 were discovered only after the asteroids had passed by. Nevertheless, the astronomers feel it is time for some action to be taken.

This is the kind of paragraph that would be written by a journalist who was supposed to report the facts and not really express her personality in the writing. It doesn't indicate, through its word choice, sentence structure, or selection of details, either approval or disapproval of the astronomers' proposal. But the paragraph does suggest, especially through its formal wording and complete absence of humor, that the situation is important enough to be taken seriously by the reader.

The same paragraph can be rewritten to make it less serious and more playful, to create a tone of amusement, to poke fun at these alarmist astronomers:

Some worrywart astronomers feel it is time for the U.S. government to create an outer space early warning system to detect large asteroids before they smash our little old planet to smithereens. After all, they estimate a 1-in-10,000 chance that an asteroid large enough to end civilization will strike during the next fifty years. (Don't hold your breath waiting for that one.) One big bruiser of an asteroid whizzed by within a measly 2.2 million miles of the planet in 1992—to a lonely astronomer, that's the equivalent of a slow dance in terms of distance. Another piece of space debris large enough to be seen on earthbound telescopes—about the size of TV's Roseanne and Dan Connor doing that slow dance—scooted past later that same year. The smaller of the two—Roseanne and Dan—was still big enough to destroy a major city, while the larger one could have easily made humans the dinosaurs of the 90s—fossil city in an instant. The purpose of the early detection system would be to alert our government to launch rockets with atomic bombs—sort of paranoid welcome wagons—

which would surely blow up the space invaders or at least discourage **185**
them. Not! Because no one is certain we can build any system accurate
enough to detect a potential collision in time to launch the rockets. "By the
way," they tell us, "we noticed those near-misses in 1992 only after the
asteroids had passed by." Oh, great. Like getting onto the dance floor
while the band is taking its break. Thanks for the terrific idea, guys!

The revised paragraph has a satirical tone because, obviously, the writer
does not want readers to take the situation seriously. The scientists are
now described as **some worrywart astronomers,** making it seem as if
they are few in number and slightly out of control of their emotions. The
asteroids **whizzed by** and **scooted past,** informal language that minimizes the seriousness of their passage. Serious comparisons are reduced
to jokes to diminish the importance of the subject—notice the reference
to **lonely astronomers** and **a slow dance** and to the extinction of the
human race as **fossil city in an instant.** The 2.5-mile-wide asteroid is
made less threatening when it is called a **big bruiser,** and the 2.2 million
miles is described as **measly,** showing how little danger there really was.
The comparisons to TV's Roseanne further belittle the seriousness of the
astronomers' concerns. Less formal sentence structure makes the paragraph more conversational too (notice the sentence fragment **Not!**). The
phrasing itself is consistently informal as well, from the early parentheti-
cal comment **Don't hold your breath** to the final sentence, which
undermines all respect for the astronomers by referring to them as **guys.**
Clearly, readers have little to worry about; it's time for a smile and a
chuckle at someone else's expense.

Of course, it's quite possible to view the destruction of our planet as
a matter of great concern. In that case, rather than poking fun by creating a satirical tone, the writer would want to be more formal and add
details that make clear the seriousness of the situation, as in the next paragraph:

A number of concerned astronomers argue that it is time for the U.S. government to take action and create an outer space early warning system to
detect large asteroids before they collide with Earth. They estimate a 1-in-
10,000 chance that an asteroid large enough to end civilization will strike
during our lifetimes. In 1992, Toutatis, a 2.5-mile-wide asteroid skimmed
closer to the earth than our nearest planetary neighbor. Another piece of
space debris large enough to be seen on earthbound telescopes passed
by later that same year. The smaller of the two was 100 yards wide, massive enough to destroy a city the size of Cleveland, while the larger one

could have easily extinguished human life on Earth in much the same way a collision with an asteroid ended the 65-million-year reign of earth's most successful animals: the dinosaurs. The astronomers' hope for the early detection system is that it would alert the government in time to launch rockets with atomic devices to destroy or at least deflect the alien intruders. Unfortunately, they cannot be certain that a detection system will have sufficient accuracy to detect a potential collision early enough to allow time for a preventive launch. Both near-misses in 1992 were discovered only after the asteroids had threatened our planet and passed by. Still, now is the time to begin searching for solutions to the potential threat posed by our neighbors in space.

There is nothing amusing or satirical in this paragraph; in fact, the writer's tone has become quite serious. Notice how the writer describes the astronomers in such a way as to sound as if there is strong support for this view by respectable scientists: **a number of concerned astronomers.** Their position is a stronger one as they now **argue** rather than **feel.** The writer also uses more vivid words to convey the degree of danger for our planet: the asteroids **skimmed** the earth, suggesting that they came very near; the smaller asteroid was still **massive,** suggesting great weight and size; human life might have been **extinguished,** suggesting death; the asteroids **threatened** the earth, suggesting grave risk; these threatening asteroids are **neighbors,** suggesting their nearness. The writer has also added details to heighten the sense of importance of the astronomers' concern by suggesting that a collision might occur during the reader's lifetime, by naming a familiar city that the smaller asteroid might have destroyed, by showing how close the asteroid came to Earth, and by emphasizing that even the long reign of the dinosaurs came to an abrupt end after an asteroid collision. The writer also chooses to emphasize the need for action at the end of the paragraph rather than the uncertainty of developing a successful solution to the problem.

The following paragraph has yet another tone, an angry tone. This writer mistrusts the astronomers, whose poorly thought out response overlooks other important issues.

A few panic-stricken astronomers feel it is time for the U.S. government to create an outer space early warning system to detect large asteroids before they collide with Earth. They estimate a 1-in-10,000 chance that an asteroid large enough to end civilization will strike during the next fifty years. Of course, it isn't the earth they want to save; it's their own skins,

whatever the cost. Evidently, two asteroids sailed by the earth in 1992, **187**
both large enough and close enough to cause grave concern. The purpose of the early detection system would be to alert our government in
time to launch rockets with atomic devices to destroy or at least deflect
any alien visitor. But no one is certain about the effects of atomic detona-
tions in outer space. Would the explosions cause damage to the Earth? If
they did destroy these asteroids, what damage would the debris cause?
Not only have the astronomers ignored these issues, they also cannot be
sure whether any system could be accurate enough to detect a potential
collision in time for a preventive launch; both asteroids in 1992, after all,
were discovered only after they had passed by. And, of course, the
astronomers assume that the United States needs to police the galaxy.
This kind of ill-conceived alarmist reaction serves no useful purpose,
promising only to gamble with taxpayers' money and perhaps worsen the
situation the scientists hope to address.

This writer wants to minimize the threat of collision, not to poke fun at
it but to raise some other issues of importance. The paragraph begins by
criticizing the astronomers (**panic-stricken astronomers**) and by making them seem to be in a minority (**a few** rather than **several** or **a number of**). The writer wants to diminish the threat posed by the asteroids,
describing them as having **sailed by,** suggesting that they weren't very
close. Notice that the details about the damage they might have caused is
referred to in a very general way (**both large enough and close
enough to cause grave concern**). The writer wants to emphasize
other considerations and stresses the potential cost to the environment
and to taxpayers; the anger is clear in the belittling comment about the
astronomers' motivations: **saving their own skins, whatever the
cost.** The unlikelihood of such a collision is suggested in the phrase
gamble with taxpayers' money. Even the expertise of the
astronomers is questioned in the bitter use of **after all** and **only** to
describe their inability to find threatening asteroids before they pose a
threat. The writer also uses questions but provides no answers, suggesting the shortcomings of the astronomers' views.

These four paragraphs on potential threats to the earth illustrate some
of your options for changing tone. In each case, the tone was different
because the writer's purpose, sense of audience, and attitude toward the
subject was different. The writer might have changed the paragraph
again into still another tone if she were to write to a new group of readers with a new purpose in mind. You'll also find that you can change
tone to suit your own purpose in writing.

 **188** **SUMMARY**

In this unit, you learned about tone, the aspect of a writer which readers can hear as they read. Writers must select words, structure sentences, and choose details to make their tone consistent with their purpose, their readers' expectations, and their own attitudes toward their subject matter. Since all writers can use many tones, they must learn to control the tone in their writing. In the series of sentences about vitamin E, you learned how a writer can change tone by using different words and altering sentence structure. In the series of paragraphs about asteroids passing near the earth, you observed how a writer can use word choice, sentence patterns, and details to change the tone of the writing. In the exercises that follow, you will have an opportunity to practice creating and controlling that valuable tool of the writer—tone.

CONTROLLING AND CREATING TONE

Each of the following paragraphs has a particular tone. By using different words, reconstructing sentences, adding and omitting details, or making any other changes, rewrite each paragraph to give it the tone suggested by the directions.

EXAMPLE

"Lennonizing," the **ruthless and tasteless exploitation** of Beatle John Lennon's death for the sale of records, books, and mementos, became a **lucrative** industry overnight. It inspired such **quickie** song tributes as "We Won't Say Goodbye, John" and "Elegy for the Walrus." Book publishers **cashed in on the bonanza** with **instant masterpieces** like *John Lennon: Death of a Dream,* published within days of—**but written weeks or months before?**—Lennon's assassination. Even the *National Enquirer* **got into the morbid act** by publishing—**with its usual vulgar taste**—a four-color photograph of John Lennon at the morgue. [Rewrite the paragraph to create a friendlier tone.]

"Lennonizing," the **commemoration** of Beatle John Lennon's death by the sale of records, books, and mementos, became a **popular** industry overnight. It inspired such **spontaneous** song tributes as "We Won't Say Goodbye, John" and "Elegy for the Walrus." It **prompted** book publishers **to respond immediately** with **biographies** like *John Lennon: Death of a Dream,* published within days of—**though evidently researched weeks or months before**—Lennon's assassination. And even the *National Enquirer* **paid its tribute** by publishing a four-color photograph of John Lennon's body **as mourners said their last farewells** at the morgue.

A. An inability to spell could cost you your self-respect. Scientists believe that spelling ability has little to do with basic intelligence, yet poor spellers are viewed as ignorant or sloppy in their writing even though the true cause of poor spelling may be dyslexia or just our inconsistent English language. Of course, some poor spellers turn to the dictionary, yet there is little hope for a person who does not know the first letter of "psychological." Some people turn desperately for help to computer spell-checking programs which unfortunately cannot decide whether the writer means "there," "their," or "they're." Others hold out for an impossible future of simplified spellings like "thru" for "through" or "hav" for "have:" In the end, spelling will always be a way to exclude and distinguish—those who can spell are "in," those who can't are "out." [Rewrite the paragraph to make the tone more playful and optimistic.]

B. Of course, it's possible that some of the sightings of flying saucers are actually close encounters of the third kind—encounters with extraterrestrial life. Scientists do believe that eighty of the 300,000 planets in our galaxy have intelligent life. It is even likely that forty of them have civilizations more advanced than our own. But each of those forty planets is at least 11,500 light-years from Earth. So besides the time—a lot—it would take the energy equivalent of 139,000,000,000,000,000,000 kilowatt-hours of electricity to move an alien spaceship to our planet in order to fly around a swamp and excite earthlings. And that's just for a one-way trip. In other words, it's more probable that flying saucer sightings are close encounters of the fourth kind—close encounters with swamp gas. [Rewrite the paragraph to make the tone more serious and less skeptical.]

C. Each year, fraternities and sororities subject potential new members to a demeaning process known as "rush," more accurately called "hazing." Supposedly a series of open houses and parties for the purpose of making friends and learning about the Greek system, rush is above all else a screening process for weeding out unacceptable pledges. It is a procedure whose escapades are bound by tradition, allowing the victims to be closely scrutinized in a variety of embarrassing and sometimes dangerous social situations. The brothers and sisters humiliate the newcomers, from the first beer bash through the final dinner party, seeking people who are willing to make fools of themselves for the sake of acceptance. These mindless carbon copies of themselves are tendered an invitation to join the fraternal organization after Hell Night, the traditional climactic close of rush activities. [Rewrite the paragraph to make the tone more favorable toward fraternities and sororities.]

THE DASTARDLY DUCKS

Combine the sentences below into a short essay with a humorous tone by choosing the funniest of the words given in parentheses. You may add or delete details as well as change any words, phrases, or sentence constructions.

1. There are (people, dedicated souls, busybodies).
2. They (are opposed to, fight, wage holy war on) pornography and vice in the media.
3. They should (take a closer look at, scrutinize, feast their eyes on) the Donald Duck comic books.

4. These (disgusting, deceptively innocent, unwholesome) books present a picture of the family and of American capitalism.
5. The picture is (dirty, sordid, "fowl").

6. The Duck family itself is (fragmented, suspiciously incomplete, motherless).
7. Donald Duck raises three ("nephews," kids he tries to pass off as his nephews, young boys who are obviously illegitimate).
8. (Moreover, Not only that, If that weren't bad enough), the kids' upbringing is (hurt, tainted, poisoned) by Donald's relationship with Daisy.
9. Daisy is a (loose, sexually active, promiscuous) duck.

10. In fact, you can't turn a page in the comic book without (observing, seeing, coming across) a duck (in its birthday suit, without any clothes on, completely naked).
11. Even the ducks that (dress, are attired, have the decency to wear clothes) cover only their tops.
12. They never cover their more (essential, private, significant) (bodily areas, parts, places).

13. The only example of a successful (business executive, business-duck, capitalist) is Scrooge McDuck.
14. Scrooge McDuck is (frugal, miserly, money-grubbing).
15. Scrooge McDuck is a (millionaire, tycoon, rich duck).

16. (All in all, If everything is taken into account, Thus), Donald Duck comics (have, offer, market) vice and corruption.

17. It is as much vice and corruption as a(n) (average, representative, typical) (copy, issue, volume) of (the *National Enquirer, Penthouse, Reader's Digest*).

REVISING FOR A CONSISTENT TONE

Each of the paragraphs below is confusing because its tone is inconsistent. Following the specific directions, make the feelings and attitudes clear by revising each paragraph to create a more consistent tone.

EXAMPLE

Machiavelli is often blamed for originating the unwholesome opinion that the end justifies the means. Now, true, he would have his prince friends sock it good and hard to anyone challenging their power. But, really, he didn't mean for rulers to do whatever they pleased no matter who got hurt. In a world where wickedness and intrigue abounded, he was trying to teach some practical skills in governing well. Princes, he reasoned, should be good guys, upholding values such as truth, humanity, and religion, but they should also be ready to play the "fox" and lower the boom when necessary. Did the end justify the means for Machiavelli? Yeah, sort of, but he also saw the necessity for limiting those means. [Rewrite the paragraph to make the tone more consistent and mature.]

Machiavelli is often blamed for the **controversial view** that the end justifies the means. **While he advised princes to be firm with those** challenging their power, **he prescribed limits for that firmness.** In a world where wickedness and intrigue abounded, he was trying to teach some practical skills in governing well. Princes, he **argued,** should uphold values such as truth, humanity, and religion, but they should also be ready to play the "fox" or **assert their authority** when necessary. **Thus** the end justifies the means for Machiavelli, but he also saw the necessity for limiting those means.

A. True to itself, the government obviously resorts to paranoid secrecy whenever its agencies conduct research that the public has good reason to suspect is either cruel or unethical. Since dogs are only animals, why not let them suffer? The Army has secretly subjected pooches to torture-endurance tests, and, in the 1950s, hid from the public its testing of LSD and other dangerous drugs on unsuspecting American soldiers. I can't believe that they would do anything like that. Not to be outdone, even the Department of Transportation has admitted using human bodies in auto crash tests for years to study the effectiveness of airbags. I tend to believe, and so do many of my buddies that I've talked with, that it would be in the public interest for the government to announce the nature and purposes of any experiment that might conceivably prove questionable. [Rewrite the paragraph to eliminate the immaturity that makes the tone inconsistently sarcastic.]

B. The national parks, which were set aside by an Act of Congress to keep the American wilderness wild, have become tame and polluted, little more than drive-in Holiday Inns complete with newfangled, computerized reservation setups. Trails that were once loads of fun to explore have been paved over for the convenience of tenderfeet. Park rangers now spend more time picking up litter and putting out fires than caring for Yogi Bear, Boo Boo, and all their friends and relatives. Walking among the Snickers wrappers, beer cans, and spray-painted boulders—some of them decorated with really interesting designs!—campers smell gas fumes more often than the scent of pine. Even the whispering wind is likely to be drowned out by the roar of trail bikes or by the chatter of portable radios. When will Americans shape up? [Rewrite the paragraph to give it a consistent voice. Decide whether to make the tone formal and serious or informal and playful.]

C. My dentist tells me that I'd better get on the stick about my gums. Over 84 percent of Americans have some form of periodontal, or gum, disease. It's the main reason people lose their choppers, she tells me. Gum disease is caused by dental plaque, that sticky, icky white stuff that forms on your teeth. Plaque is a mixture of food debris, bacteria, and saliva. If you don't remove plaque daily, it builds up on the teeth and inflames the gums, a condition called "gingivitis." And if you don't do something about it, your mouth just heads straight downhill. Unchecked, gingivitis leads eventually to loose teeth. However, my helpful dentist tells me, it's not all that hopeless. All I have to do is brush the pearly whites twice a day and use dental floss, that minty string stuff that you saw back and forth between the teeth. I need a new toothbrush every three months and dental checkups every six months. Hey! I'm no dummy. I don't want to be gumming oatmeal and creamed corn the rest of my life. [Rewrite the paragraph to make the tone either consistently formal, scientific, and sober-sounding or informal, nontechnical, and light-hearted.]

CHOOSE ME

Selecting from the facts below (you may change the structure and diction in any way you choose), construct two pieces of writing, each no longer than 300 words. Make sure that your tone in the first piece is suitable to the writing situation described in A and in the second to the situation described in B.

A. A required autobiographical statement to accompany your application for a college scholarship.

B. A letter to your new college roommate. The purpose of your letter is to introduce yourself.
    1. I am 18 years old and have just graduated from Fuertado High.
    2. I applied to four other colleges: Beloit College, University of Minnesota, Purdue University, and East Carolina University.
    3. I plan to major in history.
    4. I played the clarinet in my high school orchestra, and I received the music award in my senior year.
    5. In my junior year, I started in my school's production of the play *Tea and Sympathy*.
    6. I jog daily, and I occasionally play tennis and volleyball.
    7. My favorite sports are swimming and waterskiing.
    8. I broke both my ankles last fall.

9. To relax outdoors, I like to read books of travel or history **195** under a tree and to go fishing at the creek; to relax indoors, I play ping pong and watch TV. My favorite programs are *60 Minutes, The Simpsons,* and *Northern Exposure.*

10. Sponsored by Buzz Auffenneuter's Central Electronics, I participated in a dance marathon last year which raised $235 for the volunteer fire fighters' fund.

11. I am allergic to cats.

12. I founded the Young Historians Club, and I edited the only issue of the club magazine *Historiana.*

13. I was recently named president of the local chapter of the Young Democrats club. Last fall, I campaigned in my neighborhood for State Representative Chin.

14. For the past three summers, I've supervised the delivery and distribution of magazines, newspapers, and paperback books for Edna's News and Novelties.

15. My analysis of Lincoln's Gettysburg Address, entitled "A Mirror for Gettysburg: Lincoln and His Archetypes," won the annual R.F. Davis Award for the best essay by a senior.

16. I like to dance to all kinds of music as long as it has a beat.

17. I don't smoke.

18. One of my goals is to teach high school history; another is to enter local politics and eventually run for the state senate.

19. I do not intend to marry and settle down until after I have earned my college degree.

20. I have an older brother, Vince, who lives in Detroit, and two younger sisters—Alice and Connie—who live at home and attend junior high school.

21. Based on my past performances, my teacher and coaches predict success for me in the future. They often compliment me on my diligence, my perseverance, and my good sense.

22. I not only love hot Mexican food, but spicy Thai food is my newest dining passion.

UNIT 12

PARAGRAPH PATTERNS

All the structures and strategies we discuss in this book occur not only in writing but also in speech—except paragraphs. Paragraphs exist only in writing. They are necessary in writing both to help readers follow a text and to help writers support and develop an essay's controlling idea. Since each paragraph begins with white space that a writer creates by indenting or skipping a line, a new paragraph provides a brief rest for the reader's eye and brain. Even more important, the start of a new paragraph signals the reader that a change is taking place—perhaps in place or time, perhaps from one idea to another or from a generalization to an example, perhaps from the body of an essay to its conclusion.

In explanatory and persuasive writing, paragraphs develop a controlling idea; they also help to inform or persuade the reader. Of all the ways you might organize explanatory paragraphs, four are especially useful: the direct pattern, the climactic pattern, the turnabout pattern, and the interrogative pattern.

 ## THE DIRECT PARAGRAPH

The DIRECT PARAGRAPH opens with a direct statement of its topic sentence. The sentences after the opening develop the paragraph's controlling idea by

defining it, qualifying it, analyzing it, and—most frequently—illustrating it. **197**
For example, you might have collected for an anthropology class the following information on how people wait in line in different countries:

> In Arab countries, where women and men do not have equal rights, men
> commonly cut in front of women at ticket windows.
>
> In Britain and the United States, where "first come, first served" is almost
> an obsession, many businesses have customers take numbers to insure
> that "first come" is really "first served."
>
> In southern Europe, where people don't like businesses regulating their
> behavior, lines are disorderly, with lots of pushing and shoving for the best
> position; the strongest or most aggressive win.

Since each of these illustrates a central point—that the way people
wait in line reflects cultural values about fairness and equality—you can
write a direct paragraph, with this central point as the opening sentence:

> **After studying line-forming behaviors, anthropologists have con-
> cluded that the way people wait in line reflects cultural values about
> fairness.** In Arab countries, where women and men do not have equal
> rights, men commonly cut in front of women at ticket windows. In Britain
> and the United States, where "first come, first served" is almost an obses-
> sion, many businesses have customers take numbers to insure that "first
> come" is really "first served." By contrast, in southern Europe, where people
> don't like businesses regulating their behavior; lines are disorderly, with lots
> of pushing and shoving for the best position; the strongest or most aggres-
> sive win.

If you want to "drive home" your controlling idea, you can use your
final sentence to do more than add another illustration. In the next paragraph, the last sentence suggests an imaginary variation on actual
omelettes in order to emphasize the controlling idea—that you can mix
so many things with eggs:

> **The wonder of omelettes is that so many things can be put into
> them.** Take cheese, for example. All sorts of cheese, like Swiss or pro-
> volone, American or mozzarella, slide deliciously into the omelette's fold,
> enhancing the texture of the eggs. And vegetables, from the predictable
> onions and mushrooms to the less common spinach and kohlrabi, add vital
> flavor. Still more lavish, for those who are not vegetarians, is the addition of

a meat, possibly pepperoni or bacon or ham. But the omelette's most exotic components might be the fruits that give it tang: raisins and avocados. **Maybe someday an enterprising chef will figure out how to mix liquor and candy with eggs to produce a vodka-and-fudge omelette.**

Another way to emphasize the controlling idea is by restating it in the final sentence. Restating the topic sentence is especially useful when your controlling idea is complex. In the following paragraph, the idea that the free road map is extinct relies on explaining how oil companies justify their changing priorities. To relate the two points more clearly, the writer states the main idea in the opening sentence and then repeats it in the closing sentence:

> **The free road map has become a fossil of an earlier age—a dinosaur killed by changing priorities.** Until recent years, service stations dispensed road maps as freely as they washed windshields. In the 1960s, one oil company official boasted that "free road maps are an institution peculiar to Americans." Well, the institution peaked in 1972 with the production of 250 million maps and then began its decline. If you ask for a road map in a service station today, you'll have to pay for it. Citing higher production costs and increased charges for foreign crude, oil companies claim that eliminating road maps was actually patriotic. After all, they explain, maps promote travel and travel burns fuel, multiplying the nation's trade imbalance. **With this logic, it's no wonder that the free road map is extinct.**

The direct paragraph occurs more frequently than any other pattern. It has an obvious advantage over all other paragraph patterns: it is well suited to inform and clarify because, from the start, it lets readers know where they're going. For this reason, the direct paragraph minimizes the chances for misunderstanding. But while the direct paragraph is often the best pattern for informing and for clarifying, it is not always as effective for persuading as the other common paragraph patterns—the climactic paragraph, the turnabout paragraph, and the interrogative paragraph.

THE CLIMACTIC PARAGRAPH

A CLIMACTIC PARAGRAPH is like a direct paragraph turned upside down. It begins with illustrations and closes with the topic sentence. Notice what happens if you move the topic sentence to the end and make the **199** direct paragraph about standing in line into a climactic paragraph:

> In Arab countries, where women and men do not have equal rights, men commonly cut in front of women at ticket windows. In Britain and the United States, where "first come, first served" is almost an obsession, many businesses have customers take numbers to insure that "first come" is really "first served." By contrast, in southern Europe, where people don't like businesses regulating their behavior, lines are disorderly, with lots of pushing and shoving for the best position; the strongest or most aggressive win. **After studying line-forming behaviors, anthropologists have concluded that the way people wait in line reflects cultural values about fairness.**

By withholding the statement of its controlling idea until the end, you build an element of surprise and drama into this climactic version. You also prepare your readers, one illustration at a time, for the idea you want them to accept—the controlling idea in the final sentence.

In the paragraph below, for example, there are three instances of recent animated films that have been commercial successes before the controlling idea itself is actually stated in the paragraph's concluding sentence:

> In 1990, Disney's *The Little Mermaid* earned $84 million in North America. In 1991, an even more profitable *Beauty and the Beast* became the first cartoon feature to take in $100 million at the box office. And it's not just the new animated films that are making waves: the 1961 film *One Hundred and One Dalmations* took in nearly $60 million in clear profits when it was revived in 1991. **Not since the 1940s, when Disney released *Pinocchio* and *Dumbo*, have movie-length cartoons been so profitable.**

The climactic paragraph tends to be more persuasive than the direct paragraph. This may be because the pattern of the climactic paragraph corresponds more closely to the pattern of much of our thinking: we often begin by collecting data—an example or two here, an instance or two there—until we have enough evidence to make a generalization or reach a conclusion. By contrast, the direct paragraph presents the conclusion first and the evidence which supports that conclusion later; this pattern makes the direct paragraph clearer but perhaps less convincing. At its best, the climactic paragraph leads your readers, step by step, to a conclusion that seems to follow naturally from the examples and illustrations:

200   There is no such thing as the "Public Affairs Act." Yet one out of three Americans in a recent poll offered opinions about the act as if it really did exist. Pollsters found that these same people who offered opinions about the nonexistent act are more likely than others to offer strong opinions about real issues, like foreign affairs and education. In the 1960s, pollsters found that two-thirds of all Americans thought that the Soviet Union was a member of NATO (rather than its chief adversary), and only one-fourth knew that Mainland China was governed by communists. **Given such ignorance of world and national affairs by the general public, government policymakers must be careful not to rely too heavily on public opinion polls before they decide important issues.**

By the time they move through one example after another which shows that most people know little about national and international issues, your readers should be more likely to agree with the conclusion of the topic sentence—that policymakers would be advised not to depend on polling before making decisions.

 ## THE TURNABOUT PARAGRAPH

Unlike direct or climactic paragraphs, which move in one direction only, TURNABOUT PARAGRAPHS first move in one direction and then "turn about" in another. The turnabout paragraph begins with an idea that is often the opposite of its controlling idea. That is, if the topic sentence of a turnabout paragraph states that "ballet dancing demands as much strength, stamina, and athletic skill as professional football," the paragraph is likely to begin by suggesting the opposite: "Most people wouldn't equate the National Football League players who slam and bash each other on Sunday afternoons with American Ballet Company dancers who perform in *Swan Lake* and *The Nutcracker.*" The turnabout paragraph below, which develops the controlling idea that "our genes determine who we are much more than does our environment," appropriately begins with a different idea:

Most people believe that how we are brought up determines how we will act. We think that environment plays a greater role in determining our personalities than inherited characteristics. But psychologists studying identical twins who were separated at birth and raised in different households suggest otherwise. They point to story after story of separated twins who lived strangely similar lives. Take the "Jim Twins," for instance, who did not meet until age thirty-nine. Each had married a woman named Linda. Each had owned a boyhood dog named Toy. Each worked as a deputy sheriff. They had done well in the same subjects at school and even shared a common slang. Repeated stories like this lead researchers to claim that **our genes determine who we are much more than does our environment.**

To signal readers that your paragraph may not be leading them where they expect, you generally suggest that the first statement may not be correct, and then you clearly mark the turn in ideas. As another aid to readers, you often conclude a turnabout paragraph with a statement or restatement of its controlling idea. The turnabout paragraph below employs all three ways to help the reader follow its movement. The word **seem** in the first sentence encourages readers to doubt the observation by "those of us tied to routine jobs" that truck drivers are "independent rogues." The word **but** in the second sentence clearly signals the turn-about. And the controlling idea—that truckers too are bound by business conditions—is plainly stated in the final sentence.

To those of us tied to routine jobs in offices or factories, truckers **seem** to be tough, independent rogues of the open road, driving their own rigs and setting their own rules, like the cowboys of old who rode the open range on horseback, beholden to no one. **But** truck drivers themselves will tell you that—the public's perception be damned—trucking is a business and a not very good one at that for the small, independent operator. Since the 1970s, it seems, most independent truckers have been forced out of business by skyrocketing costs and changing commercial situations that favor large trucking outfits. **So the truckers you see on the road now generally work for large national corporations and are as tied to routines and regulations as office or factory workers.**

Carefully constructed turnabout paragraphs tend to be persuasive. If you want to persuade or move your reader from one idea to another, then the turnabout paragraph may be the most effective pattern. Because it presents one point of view before advancing another, the turnabout paragraph suggests that you have examined both sides of an issue. Once you have convinced your readers of your sense of fairness, you will find them more willing to accept your viewpoint. In your next persuasion paper, try using the turnabout pattern in a paragraph intended to refute a commonly held opinion.

THE INTERROGATIVE PARAGRAPH

The INTERROGATIVE PARAGRAPH differs from the other types of explanatory paragraphs because it opens with a question. The opening question is used either as an introduction to its controlling idea or as a transition from one idea to the next. The opening question of the following paragraph introduces the controlling idea, that de Camp's book **explores what many consider to be the 'secrets' of the ancients, which turn out not to be so secret after all**.

> **Have you ever wondered how ancient peoples created such marvelous feats of engineering as the pyramids, the Great Wall, and the fabled Tower of Babylon?** If you have, then you should read *The Ancient Engineers,* by L. Sprague de Camp. **The book explores what many consider the "secrets" of the ancients, which turn out not to be so secret after all.** While the ancient Egyptians, Chinese, and Babylonians did not have engineering know-how equivalent to ours, they were able to make optimal use of what they did know, largely because they had an unlimited source of labor and—what may be more important—infinite patience. De Camp discloses that the Egyptians used 100,000 laborers over a twenty-year period to build the Great Pyramid. He also shows that the Chinese labored for centuries on the Great Wall, as did the Babylonians on the Tower.

Because questions have a strong psychological hold on us, paragraphs that begin with them tend to involve readers more directly in your writing than do other paragraph patterns. Notice how the opening sentence of the next paragraph almost gets you responding silently, with your own question, "O.K., why *do* track coaches watch so carefully as students walk by in the corridors?" The opening question not only introduces you to the controlling idea, it demands your response.

> **Why do high school track coaches watch so carefully as students walk by in the corridors? To look for youngsters who are pigeon-toed, bowlegged, or flat-footed, of course.** It seems that such youngsters make the best sprinters. Coaches know that a normal gait, with toes pointed outward, slows you down. A normal gait forces your heels to slip forward as you raise up on your toes, detracting from the force of your pushoff. Those odd gaits, though, give you a firmer landing and kickoff, helping you run faster.

In the two-paragraph passage below, the opening question of the second paragraph is used as a transition. The passage argues that the risks of changing the characteristics of vegetables through genetic and chemical research outweigh the benefits of tastier supermarket produce. The first paragraph shows how several companies have, in fact, produced high-quality vegetables by altering their genes. Then, to turn the reader's attention to the main argument—that the risks of genetic research are greater than the gains—the second paragraph opens with a question about the benefits of these developments:

> Advances in agricultural technology are changing the kinds of food we eat. Grocery stores will soon stock genetically altered tomatoes that are fully ripe and rot resistant. By 1995, the Monsanto Company plans to market corn that can withstand insects, diseases, and weed-killing chemicals. Frito-Lay is at work growing potatoes that resist pests and that fry better. Many researchers and investors eagerly await these developments.

> **Are these developments really advances, though—signs of progress that will benefit consumers?** Some environmental activists, along with growers and restaurant owners, say no! The National Wildlife Federation argues that this research will prolong the use of dangerous chemicals that we must eliminate from our farm production. Botanists and consumer advocates caution that toying with plant genes will create unsafe foods. Growers worry that consumers will stop buying their vegetables altogether. And restaurant owners fear the consequences of customers getting sick after meals.

Whether or not it resembles the turnabout paragraph, the interrogative paragraph can help you persuade your readers to accept your viewpoint. For instance, if you want to convince your readers to take up jogging, you might try an opening question like this: "Would you like to firm up flabby muscles, lose weight, handle stress better, and have more energy, too?" Before they can read the next sentence in your paragraph, "Then you should take up jogging," many of your readers will be responding affirmatively to your question and be more open to your point of view.

 **SUMMARY**

In this unit, you learned about four different kinds of explanatory paragraph patterns—the direct pattern, the climactic pattern, the turnabout pattern, and the interrogative pattern. The direct pattern states a control-

204   ling idea in its opening sentence and illustrates that controlling idea in the following sentences. The climactic paragraph inverts the structure of a direct paragraph, building a series of illustrations to the topic sentence, which comes at the end. The turnabout paragraph states one view in its opening sentence, then "turns" to a different view. The interrogative paragraph draws the reader into a controlling idea by asking a question that is answered later in the paragraph.

The direct paragraph occurs more often than the rest, and it is the best for informing or clarifying. The others can often be more effective for persuading. They also add variety and drama to your writing. The exercises that follow will help you practice constructing and understanding all four paragraph patterns. The goal of this chapter is for you to try the paragraph patterns in your own explanatory writing.

CONSTRUCTING PARAGRAPH PATTERNS   **205**

The sentences are out of order in the groups below. Read through them to get the sense of their meaning. Then organize each group of sentences into an effective paragraph of the pattern indicated. Be sure to write out each paragraph.

EXAMPLE

ALPINE SLIDE
Organize these sentences into a *direct* paragraph.

1. Covering anywhere from 2,000 to 4,000 feet of mountainside, the ride lasts four minutes and costs only a few dollars.

2. Riders cruise down curving chutes of asbestos cement in a fiberglass sled whose speeds, reaching twenty-five miles per hour, are regulated by a control stick, which can be pushed forward to accelerate or pulled backward to brake.

3. Once deserted during the snowless summer months, ski resorts now attract visitors with a new sport—the Alpine Slide.

Once deserted during the snowless summer months, ski resorts now attract visitors with a new sport—the Alpine Slide. Riders cruise down curving chutes of asbestos cement in a fiberglass sled whose speeds, reaching twenty-five miles per hour, are regulated by a control stick, which can be pushed forward to accelerate or pulled backward to brake. Covering anywhere from 2000 to 4000 feet of mountainside, the ride lasts four minutes and costs only a few dollars.

ON ICE
Organize these sentences into a *turnabout* paragraph.

1. Players feel pressured by their organization to put on spectacular shows, a practice that translates into more violence.

2. We assume that players almost instinctively react to a push or shove with fists flying.

3.   In fact, one team's publicity agent admitted that his organization stresses violence as a major attraction to spectators.

4.   Yet, according to a Canadian criminologist who has studied fighting in hockey games, violence reflects not the killer instincts of players but the greedy policies of owners.

5.   Violence is so common to hockey that we can't help believing that players crave nothing more than a good fight.

NAME CALLING
Organize these sentences into a *direct* paragraph.

1.   There was a time when parents honored their newborn children by naming them after figures in the Old Testament, like Esther and Ezekiel.

2.   During the years following World War II, most parents thought twice before naming a son Adolph or a daughter Rose, lest they be associated with Adolf Hitler or Tokyo Rose.

3.   Like clothing and hairstyles, the naming of children has always reflected the fads and fancies of culture.

4.   And when President Nixon resigned from office rather than risk impeachment for Watergate-related crimes, it's a safe bet that the name Richard became less popular.

5.   Back in seventeenth century Ireland, after the Protestant army of William III defeated the Catholic army of James II, loyal Catholic parents stopped naming boys William.

6.   The fashion passed, but parents have continued to be influenced—often negatively—by the reputations of famous men and women.

BIGFOOT
Organize these sentences into a *climactic* paragraph.

1.   Despite its variety of names, in every case it is an eight- to ten-foot-tall man-ape, a strange and hairy being that flees at the sight of humans.

2.   In the Pacific Northwest, where it roams the great forest, it is commonly called Bigfoot.

3.   Native Americans refer to it as Sasquatch, which means "the wild man of the woods."

4. Whether the creature exists or not, the proliferation of stories **207** about it surely points to the human need to believe in the strange, the mysterious, the unknown.

5. To the Russians, it is the final descendant of the Neanderthals and is known as Alma.

6. In Nepal, it is Yeti, the Abominable Snowman, a feared yet revered creature who wanders in the snows of the Himalayas.

POETS
Organize these sentences into an *interrogative* paragraph.

1. In the nineteenth century, poetry was just about the most popular literature, and some poets—like Byron, Shelley, Keats, and Tennyson—even became celebrities.

2. Can you associate the names Kenneth Koch, Adrienne Rich, Ted Hughes, or Leonard Cohen with an occupation?

3. In their own time, they were as well known as movie stars like Paul Newman, Madonna, Tom Cruise, or Meryl Streep are today.

4. But such was not always the case.

5. You probably don't know that Koch, Rich, Hughes, and Cohen are among the most respected contemporary poets, because few people today read poetry or pay attention to living poets.

THE BEAR FACTS

Combine the sentences below into an explanatory essay about how and why teddy bears became popular. Since this is a subject most of us can relate to personally, you may add details from your own experience that make the essay more engaging and more individual. Be sure to construct at least one paragraph like those discussed in this unit—direct, climactic, turnabout, or interrogative.

1. Winston Churchill, Radar O'Reilly, and Christopher Robin have something in common.

2. The great WWII leader was an arctophile.

3. The company clerk in *M*A*S*H* was an arctophile.

4. And the protagonist of the *Winnie the Pooh* books was an arctophile.

5. An arctophile is a lover of teddy bears.

6. And they're not the only ones.

7. This is so if recent statistics are a true indication of bear popularity.

8. The "bear" facts are these.

9. Toy bear sales rose to several hundred million per year in the 1980s.

10. Over 40 percent of those sales were to adults.

11. The teddy bear mania began with a hunting trip.

12. President Theodore Roosevelt took it in 1902.

13. It seems that [this happened].

14. The president refused to shoot a bear under unsportsmanlike conditions.

15. A political cartoon popularized the scene.

16. A Russian immigrant received permission from T.R. to call the stuffed bears teddy bears.

17. He sold the stuffed bears in his Brooklyn candy store.

18. He was named Morris Michton.

19. Michton eventually founded the Ideal Toy Corporation.

20. Bears may have become popular because [of this].

21. They were associated with a popular president.

22. But they have remained popular because [of this].

23. They fill a need in people's lives.

24. Bears are comforting to hug.

25. And bears are comforting to talk to.

26. So people of all ages learn to rely on them.

27. Olympic athlete Greg Louganis talked to his bear.

28.   This was during his gold-medal dives at the Los Angeles   **209**
      Olympics.

29.   Bears have accompanied fighter pilots.

30.   Bears have traveled with Arctic explorers.

31.   Bears have driven with daredevil racers.

32.   And we all remember hugging our own teddies.

33.   This was when things got tough at nursery school.

34.   It is not unusual to rely on stuffed bears.

35.   Marc Stutsky summed it up nicely.

36.   Marc Stutsky is a noted psychiatrist.

37.   He said teddies "make scary things manageable."

38.   Life might be "unbearable" without stuffed animals.

REVISING PARAGRAPHS

The paragraphs below are written as either direct, climactic, turnabout, or
interrogative patterns. Rewrite each as a different type, changing sentences
where appropriate. Make sure you write out the complete paragraphs.

EXAMPLE

Is romance a thing of the past? It is, according to one Michigan State psychologist, who claims that romance is going out of our lives. According to
him, the conditions for romantic love no longer exist, replaced in men and
women today by a pragmatic cynicism in which they view each other with
a cool and objective eye. He says that freer attitudes toward sex and contraception have also helped kill off romance. Would-be Dantes can have
affairs with would-be Beatrices rather than mope and pine away in poetry. [Interrogative paragraph]

210   A Michigan State psychologist confirmed what most of us already know—
that romance is going out of our lives and that the conditions for romantic
love no longer exist. According to him, those conditions are replaced in
men and women today by a pragmatic cynicism in which they view each
other with a cool and objective eye. The psychologist claims that freer attitudes toward sex and contraception have also helped to kill off romance.
It seems that would-be Dantes can now have affairs with would-be Beatrices rather than mope and pine away in poetry. [Direct paragraph]

A.   In the quiet 1980s, students were supposedly dull and conform-
ing. But they may in fact have been as imaginative and rebellious
as their counterparts in the 1960s and 1970s, if the behavior of
Cal Tech students is indicative. A group of them disassembled a
senior's Porsche and left it in his room, completely reassembled
and with the engine running. When McDonald's ran a promo-
tional contest in California, Cal Tech students found a loophole
in the rules and programmed a computer to spit out 1.2 million
entries, winning thousands of dollars in prizes. A senior physics
major created a quantum mechanics problem for some undergraduates as a prank and ended up with a puzzle that stumped
even a Nobel Prize–winning physicist. Some dullards! Some
conformists! [Turnabout Paragraph]

B.   Children in Northern Ireland, the scene of a long, bitter, and
bloody civil war, have been studied by a group of psychologists.
They tell us that 75 percent of the ten-year olds believe that any
unknown object found in the street—like a cigarette pack, a letter, or a package—is likely to be a bomb. Moreover, 80 percent of
the children believe that shooting and killing are acceptable ways
of achieving political goals. In effect, terrorism seems to have a
powerful psychological effect on children. [Climactic Paragraph]

C.   Have people really progressed since primitive times, or does civilization simply cover our innate savagery? A British Broadcast-
ing Corporation documentary indicates that we may not be as
civilized as we think. To film a documentary on life in the Iron
Age, the BBC hired a group of ten men and ten women to live
in an ancient village just outside Stonehenge. There, the men
and women had to live as their distant ancestors did: they wove
cloth, made tools, farmed in ancient ways, and practiced the
Celtic religion. After a year, their behavior changed. They
walked more slowly, and they talked more slowly. They slept

longer and were less inhibited about nudity. They were more self-sufficient but also less civilized. At the planting ceremony, for instance, they forced one member of the group to be lashed as a sacrifice to ensure a good harvest. [Interrogative Paragraph]

D. Toy fads have their own peculiar logic, which manufacturers are seldom able to predict or even to explain. So Coleco Industries— the makers of Cabbage Patch Kids, those ugly, lovable urchins who came complete with adoption papers, names, and birth certificates—wasn't surprised when its cuddly creations took the trade by storm a few years ago. It was simply one of those hysterias that sweep the volatile toy market from time to time. Nor was Coleco surprised—though it was disheartened and disappointed—when Cabbage Patch sales plummeted, plunging the company into near bankruptcy. After intensive market analysis, Coleco still has no idea why the Kids faded quickly from the scene like Pet Rocks and Davy Crockett hats rather than retaining their popularity like Barbie dolls and Raggedy Andys. [Direct Paragraph]

THE HOME FRONT

Combine the following sentences into an explanatory essay about how civilians lived during World War II and how they produced the weapons of war. Be sure to create at least one paragraph like those discussed in this unit—direct, climactic, turnabout, or interrogative. If you can, add details from movies or TV shows you've seen, from books you've read, or from what your parents or grandparents have told you about those times.

1. Large numbers of the civilian population took to the streets during the Vietnam War era.

2. This happened in protest against our most unpopular war.

3. Civilians stood firmly behind the government to help defeat Germany and Japan.

4. This happened a generation before the war in Vietnam.

5. This happened during World War II.

6. Most of the young men were in the military.

7. So women had to replace men in industrial jobs.

8. The women were symbolized by "Rosie the Riveter."

9. The women left their homes to work in the factories.

10. "Rosie the Riveter" was a cartoon figure.

11. She wore coveralls and carried a pipe wrench.

12. And she urged workers to greater production.

13. Women like Rosie learned how to solder.

14. They learned how to run lathes.

15. And they learned how to rivet metal parts together.

16. The civilians on the homefront did without new cars.

17. They did without new refrigerators.

18. They put up with shortages of certain foods.

19. And they put up with shortages of luxury items.

20. They bought gas and tires only when they had saved enough ration coupons.

21. They carpooled to work in broken-down Studebakers and Nashes built before the war.

22. The civilians put up blackout curtains at night.

23. And they turned on the radio to hear Gabriel Heatter or H.V. Kaltenborn.

24. Heatter and Kaltenborn announced the latest news from the European and Pacific theaters of operation.

25. This was how millions of Americans spent the war years.

26. They waited for loved ones in uniform.

27. They listened to the radio.

28. And they took part in the greatest production effort a people has ever made.

29. All the civilians pitched in.

30. Women like Rosie pitched in.

31. And men exempt from the draft pitched in.

32. High school kids spent evenings in tank factories and steel mills.

33. Old people in retirement took up half-forgotten trades.

34. Together they produced the weapons that fought the Axis.
35. They produced 296,029 airplanes.
36. They produced 86,333 tanks.
37. And they produced 319,000 artillery pieces.

38. They saved tin cans.
39. They brushed their teeth with half brushfuls of toothpaste.
40. And they volunteered their time at the local USO.

41. They walked the darkened streets in the evenings as air raid wardens.

42. Or they strained their eyes.
43. They peered through the night skies as aircraft warning watchers.

44. They waited.
45. They worked.
46. They lined up for hard-to-get items.
47. They had ration coupons in hand.
48. Sugar was a hard-to-get item.
49. Nylon stockings were hard-to-get items.
50. Tires were hard-to-get items.
51. And coffee was a hard-to-get item.

52. They were unlike the civilians during the Vietnam War.
53. They were a people united against a common enemy.
54. They were united in their desire to win a war they believed in.

PART THREE

WRITING STRATEGIES

PART THREE
AT A GLANCE

UNIT 13

PREWRITING

DISCOVERING AND GENERATING IDEAS

Perhaps the most intimidating aspect of writing is facing that empty white page (or blank computer screen), knowing that you have to fill it with words, sentences, and paragraphs. Where will you find those words? This unit describes four strategies that you can use to discover and generate ideas before you write your first draft: listing, focused free writing, the reporter's formula, and cubing.

LISTING

The simplest strategy for discovering and generating ideas is LISTING. Lists can help you find a suitable topic for an assigned paper or remember and collect information about that topic.

LISTING TOPICS

The best way to generate a list of possible topics is to go quickly without stopping to ponder whether your list is a good one or not. At this early writing stage, just suspend your judgment: the idea is to make as long a list as you can. After you've finished, you can go back over the list and cross out the silly, vague, or unproductive topics.

Begin by writing as rapidly as you can any subject that you might conceivably like to write about. Be sure to write down every possibility, even those that may initially seem ridiculous. Take no more than five or ten minutes for this exercise, but be sure to list at least ten items.

Your list might look like this:

fortune-tellers

being picked on by the school bully

Sherlock Holmes mysteries

special effects in outer space movies

my great aunt Etta

lifeguarding at the shore

Margaret Sanger

the Model UN at school

no more frog dissecting for me

Charles Lindbergh

my favorite MTV videos

neighborhood crime watch

Remember that you'll have great difficulty interesting your readers in any topic that you're not genuinely interested in yourself, so look back over your list and pick a topic that seems promising to you.

LISTING TO COLLECT NOTES

Suppose you included the topic "Charles Lindbergh" on your list because you had studied aviation pioneers in an American history course and were interested enough in Lindbergh to do some additional reading about him in the library. You might find it valuable to compile a new list of what you know about Charles Lindbergh in the form of random notes—just to make sure you don't forget any information or ideas you have run across in books and articles. It doesn't matter what your list of notes looks like because your goal in listing at this point is to capture any facts, details, or impressions that could possibly be useful when you begin to select and organize your material.

You might list a set of notes like this about Charles Lindbergh:

Lindbergh was 25 years old when he flew from New York to Paris.

The solo flight was from Roosevelt Field on Long Island to Orly Airport.

It took 33 hours.

Onlookers thought he was doomed to failure.

He had flown and navigated mail planes for years.

He had been a stunt pilot on the barnstorming circuit.

He had set out to win the $25,000 prize offered for the first nonstop flight across the Atlantic.

He had studied all the planes available, and he chose the Ryan monoplane.

He had it modified and supervised all the modifications.

The original wingspan was extended 10 feet for more lift.

He added stronger landing gear.

The fuel capacity was increased from 50 to 450 gallons.

He had enough fuel for a 300-mile navigational error.

He had replaced the original seat with a cane chair to save weight.

He installed a 200-horsepower radial air-cooled Wright Whirlwind engine.

The plane had a 130-mile-per-hour top speed.

He had no radio.

He navigated with a magnetic compass and mariner's sextant.

He flew 10 feet above the waves to keep track of wind direction and wind speed.

He had a bottle of water and five sandwiches—two ham, two beef, and one egg with mayonnaise.

His first landsight was Ireland, just as he had planned.

After the flight, he was made a hero, and songs were written about him.

One song was "Lucky Lindy."

At this point, your list probably gives you enough to say about Charles Lindbergh to write a detailed short paper. However, if listing to collect notes doesn't work for your topic or if you are simply tired of listing, you might try to generate ideas by using one of the other prewriting strategies, discussed below.

 FOCUSED FREE WRITING

FOCUSED FREE WRITING is a quick, efficient way of generating and discovering ideas and getting them down on paper. Focused free writing is nonstop writing for a specific period of time: five minutes? ten minutes? until you fill one page or two pages?

Focused free writing is based on three principles:

1. *Don't stop writing.* During the time you are free writing, try to write as rapidly as you can. The technique is called "free writing" partly because it relies upon "free association." If you "blurt out" whatever pops into your mind, you will probably make some surprising and interesting associations between ideas. But that won't happen if you agonize over what to write next, so just keep writing quickly. If you run into a block and you can't think of what to write next, write whatever you are actually thinking ("I'm stumped here. I can't go on. My hand is killing me. Isn't my ten minutes up yet? Can't I stop?") until you get back on track with your topic. Or you can simply write the last word you've written over and over again (". . . bright sunny smile. Smile, smile, smile, smile, smile . . .") until a new idea comes up. Just don't stop that pen from moving across the page or that cursor from scrolling across the computer screen.

2. *Don't edit.* A second reason why the technique is called "free writing" is that it frees writers from the burdens of editing. When you write, you play two roles: creator and critic. The creator fills up blank pages with new ideas that the critic looks at later and revises. If you let the critic loose too soon, sometimes you paralyze the creator. Have you ever spent two hours on a

piece of writing and concluded with a mountain of crumpled up **221** paper, a monumental headache, and only two sentences of actual writing? That's because the critic in you demanded correct, well-thought-out language before the creator in you had produced any language. If you turn off the critic by refusing to edit as you free write, that kind of agony won't happen. Don't worry about spelling, punctuation, and other usage issues when you're free writing. The goal is to generate ideas at this point and not to create polished prose.

3. *Don't stray from the topic.* The reason the technique is called *"focused* free writing" is that your nonstop writing focuses on a specific topic. If you keep focused on your topic, you have a better chance of finding more things to say about it.

Here is the result of five minutes of focused free writing in which the author was thinking about a book he had just read:

March 20

Koko's Kitten—the book about the gorilla who learned sign language—is fascinating. "In December, I made a list for Koko. I drew about twenty pictures—fruits, vegetables, nuts, dolls, combs, & blankets. Every year, Koko gets a stocking & lots of presents. She loves Christmas." Does this make Koko a Christian? If she is capable of signing abstractions (like "love"), in what sense is she less than human? Has she a soul? What if she learns the sign for "soul" & claims to have one? Who could deny it to her? There's a short story in here I think—about the power of language to create reality. Reality, reality, reality. Now that we know that Koko thinks, she is. "I think, therefore I am" becomes "If I let you know that I think, therefore I am." Francine Patterson wrote an article called "Conversation w/a Gorilla" for *Nat'l Geographic.* Read it to get a better feel for Koko's speech patterns & 500-word vocabulary. If she uses our language, why isn't she a "person"? "When Koko was asked whether she was an animal or a person, Koko answered, 'Fine animal gorilla.' " But what if she had signed, "Person"? On what grounds would she be wrong? I mean, of course, she'd be wrong, but how would we tell her? This fascinates me. I need to write more about Koko.

After you finish a focused free writing, you need to read over what you have written. It's likely that some—or much—of it won't be terribly helpful, but you want to look for ideas that surprise you, that interest

222 you, that help you understand your topic more fully. Look for any ideas
you felt were important enough to repeat; see if any pattern of ideas has
developed. Sometimes one of your ideas can even lead you to another
round of focused free writing; the writer above might free write later on
Koko's very positive self-image ("fine animal gorilla"), perhaps contrasting that with the negative self-image of many human beings he knows.

Some people think that free writing is the single most effective way of
generating and discovering material to write about. For others, however,
free writing never really becomes a comfortable technique. In that case,
there are other ways to generate ideas, such as the reporter's formula.

 THE REPORTER'S FORMULA

Once you've settled on a topic, you can ask the questions that newspapers reporters use to generate ideas:

Who?

What?

Where?

When?

Why?

How?

These questions, which reporters call the 5 Ws plus H, are designed
to accumulate information about a specific topic. When you ask these six
questions, go slowly; spend at least several minutes considering each of
them and writing down your responses. Don't worry if the questions
seem to overlap. After all, the purpose of the REPORTER'S FORMULA is to
generate material; organizing it comes later. Finally, keep in mind that—
depending on your topic—some questions are likely to produce more
interesting answers than others.

By applying the six questions of the reporter's formula to the topic
"Nursing as a Career," one writer generated the following information:

Who?   Who goes into nursing? Well, women still do in great num-
         bers. However, a lot more men are entering nursing now.

Many of them begin as paramedics or as army medics and **223** then decide to become nurses. Many of them see nursing as a stable, secure career with reasonable financial rewards. Of course, that's why women go into nursing as well. Most nurses also want to help other people, to work with others.

What?   Nursing now defines health as more than just the absence of illness. Nursing focuses on bringing the potential of humans to the maximum. Health should be defined by each person himself or herself, making the nurses's job to help people achieve a state of health that they feel is the best they can reach. For example, someone with kidney disease would define "best health" differently than someone who doesn't have kidney disease but instead has a family history of heart disease. The nurse assists people in determining and reaching their maximum health potential.

Where?   Since the focus of nursing is people, then nursing can take place anywhere there are people, including such obvious locations as hospitals and nursing homes. Other sites for nursing also exist: community health (home care), hospice care (nursing care for the terminally ill), outpatient clinics, nurse practitioners (such as nurse midwives, who may have their own offices), and industrial nursing (in a corporation).

When?   When do people go into nursing? Nurses are no longer just young women who enter nursing right after high school. Many are now studying to be nurses at later ages. Women returning to college in their thirties and forties have increased in number. So have male students in their twenties after serving as Medics in the Army.

Why?   Society needs nurses. People usually require help from trained practitioners in order to achieve their maximum health potential. Another reason to go into nursing is to pursue an interest in science; ongoing nursing research is developing a scientific base for nursing practice. In fact, a number of major universities have instituted Ph.D. programs to educate nurses in research methodology. Many nurses enter the profession out of a desire to help people, and an increasing number of people choose nursing because of the job security it offers.

How?   Nurses receive their education in two-, three-, and four-year programs. Two- and three-year programs cost less to the student and offer a faster preparation for employment. But some national nursing organizations now recommend four-year baccalaureate degrees because of the increasing complexity of the health-care system, people's needs, changes in science and technology. After completing their education, nurses must pass a state licensing exam to become a Registered Nurse (RN). More and more states are requiring continued education for nurses in order to renew their licenses, similar to the requirements for public school teachers.

The six questions of the reporter's formula can generate a wealth of material, whether it is information you are trying to remember or information you have researched at the library. But sometimes this strategy doesn't accomplish what you'd hoped it would; you might consider another prewriting strategy: cubing.

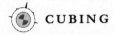 **CUBING**

The strategy of CUBING contains elements of focused free writing and the reporter's formula. Like focused free writing, cubing asks you to write nonstop about a specific subject, but like the reporter's formula, cubing asks you to look at your subject in more than one way. Just as a cube has six sides—think of dice—cubing provides six different angles from which to view your subject:

1. Describe your subject. (What does it look like? What are its distinctive characteristics? How does it appear to you?)

2. Compare your subject. (What is it like? What is it not like?)

3. Connect your subject. (What can you connect it with? What does it remind you of? What else does it make you think of?)

4. Analyze your subject. (What makes it like it is? What aspects of the subject are most notable?)

5. Apply your subject. (How can it be used? What purpose does it serve? What is its function?)

6. Argue for or against your subject. (Define an issue and take a position.)

To use cubing, make sure you try each of the six operations listed. Free write for five minutes (or ten minutes or however long you wish), describing your subject. Then move on to comparing your subject, and **225** so on. Here's an example of cubing applied by a student to her subject, England:

1. Describe England

   I think of England in terms of London. Which I assume is rather cold misty foggy. That's how it always was in Sherlock Holmes stories anyway. I think of the London Bridge & Big Ben. I remember Chevy Chase driving his family around and around in that movie saying, "Look kids, Big Ben, Parliament." I think of Sarah & Guy. I think of punks & purple Mohawks. I like England because it is somewhere else, somewhere I've only heard of, may only visit. Just like Londoners think of America that way. I like British music, I like the Beatles, I know they are not from London so I think of Liverpool when I think of England too. I see pictures from "Howard's End." I see Stonehenge and strawberries at Wimbledon and those guys with the high fuzzy hats guarding the palace and I hear those Cockney accents like in "My Fair Lady."

2. Compare England

   I'll compare England to America. I haven't been to England—yet, so these are just assumptions. I think of it as vintage & proper. America seems newfangled. We've slaugtered their language. We say "truck" and they say "lorry"; we say "in the hospital" and they say "in hospital." They spell all those words with "u" (like "colour"). We used their traditions, I don't know. What to say here? Here here here here. English is considered our mother country. So what does that make America? Maybe a teenager who thinks she knows everything but goes running back to the mother? Then in another perspective—with the power America does have, I think of America as superior to England. Like America is a Yuppie & England is older. We still have problems between racial groups & they have problems with the Irish Republican Army.

3. Connect England

Beatles	Mary Poppins
Sarah	Guy
WWII bombing runs	Winston Churchill
George Michael	pounds and shillings
Live Aid	Wembley Stadium

Prince's Trust concert	Paladium
Newcastle	Birmingham
London	Liverpool
Lennon	next summer?
chim chim charee	Fergie and Di
Sid & Nancy	Surrey
scones and high tea	Dickens
Carnaby Street	9th grade English class
Piccadilly	fog
Yorkshire pudding	English muffins
Manchester United	Magna Carta
Robin Hood	jousting
the Round Table	The Sword in the Stone
swimming the Channel	white cliffs of Dover
the Pilgrims	Tower of London

4. Analyze England

I have been attracted to England since I first saw Mary Poppins. The accents fascinate me. I once met a little boy from Birmingham who had a full-fledged British accent and I thought how clever of him to have learned it at his young age! How silly since we all have whatever accent we hear as we grow up. Up up up up. What now? Now that I have friends in England and plan to go there next summer, that's all I think about. I listen to British music—which I've always done but even more so lately it seems. I'm stumped here. What should I write? It's the history of England that really grabs me. There are buildings there 800 years older than the United States. It's an old country. I don't mean the land itself, of course, because our land is just as old but the country has existed forever it seems like. When was Robin Hood and Richard the Lion-hearted and all of that? Probably long before the Pilgrims ever came to Massachusetts.

5. Apply England

This one is hard. England exists because the earth exists—there you go that should clear things up. I could say England exists because someone somewhere knew that someday *I* would want to go there. So basically after I visit there next summer, there will be great destruction because its reason for existing will be over. That is pretty realistic. England exists so people like Sher-

lock Holmes & Mary Poppins will have a place to live. And the
Beatles could come from Liverpool. More seriously? Hmmm.
What else? England can help Americans understand our own
roots as a country, maybe? If we go there and see things like the
Magna Carta maybe our own democracy will seem different. It
would be weird to hear them sing "God Save the Queen"
when I'm used to "My Country, 'Tis of Thee" with the same
tune.

6.   Argue for or against England

I am for England—my heroes & heroines throughout my life have
come from there—which, incidentally, I didn't realize until this
writing exercise. Mary Poppins, the Beatles, Robin Hood, Monty
Python—at one time were heroes of mine, God only knows why.
And some of my best friends live in England like Sarah and Guy.
Now this attitude may change after I return from there but I'm
not counting on it. What about an issue about England? I read
somewhere that more U.S. property is owned by England than
even by Japan. I don't think I'm much in favor of that. I'd like to
go to England not have England come here! Wouldn't that be
something if England bought up the whole U.S. piece by piece?
Sort of undo the whole American Revolution. No thanks,
guv'nor.

After you've finished cubing, the final step is to read over the ideas
you've generated. Look for patterns of thought or for significant repeti-
tions of ideas. You may discover surprising ideas or meaningful ones
buried as if in code. For instance, the student chose to make a list when
she was connecting her subject; she mentions the names of several people
like "Sarah" and "Guy." These are people whose names don't mean very
much to us as readers, but to the writer they have much greater significance. Perhaps she might expand on those names, even developing an
entire paper about having close friends who live across the ocean in England. The writer also tends to think about movies—*Howard's End, Sid and
Nancy, Mary Poppins*—some of which you may not have seen, but for this
writer, movies themselves might prove to be a subject worth further
development. Most times, cubing produces much information; you'll
need to sift through it, looking for the ideas that you find most worth
developing.

228  **SUMMARY**

In this unit, you read about four major strategies for discovering and generating ideas: listing, focused free writing, the reporter's formula, and cubing. In listing, you make a quick list of ideas, while in focused free writing, you write full sentences and paragraphs but ignore the impulse to edit as you go. By asking "who? what? where? when? why? how?" you can use the reporter's formula to generate ideas. You can generate ideas through cubing by looking at your topic from six different angles. Each of these strategies has its own advantages; you will find that some may work better for you than others, depending upon what you are writing.

LISTING

1. *Listing topics.* In no more than ten minutes, write down a list of at least twenty topics that you might possibly like to write about someday. Go quickly, writing down any topic that comes to mind, and don't reject any possibility. After completing that list, select the two or three topics that strike you as most promising. For each of those topics, write down a list of three or more possible paper titles.

2. *Listing to collect notes.* In the preceding exercise, you made a list of possible topics and then selected two or three that were most promising. In this exercise, choose one of these promising topics and jot down, in the form of a list of notes, at least fifteen facts or observations about that topic. Write down anything that occurs to you or that you discover by checking written sources.

FOCUSED FREE WRITING

Give yourself exactly ten minutes, and during that time write down—without stopping for any reason—whatever comes into your head on *one* of the following topics:

a topic generated by your listing activities

what you most vividly remember from junior high school

the person you care for most in the world

what you think you'll be doing a year or two from now

the one thing you'd most like to see changed

a topic of your choice

THE REPORTER'S FORMULA

Use the reporter's formula—the questions "who?" "what?" "where?" "when?" "why?" and "how?"—to generate material about one of the following topics:

a topic generated by your listing activities

a current environmental issue that concerns you

breaking up is hard to do

the difference between right and wrong

being made to feel different from everyone else

what I enjoy more than anything else in the world

a topic of your choice

When you have answered each of the six questions, go through your material carefully in order to decide on a focus or central idea for a paper.

CUBING

Use the six operations of cubing—describing, comparing, connecting, analyzing, applying, arguing for or against—to generate material about one of the following topics:

a topic discovered by your listing activities

the last time you hit someone or were hit by someone

the double standard for males and females in sexual behavior

your favorite movie, TV show, or compact disc

The Awakening, Great Expectations, or any other book

loneliness

a topic of your choice

When you have applied the six operations of cubing to your subject, go through your material carefully to decide on a focus or central idea for a paper.

U N I T   1 4

DRAFTING

 SELECTING AND ORGANIZING IDEAS

Once you've chosen a topic and collected materials for that topic, you can move ahead to the next stage of your draft: selecting and organizing the ideas you have generated.

Let's return to the list of details that appeared in Unit 13 about Charles Lindbergh's historic transatlantic flight in 1927:

Lindbergh was 25 years old when he flew from New York to Paris.

The solo flight was from Roosevelt Field on Long Island to Orly Airport.

It took 33 hours.

Onlookers thought he was doomed to failure.

He had flown and navigated mail planes for years.

He had been a stunt pilot on the barnstorming circuit.

He had set out to win the $25,000 prize offered for the first nonstop flight across the Atlantic.

He had studied all the planes available, and he chose the Ryan monoplane.

He had it modified and supervised all the modifications.

The original wingspan was extended 10 feet for more lift.

He added stronger landing gear.

The fuel capacity was increased from 50 to 450 gallons.

He had enough fuel for a 300-mile navigational error.

He had replaced the original seat with a cane chair to save weight.

He installed a 200-horsepower radial air-cooled Wright Whirlwind engine.

The plane had a 130-mile-per-hour top speed.

He had no radio.

He navigated with a magnetic compass and mariner's sextant.

He flew 10 feet above the waves to keep track of wind direction and wind speed.

He had a bottle of water and five sandwiches—two ham, two beef, and one egg with mayonnaise.

His first landsight was Ireland, just as he had planned.

After the flight, he was made a hero, and songs were written about him.

One song was "Lucky Lindy."

Which ideas and details you select and how you arrange them depend on your focus. Imagine yourself in the Arizona desert photographing a giant saguaro cactus with distant purple mountains behind it. If you focus tightly on the cactus, the mountains in the background will be out of the picture; if you use a telephoto lens to focus on the faraway mountains, the cactus will disappear. When you sharpen your focus as a writer, something similar happens. You begin to decide which of the details you've accumulated to include and which to leave out; change the focus, and your selection of details will also change. When you decide what the purpose of your photograph is, you can determine whether to focus on the cactus or the mountains. When you decide what the purpose of your writing should be, you can begin to determine which idea to focus on.

We might call the focus of a written piece its thesis or its controlling idea. If, for example, your controlling idea about Charles Lindbergh is

234   that he succeeded because of his knowledge, experience, thoroughness, and luck, you will probably see at once that some of your collected notes are irrelevant and should be discarded. The fact that Lindbergh had no radio and that he took along five sandwiches is not clearly connected to the reasons for his success. In the same way, the fact that the flight took thirty-three hours, that it began at Roosevelt Field and ended at Orly Airport, or that it won Lindbergh $25,000 is not directly related to knowledge, experience, thoroughness, and luck. By omitting such irrelevant material and including only details that develop the controlling idea, you can construct a sharply focused, unified, and effective paragraph:

> **Lindbergh was successful in flying nonstop across the Atlantic because of his knowledge, his experience, his thoroughness, and his luck.** He knew airplanes both as a pilot and a navigator. He had gained extensive flying experience from mail runs and the barnstorming circuit. He carefully selected his own plane and thoroughly modified it for the arduous flight by extending its wingspan, installing stronger landing gear, and increasing its fuel capacity. And, as popular songs like "Lucky Lindy" made clear, he had plenty of luck.

Whenever you have difficulty finding a controlling idea, it's helpful to start asking questions about the information you've gathered. For example, one of your notes says that Lindbergh was "made a hero" after his flight. A question you might ask yourself and then try to answer is whether Lindbergh really deserved to be made into a hero. The question itself indicates the topic of a potential paragraph or essay, and your answer to it helps define a controlling idea. If you answer that "Lindbergh deserved his status as a hero" and choose that statement as your controlling idea, the next step is to select from your notes those details that are relevant and discard those that are not. The most relevant details for establishing Lindbergh's heroism relate to the length and difficulty of his journey, to his primitive flight instruments, and to the uniqueness of his achievement. Those details might be organized into a paragraph like this:

> Charles Lindbergh was hailed as a hero when he landed safely in Paris because, by flying nonstop across the Atlantic, he had done what no one had done before. And he did it under almost impossible conditions. He piloted a single-engine Ryan monoplane capable of flying no faster than 130 miles per hour. He flew alone for thirty-three hours, without a radio and with only a sextant and magnetic compass for navigational help. He

often cruised but ten feet above the ocean waves to estimate wind speed and wind direction. Because his was truly a heroic feat, **Lindbergh deserved to be considered a hero.**

Details in the earlier paragraph explaining why Lindbergh succeeded were deliberately omitted from this paragraph because they were no longer relevant. The details about Lindbergh's knowledge, experience, thoroughness, and luck did not directly support the controlling idea that "Lindbergh deserved to be considered a hero." As always, it is your controlling idea that determines which details are relevant and which are not.

If you had asked how Lindbergh modified his plane instead of why he succeeded or whether he deserved to be a hero, still another paragraph with a different controlling idea could have grown out of your notes. By focusing on the details about the plane's wingspan, landing gear, engine, fuel capacity, and seat, you might write a paragraph developing the idea that after Lindbergh modified the plane, even its manufacturers wouldn't recognize it.

The plane Charles Lindbergh flew nonstop across the Atlantic only began as a Ryan monoplane. That was before Lindbergh started modifying it. First, he extended the wingspan by ten feet and added stronger landing gear. Then he increased its fuel capacity from 50 to 450 gallons and installed a 200-horsepower Wright Whirlwind engine. Before he was through, he even replaced the original seat with a lightweight cane chair. **When he was done, the original builders probably wouldn't have recognized their own creation.**

Once again, the controlling idea governed the selection of details. Because the details of Lindbergh's difficult flight and primitive instruments did not help develop a controlling idea about plane modifications, they were not included in the paragraph.

Sometimes your controlling idea and even the purpose of your paragraph become clear to you only after you have begun writing. Just as often, what you have written may give you new ideas for developing the paragraph. Here is a paragraph you might have written to support the controlling idea that Lindbergh was a skillful planner, pilot, and navigator:

When twenty-five-year-old Charles Lindbergh took off from Long Island to claim the $25,000 prize for flying nonstop to Paris, most of the onlookers thought he was just another ex-barnstormer doomed to failure. They didn't know that **"Lucky Lindy" was a skillful planner, pilot, and navigator.** He had carefully chosen the Ryan monoplane and supervised its modification. He had installed a 200-horsepower radial air-cooled engine that gave him a top speed of 130 miles per hour. He had the wingspan extended by ten feet for more lift. And he had the normal 50-gallon fuel tank increased to 450 gallons. He was an excellent navigator and pilot who kept track of wind direction and wind speed by flying ten feet above the ocean. When he sighted land, it was precisely where he expected—in Ireland.

But after completing such a paragraph, you might begin to see a new idea emerging—the contrast between the nickname "Lucky Lindy" and the facts indicating that Lindbergh had prepared for his flight with great care and skill. To develop this contrast as the controlling idea of a revised version of your paragraph, you would first want to return to your notes for additional supporting information. There you would find two further details to illustrate Lindbergh's careful preparation—his experience as a pilot of barnstormers and mail planes and his carrying enough fuel for a 300-mile navigational error. By incorporating these details and excluding others, by revising and rearranging sentences, but especially by emphasizing in both your first and last sentences the contrast between luck on one hand and care and skill on the other, you are now able to construct a new and highly effective paragraph:

> **Though the world called him "Lucky Lindy"** after he became the first person to fly nonstop across the Atlantic, twenty-five-year-old **Charles Lindbergh had actually depended on skill and careful preparation** for the flight. He was an expert pilot and navigator with years of experience flying barnstormers and mail planes. He carefully selected the Ryan monoplane from among the available aircraft as the best suited for his difficult task. And he personally supervised its modification, which included extending its wingspan by ten feet and increasing its fuel capacity by 400 gallons in order to allow for a 300-mile navigational error. When "Lucky Lindy" touched down in Paris thirty-three hours after leaving Long Island, it was because he had left little to luck.

Because there are many ways to focus on a given subject, it is almost always possible to use the same information in different ways to accomplish a variety of purposes. All of theses different paragraphs have their roots in the same list of details generated about Lindbergh's flight; how you select and arrange those details depends on what your controlling idea is going to be.

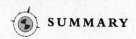 **SUMMARY**

Once you determine your purpose in writing, you can sharpen your focus and decide which details to include and exclude from your draft. Sometimes you discover your purpose as you write. If you ask yourself questions about your material, you can create a controlling idea that will hold your writing together. While you select and arrange your ideas, be open to the possibilities offered by the material, because you can usually present the same information in more than one way to suit different purposes.

SELECTING AND ARRANGING IDEAS

GAME SHOWS

Select from the list below all the notes that support the controlling idea that "game shows exploit sex and greed to create excitement." Then organize those notes into an explanatory paragraph unified by the controlling idea.

1.   Game show hosts are usually young and attractive.

2.   They dress in the latest fashions.

3.   Game show sets are alive with flashing lights and gaudy colors.

4.   Women assistants on shows like "The Price Is Right" and "Wheel of Fortune" are dressed in revealing outfits.

5.   On "The Price Is Right," contestants called down from the audience are told to run from their seats to the stage.

6.   They often exhibit no regard for others sitting in their areas.

7.   Contestants on all the shows are encouraged to use cutthroat tactics to eliminate their competition.

8.   Prizes like cars, boats, and furs are displayed in the flashiest way possible to make them appear more exciting.

9.   Contestants display their greed when they consider the value of their prizes or decide which door to choose.

10.   Many of the game shows are gimmicky.

11.   Game shows like "The Love Connection" and "Studs" encourage contestants to reveal intimate information about themselves.

12.   When contestants win prizes, they often become hysterical and cry.

13.   Hosts take advantage of contestants' peculiarities to make them look ridiculous.

14.   Dating game shows send strangers on exotic dates to expensive resorts.

15.   Many of the shows ask very simple questions.

16.   Hosts often make sexual puns.

17.   The prizes are usually donated by manufacturers in return for free publicity.

18. Cars are usually the most difficult prize to win.
19. Some contestants are so nervous they can hardly speak.
20. The studio audience often moans with excitement at the prizes.

MOUNT RUSHMORE

Construct a unified and ordered paragraph by picking one of the three statements below to serve as a controlling idea and then choosing appropriate supporting details from the notes.

A. Some Americans view Mt. Rushmore as a priceless American tribute to national ideals.

B. Some Americans view Mt. Rushmore as a symbol of some disturbing aspects of American life.

C. Creating and repairing the Mt. Rushmore monument illustrate how difficult it is to overcome natural forces.

1. Mt. Rushmore is the world's largest piece of sculpture.
2. The Black Hills are sacred land to the Sioux.
3. Doane Robinson wanted a permanent tourist attraction for South Dakota.
4. Robinson (1924) suggested a "colossal monument" of Buffalo Bill or Chief Red Cloud.
5. John Gutzon de la Mothe Borglum was chosen to be the sculptor.
6. Borglum had worked on a quarter-mile-long bas relief of Confederate soldiers at Stone Mountain, Georgia.
7. Borglum argued with the Stone Mountain planning group, destroyed his work, and fled Georgia before he could be arrested.
8. Mt. Rushmore has a near-vertical granite wall 500 feet long and 400 feet high.
9. Sioux Indians claim the land on which Mt. Rushmore is built.

10. The workers had to build a staircase of 504 wooden steps on 45 inclined ramps to get to the top.

11. The first step in repairing Mt. Rushmore was to take hundreds of aerial photographs in order to define the monument's structural features.

12. Structural cracks were overlaid on the computer model to determine where the repair work would begin.

13. Borglum initially carved Jefferson's face on Washington's right but then carved it again on the left.

14. The monument needed repairs by 1991.

15. The repairs cost $40 million.

16. The repair company used a computer model to produce a three-dimensional image of Mt. Rushmore.

17. It took Borglum 14 years to carve the four faces.

18. Borglum was a Ku Klux Klan supporter and an active anti-Semite.

19. Borglum proposed Presidents Washington, Jefferson, Lincoln, and Theodore Roosevelt instead of Wild West figures.

20. Borglum wanted to memorialize four great national leaders.

21. Native Americans feel that the four Presidents "committed acts of atrocity against our people"—Tim Giago, Oglala Sioux spokesperson.

22. Borglum's workers had to build a new road to get to Mt. Rushmore.

23. Within 500 generations, the monument will erode to the point where the Presidents look like bald little children.

24. Sioux Indian land claims date back to 1868.

25. In 1980, the U.S. Supreme Court ruled in favor of the Sioux and ordered the U.S. government to pay $263 million in fines and interest.

26. The Sioux have refused the money, which sits in a trust account; they want their land back.

27. Funding for the monument kept running out, but Borglum convinced Calvin Coolidge and Franklin Roosevelt to use government money to finish it.

28.   The Rushmore granite is eroding at a rate of 1 inch per   **241**
      10,000 years.

MARGARET SANGER: PIONEERING NURSE

Suppose your next writing assignment is a 300- to 400-word paper about Margaret Sanger, founder of the Planned Parenthood Foundation. After generating the following list, you need to think of a controlling idea that will help you decide which details to include and which ones to omit. After you have a controlling idea, write a well-organized and focused paragraph about Margaret Sanger.

Sanger trained as an OB/GYN nurse.

She worked in the slums of NY City before World War I.

She saw many victims of self-induced abortions.

She published a birth control magazine *(The Woman Rebel)*.

She was arrested for distributing obscene material.

In 1916, she opened the country's first birth control clinic.

The clinic was in Brooklyn.

Sanger had 3 kids of her own.

She founded the National Birth Control League (now called Planned Parenthood).

She toured Asia and internationalized the birth control movement.

She visited India and established teaching centers.

She retired to Tucson, Arizona.

She died in 1966.

She wrote 10 books (including *What Every Mother Should Know*).

She urged sex education.

What Every Girl Should Know distinguished between sex and love.

Sanger was born Margaret Higgins (1879), one of 11 kids.

Her mother's health was affected by bearing and raising 11 kids, which made a strong impact on Margaret.

242   She wrote in her diary about how witnessing a birth in a delivery room was "awe-inspiring."

Margaret spent 8 months in a sanitarium recovering from the birth of her first child.

The death of Mrs. Sachs—a woman who died after 2 self-induced abortions—had a powerful effect on Sanger.

Mrs. Sachs didn't know anything about birth control.

Poor women always asked Margaret for the "secret" of birth control.

UNIT 15

REWRITING 1: USING DETAILS

 ## USING DETAILS TO PAINT A PICTURE

We say that a picture is worth a thousand words because a picture paints a scene—its color, shape, and texture. But writing can paint scenes too. In fact, good writing is alive with details that capture the sights, sounds, smells, tastes, and textures of the real world. That's why, when you finish a book you enjoyed reading, you often remark, "It was so real, I felt I was there." Details make writing interesting and engaging and give it life.

Here are two papers by beginning college writers. Both are about moving into a dorm for the first time. Which paper makes you feel as if you're really there?

Meeting My Roommate

I was more anxious about meeting my roommate than about almost anything else when I first came to college. The last night of vacation was awful. I hardly slept. I worried about school and about my future roommate and about what she was going to be like. After all, I'd have to live with her for the next nine months.

That morning I got up bright and early and got ready to go to Risser College. The butterflies were fluttering around in my stomach more than ever. My family and I arrived at Risser about 3:30 P.M. I went to Klein Hall, registered, received my keys to the room and dorm, and then took some clothes and things up to my room. I found that my room was empty, and there was no sign of my roommate. That eased things a bit, although I would have liked to have met her and gotten it over with!

Then I made another trip from my room down to the car to get more clothes and things, but this time when I got to my room, there was another family! I knew it had to be her—my roommate. Actually meeting her wasn't so bad after all. We introduced ourselves and our families, said a few more words, and that was it! My first impression wasn't too bad.

After our families left for home, my roommate and I had a better chance to get to know each other and found out that we had a lot in common. It was great! I knew then that this year was going to be a good one, and all my worrying had been for nothing.

A Friendly Face

I climbed the stairs exhausted, carrying a suitcase in one hand, a lampshade in the other, my father following with two more suitcases. By the time I got to the third floor of Klein Hall, I'd had it. I was tired, frustrated—feeling lonely and a bit scared. To top it all off, Dad tripped on the landing and sent my new American Tourister suitcases flying down the hall, bumping into walls like in some mad commercial about the durability of luggage. "Damn!" he screamed, the veins in his forehead pulsing quickly. I knew trouble was ahead. Whenever Dad's veins pulse, look out!

How would I ever get him to finish unloading the car without screaming at me and making a scene in front of the girls in the dorm, the girls I would have to spend the rest of the year with? Doors were opening and heads peering out of cracks. My first year of college would be a disaster because of a torn piece of carpet and those suitcases still bouncing off the walls.

"Find the room quickly," I thought. "Get him into a chair and calmed down." But then again, would there even be a chair in 316? Or would it be an empty room? I'd find out soon enough, for the number 316 glared at me as if it were a gaudy, blinking neon sign beckoning just ahead.

Hesitantly, I turned the key in the lock and pushed the door open, with Dad still muttering about a bruised knee or something. I put my head into the space between the door and the jamb, expecting the worst. But to my **245** surprise, the room wasn't empty after all! It was furnished and decorated, with posters of Aspen and Daytona Beach on the walls, beige curtains, and an area rug. It looked like a page from *Seventeen*'s "All-American Dorm Rooms."

And there on a well-made bed sat Amy, my new roomie, dressed in starched khaki shorts and a dark blue knit blouse. "Hi, you must be Cori," she said in a soft Southern drawl. Then she turned down the Carly Simon CD on the stereo and looked over at Dad. "And of course, you're Mr. Faber," she remarked, smiling, a bright, blue-eyed smile. "Would you like a glass of iced tea?" Dad's veins shrank slightly and turned decidedly less red before he could utter a subdued "yes."

I knew then that Amy and I would be friends and my first year of college would be a success.

"A Friendly Face" evokes the scene better because it's alive with vivid images. "Meeting My Roommate" lacks the specific details that would bring it to life for the reader. It tells us how the writer felt and what she did. It tells us that she was worried, that she went to the dorm, that she took her clothes up to her room, and that she met her roommate and her roommate's family. But these generalizations are never made vivid enough for us to picture the scenes; the paper is weak because of what it leaves out. We don't see or feel or hear what the writer saw or felt or heard, so we are left unsatisfied. We don't really know the details of what went on.

In "A Friendly Face," on the other hand, the details do create a scene. Here are Cori and her father exhausted after climbing three flights of stairs carrying furnishings and suitcases. There is Mr. Faber shouting, "Damn!" Then we see the suitcases "flying down the hall, bumping into walls like in some mad commercial. . . ." We can hear Cori's mind racing: "Get him into a chair and calmed down." When Mr. Faber begins to calm down, the veins on his forehead shrink and "turn" decidedly less red before he could utter a subdued 'yes.' " Cori gives us enough details about Amy and the room to suggest what sort of person Amy is. She's blue-eyed, Southern, organized, tasteful, and not easily rattled. She certainly knows how to defuse a tense situation, by staying cool and offering Mr. Faber a glass of iced tea. "A Friendly Face" succeeds because the writer makes the characters and situations come alive with details that appeal to our senses and to our imagination: Cori paints a picture with words.

SHOW, DON'T TELL

As you can see by contrasting the two papers, it's generally better to show than to tell. The writer of "Friendly Face" doesn't tell us that Amy is neat and "preppy." She shows us Amy's "starched khaki shorts and dark blue knit blouse." She doesn't have to say that the girls in the dorm have been watching her and her dad. She shows us "doors were already opening and heads peering out of cracks." Cori doesn't tell; she shows.

You can use the same technique. Do you want your readers to know that a character is nervous? Don't say that he is nervous. Show that his hand is wet and clammy when you shake it. Does your history professor smoke too much? Don't tell the readers. Show them that his clothes stink from tobacco and that his fingers are discolored by nicotine. Were you uncomfortable sitting in the gym? Show that the bleachers were so rough that they left ridges in your rear. Did the judge at traffic court unnerve you? Show that her voice sounded like chalk squeaking on a blackboard, sending shivers down your spine.

 ADDING DETAILS TO SENTENCES

Showing sharpens and focuses impressions for your readers—either by giving characteristics, by distinguishing parts, or by making comparisons. You often start a sentence with a "telling" statement, then sharpen its focus by rewriting it with more details in the form of grammatical structures like participles, appositives, absolutes, and subordinate clauses. Notice the difference between the next two sentences:

What I first noticed when Merle walked in the door was her dress.

What I first noticed when Merle walked in the door was her dress, **rumpled and slightly frayed.**

The first sentence *tells* us that the writer noticed Merle's dress, but we do not know what about the dress caught the writer's eye. In the second sentence, the phrase **rumpled and slightly frayed** furnishes that information by giving characteristics of the dress.

In the next example, the writer first tells us that the tennis player's **247** movements around the court are arrogant. Then, she rewrites it, narrowing the focus by adding two modifiers that distinguish the parts of Connors' movements. She shows us exactly what in his movements made her come to the conclusion that the tennis player is arrogant:

> There was a touch of arrogance in the way young Jimmy Connors moved around the tennis court.

↓

> There was a touch of arrogance in the way young Jimmy Connors moved around the tennis court—**his shoulders hunched, his eyes focused on himself**.

Cori uses this technique of adding focusing details to sentences several times in "A Friendly Face." In the opening sentence, for instance, we find out she is exhausted climbing the stairs. Then we are shown the details of the scene in the modifiers added to the main clause:

> I climbed the stairs exhausted, **carrying a suitcase in one hand, a lampshade in the other, my father following with two more suitcases**.

Sometimes the details you add to sentences can sharpen the focus by showing that one thing is like something else. Usually, you make comparisons with phrases that begin with **like** or **as**:

> The children scampered onto the playground, **like** puppies out on a romp.
>
> The figure skater spun on a single blade, **as** still in motion **as** a top.

Cori says that her suitcases flew down the hall **like in some mad commercial about the durability of luggage**. And she remarks that the room number glared at her **as if it were a gaudy, blinking neon sign beckoning just ahead**.

In brief, you can sharpen and focus impressions in your writing by adding details that (a) give details or circumstances, (b) distinguish parts, or (c) make comparisons, as in the following three sentences:

1. Down the slope came Avis, **intent on keeping her balance.**
2. Down the slope came Avis, **her hands tightly clutching the ski poles.**

3.   Down the slope came Avis, **as awkward as a newborn colt attempting to walk for the first time.**

CHANGING TELLING STATEMENTS INTO SHOWING STATEMENTS

It's not always enough to add details to a sentence to make it more vivid and appealing. Sometimes you have to rewrite a telling statement to make it a showing statement. For example, the sentence "Shaquille O'Neal is unusually tall" becomes more memorable if you change it into "Shaquille O'Neal ducks his head whenever he comes through a door." The young woman who wrote "Meeting My Roommate" missed an opportunity to stimulate the reader's imagination in her first paragraph when she wrote, "I hardly slept." How much more of an image she would have created for the reader if she had written instead, "All night I tossed and turned uncomfortably, twisting my sheets and covers into a tangled mess." Cori, on the other hand doesn't miss many opportunities to write showing sentences in "A Friendly Face." Notice that she does not say, "Dad got angry" after her father tripped and dropped the suitcases. She shows you how he reacted and what she thought at the time and lets you conclude that he got angry:

> "Damn!" he screamed, the veins in his forehead pulsing quickly. I knew trouble was ahead. Whenever Dad's veins pulse, look out!

It's that sort of writing that makes "A Friendly Face" so lively and interesting.

You can choose whether to show or tell, especially when you revise early drafts of your writing. What if you were writing about a trip that you and your mother had recently taken and you wanted to indicate that the bellhop who carried your bags in a New York hotel was stiffly courteous? You could make a telling statement to that effect, leaving readers to wonder what it was about the bellhop that made you think he was stiffly courteous:

> A stiffly courteous bellhop carried our bags to the room.

Or you could show what the bellhop did, letting the readers see the bellhop's actions and even hear him speak:

"May I take your bags, sir?" the bellhop snapped, picking up my duffel in **249** one hand and—turning precisely, like a drill sergeant—reaching for Mom's suitcase with the other. At the same time, he said, "I'll bring that to your room, ma'am. Please leave it right there."

Since the readers can see and hear the bellhop being stiff and courteous in the second version, they don't need to be told how he acted. They can draw the conclusion themselves.

 **SUMMARY**

Good writing paints scenes with details that appeal to the senses. Especially as you revise, you'll find plenty of opportunities in your writing to show rather than tell. You need to keep a lookout for places where you can add details to sharpen images. And you should be especially careful to turn telling statements into showing statements so that your reader can share your experience, can see and hear and feel and taste and smell what you saw, heard, felt, tasted, and smelled.

ADDING DETAILS 1

To sharpen the focus of the following sentences, rewrite them by adding details that either give characteristics, distinguish parts, or make comparisons. Write at least two versions of each sentence, one with a single modifier, the other with several modifiers.

EXAMPLE

The coach demonstrated the reverse layup.

The coach demonstrated the reverse layup **by driving under the basket and banking the ball off the backboard.**

OR

The coach demonstrated the reverse layup, **balancing the ball on his fingertips, his upper body stretching toward the backboard as gracefully as a ballet dancer doing leaps.**

A. The boys trashed the yard.
B. Jonathan couldn't finish the marathon.
C. The janitor wore mismatched clothes.
D. A helicopter hovers over the brightly lit scene.
E. The fat woman questioned Oprah's guest expert.

HOW TO GET AHEAD

Combine the following sentences into a story that conveys the humor created when a young man has to think on his feet in order to get out of a sticky situation. Add details of your own that will make the scene more vivid. You might think about what the woman looks like, how Syd reacts, what she and Syd sound like. What do you think Syd is doing when the woman walks up?

1. A woman walked up to Syd.
2. Syd worked as a clerk at a supermarket.

3. The woman asked Syd about the price of lettuce.
4. Syd told the woman that lettuce cost 99¢ a head.

5. The woman complained.
6. She said the lettuce would spoil before she could eat it all.
7. She said she wanted only half a head.

8. Syd said he couldn't sell her half a head.
9. Even after this, she asked again.
10. Then she asked to see the store manager.

11. Syd walked to the back office to tell his boss.
12. He didn't realize [something].
13. The woman was following him.
14. "Sorry to bother you, Mr. Lumberger," Syd said to his boss.
15. "But some idiot woman wants to buy half a head of lettuce."
16. Syd turned around.
17. Syd pointed to the front of the store.

18. Then Syd saw [something].
19. The woman was right behind him.
20. "And this nice lady wants to buy the other half," Syd said.

MAKING SHOWING STATEMENTS

Rewrite the telling statements below so that they become showing statements. Make the showing statements so vivid that readers can sense the actions and ideas.

EXAMPLE

The senator spoke to the reporter defiantly.

252   The senator shouted, "Baloney," to the reporter, punctuating his remarks by sharply bashing his fist on the podium.

A. The radio blared.

B. The school halls were tense.

C. The kitten was playful.

D. The teddy bear needed repairs.

E. Mary was depressed.

F. The artist labored over the drawing.

G. The professor lectured quietly.

H. Jennifer was noisy.

I. MTV assaults our senses.

J. Susan tried to look cool and at ease.

SNOWBOY

Combine the following sentences into a narrative essay about a boy who wants to stay out in the snow while his mother wants him to come in for dinner. Add details of your own that will make the scene more vivid.

1. Barry heard his mother calling him in.

2. Her voice sounded colder in the winter wind.

3. He turned reluctantly from the frozen white walls he had built.

4. He looked hopefully to the back door.

5. His cheeks were red from hours of play.

6. His nylon snowsuit was a shade darker from melted snow.

7. No reprieve came.

8. He waved to his daylong companion.

9. His companion was the snowman.

10. He began the fifty-foot trek to his house.

11. He prolonged every step.

12. He took last glimpses of his empire.

13. He dragged his black galoshes through the snow.
14. He thought only of the day's fun.
15. He thought of the snowballs thrown.
16. He thought of the territories conquered.

17. The warm dinner seemed less inviting than the cold mouthfuls of snow.
18. His mother would insist the warm dinner was good for him.
19. He had swallowed snow while crawling through his network of tunnels.

20. His only comfort was one last wild plunge.
21. He plunged over the snowy yard.
22. He plunged through an enemy fort.
23. The walls of the fort were already weak from his earlier barrage of iceballs.

24. Barry's day was ending.
25. It had seemed to go on forever.
26. Now the games were gone.
27. The friends were gone.
28. The runny noses were gone.

29. Adam lingered awhile on the porch.
30. He stomped his boots clean.
31. He clapped his mittens free of the snow.
32. Snow was frozen in every crease.
33. He wished to return to his real home.
34. The yard was his real home.

35. His mother finally hurried him into the house.
36. She was growing impatient.
37. The house swallowed him for the evening.

ADDING DETAILS 2

To sharpen the focus of the following sentences, rewrite them by adding details that give characteristics, distinguish parts, or make comparisons. Write at least two versions of each sentence, one with a single modifier, the other with several modifiers.

EXAMPLE

The satellite went out of control.

The satellite went out of control, **pirouetting like a weightless dancer marking infinite time.**

OR

The satellite went out of control, **rising, dipping, and looping haphazardly until it re-entered the atmosphere in a fiery flash.**

A. Mick Jagger pranced around the stage.
B. The protesters stood at the entrance to the waste dump.
C. Mr. Rogers zipped up his cardigan.
D. The '57 Chevy sits rusting in the yard.
E. The crowd watched the firefighters.

LOVE AND THE ZIP

Combine the following sentences into an explanatory essay that humorously suggests a connection between love and the five-digit ZIP code. Add or change details whenever they can make your essay funnier or more informative.

1. Do this the next time you send a letter to a special someone.
2. Take a few minutes to examine the envelope.

3. It may be plain white.
4. It may be delicate pink.

5. It may be scented with her favorite cologne.   **255**

6. It may be scented with his favorite perfume.

7. There may be no return address.

8. Or you may have included a message on the envelope.

9. The message may be a cryptic private joke.

10. The message may be a cartoon.

11. It doesn't matter what message you send your loved one.

12. The most important thing on the envelope may be the ZIP Code.

13. The U.S. ZIP Code is thirty years old.

14. Still, nothing works better to get your letter where it's going.

15. Postmaster General J. Edward Day instituted the ZIP Code system in 1963.

16. In doing so, he bypassed bureaucrats.

17. Bureaucrats had been agonizing over the idea like a young man writing love letters.

18. Today the U.S. Postal Service uses ZIP Codes to sort over 100 billion pieces of mail a year.

19. Today the U.S. Postal Service uses ZIP Codes to deliver over 100 billion pieces of mail a year.

20. Most people use the proper ZIP Codes.

21. But forgetting the ZIP Code can be costly.

22. Using the wrong ZIP Code can be costly.

23. Just imagine the work that goes into that letter to your someone special.

24. Sweat is standing out on your forehead.

25. You struggle to come up with just the right words.

26. Heaps of crumpled stationery lie scattered around your desk.

27. Suddenly your eyes brighten.

28. You begin to hum.

29.   You finally know exactly what to say.

30.   It is not too serious.

31.   It is not too sentimental.

32.   You can mail it just in time for your anniversary.

33.   You carefully write the address on the envelope.

34.   You put a stamp in the corner.

35.   You grab your coat.

36.   Outside at the mailbox, you pause.

37.   You are sure you've forgotten something.

38.   Your heart starts with a leap.

39.   You realize you haven't put the ZIP Code on the letter.

40.   It might never get there.

41.   Sometimes addressing a letter properly can be serious.

42.   It can mean the difference between a happy anniversary and a lot of lonely Valentine's Days.

UNIT 16

REWRITING 2: CHANGING STRUCTURE

Beginning writers often think of revision in terms of "local" changes: cleaning up spelling and punctuation, perhaps replacing a specific word here and there to make a sentence "look better." But more experienced writers generally think of revision in more "global terms," looking at an entire draft, rethinking it, reworking its organization, improving what they have already written, even if it means taking the entire paper apart and starting over in a different way. Beginning writers revise to make their papers neater; they proofread. Experienced writers revise to make their papers more vivid, more forceful, and more interesting; they rewrite. In the process, they often are able to define more clearly for themselves and for their readers just what it is they mean to say. Sometimes, rewriting demands only that you change words, mend sentences, and restructure paragraphs. But just as often, it demands that you make radical changes in structure and content based on a new look at your text.

THE FIRST DRAFT

To give you an example of how writers can alter both structure and content after a fresh look at their work in progress, we'll take you through the revision of a paper by a student named Vicki Robinson. The paper was written in response to an assignment that asked students to describe a place that is special for them in such a way as to make their readers sense its specialness. Here is Vicki's first draft.

Indiana Memories

When I was around eight years old, my grandparents decided to build a cabin on some land they owned in Indiana. The first thing I remember about the place was the dirt roads. Where we lived, all the roads were paved. I had just assumed that all roads were paved, but these were usually dry, dusty, and full of potholes. They made riding in the back of the pickup truck an adventure. We would imagine we were escaping from the bad guys or running from the evil dust cloud. There were several turns to get to the area, and I could never understand how my parents could navigate all those roads when they were all lined up with the same-looking cornfields.

I remember being there the day the bulldozer came to build the lake. It wasn't a very big lake, probably no more than a pond in reality. I can still remember hearing the roar of the bulldozer as it moved the dirt here and there and wanting to go watch so bad. But Mom wouldn't let me get near where they were working. Being a typical mother, she said it was "too dangerous." But, as it turned out, the construction men managed to get the lake done without my help. It would take several months for the rain to fill the lake and get it ready for fishing.

Then it was time to start the cabin, and we spent many weekends there helping build it. I was so excited because I finally got to actually help. My helping was no more than picking up scrap lumber and bringing more nails, but it was helping just the same. As soon as there were enough floorboards in place to walk on, I got to be the first person to walk on the floor. Not a big deal to anyone but me, and for some reason I looked at it as a very important event. I never missed a chance to inform my sister that "I" was the first to walk on it. When the cabin was done, we spent nearly every weekend there.

There were only a couple of things that really made staying there an inconvenience. One was the outhouse, which explains itself, and the other was the water. Since there was no well, the nearest place to get water was a natural spring, which was about a quarter mile down the dirt road. The first time I went there with Nannie, I was shocked to see just a hole in the ground. Where was the familiar "old-fashioned" well with a bucket on a rope? This was an open hole with water in it. There was also a crawdad that lived in it, and it took quite a bit of convincing to get me to drink water

that had things living in it. But the water was delicious and so cold it hurt **259**
my teeth when I took a drink.

The highlight of our weekend was the Saturday night auction. We'd all
pile in the pickup truck and drive five miles to the place. It was nothing
more than a glorified barn where all the folks around that area brought
their stuff before the age of garage sales. We would sit in the bleachers
and listen to the auctioneer selling boxes of this and bags of that. It was
fun to buy a big box of stuff for 25 or 50 cents only to discover you had
purchased some broken Christmas decorations, rope that wasn't long
enough to tie anything, or a bunch of stuff that you really couldn't tell what
it was or had been at one time. When we got restless sitting there, Nannie
would take us to the "restaurant," which was in the next room. The smell
of grease would hang in the air so thick. We'd have cheeseburgers and
fries all around. They were the best I'd ever had; must have been the
atmosphere.

During the day, we'd go fishing or play in the woods that were next to
the lake. One day we found some kind of vine hanging from a tall tree.
After talking one of my younger cousins into being the safety "test pilot,"
we all took turns swinging on the vine and giving our best Tarzan yell.
Other times, we'd play hide and seek in the cornfields.

As Nannie and Papaw got up in years, they sold the cabin and moved
back to Ohio. I was too young at the time to realize what was really happening. I'd like to go and see the place sometime. I've always wondered
if my name is still on the tree where Daddy carved it for me. Someday I'd
like to have the money to buy it back from whoever bought it and keep it
in the family.

Vicki's draft has met the requirements of the assignment because
she has done a strong job of painting a picture of her favorite childhood place—her grandparents' Indiana cabin. She has a knack for
using sharp images to picture a scene: "I had assumed that all roads
were paved, but these were usually dry, dusty, and full of potholes.
They made riding in the back of the pickup truck an adventure. We
would imagine we were escaping from the bad guys or running from
the evil dust cloud."

Although she misses the old cabin, her paper is not meant to be sad
or teary, and she expresses a light, amused tone on occasion, appropriate
to this wistful remembrance of things past: "Nannie would take us to the
'restaurant,' which was in the next room. The smell of grease would hang
in the air so thick. We'd have cheeseburgers and fries all around. They
were the best I'd ever had; must have been the atmosphere."

260   But Vicki's essay sprawls. It has no direction. It meanders from memory to memory, first about the trip to the cabin, then about the cabin's construction, and then about a typical weekend visit. And the visit section is not even in chronological order. Her paper finally just ends, leaving the reader to feel that it could have ended sooner or could have gone on longer.

 PEER GROUP COMMENTS

At this point, Vicki might simply have proofread, spruced up a few sentences, and handed in the paper—clean and adequate—to her instructor. Or she might have sat down with the paper and worked on revising it on her own. But since Vicki's instructor asks students to share their papers with a peer revising group before they submit them, Vicki brought the Indiana paper to her group for their comments and suggestions. Revising groups provide writers with an opportunity to hear what others think of their drafts, to find out how readers react to their writing. The peer group members generally make brief comments on the draft itself; individuals can also give their overall reactions and suggest changes the writer might make. Writers, of course, are free to take the group's advice, modify that advice, or ignore it.

Vicki's group, Ben, Eleni, and Lynn, read her draft and wrote questions and comments in the margins of the paper. At the end of the draft, each of them wrote a longer comment, summarizing their overall reactions to "Indiana Memories." Here's what Vicki's group had to say about her paper:

Indiana Memories

I remember visiting my grandparents too when I was little.

When I was around eight years old, my grandparents decided to build a cabin on some land they owned in Indiana. The first thing I remember about the place was the dirt roads. Where we lived, all the roads were paved. I had just assumed that all roads were paved, but these were usually dry, dusty, and full of potholes. They made riding in the back of the pickup truck an adventure. We would imagine

This sentence isn't really grabbing my attention.

we were escaping from the bad guys or running from the evil dust cloud. There were several turns to get to the area, and I could never understand how my parents could navigate all those roads when they were all lined up with the same-looking cornfields.

This is a vivid image!

I remember being there the day the bulldozer came to build the lake. It wasn't a very big lake, probably no more than a pond in reality. I can still remember hearing the roar of the bulldozer as it moved the dirt here and there and wanting to go watch so bad. But Mom wouldn't let me get near where they were working. Being a typical mother, she said it was "too dangerous." But, as it turned out, the construction men managed to get the lake done without my help. It would take several months for the rain to fill the lake and get it ready for fishing.

A nice lighthearted touch.

Then it was time to start the cabin, and we spent many weekends there helping build it. I was so excited because I finally got to actually help. My helping was no more than picking up scrap lumber and bringing more nails, but it was helping just the same. As soon as there were enough floorboards in place to walk on, I got to be the first person to walk on the floor. Not a big deal to anyone but me, and for some reason I looked at it as a very important event. I never missed a chance to inform my sister that "I" was the first to walk on it. When the cabin was done, we spent nearly every weekend there.

A cute anecdote— sounds like me as a child.

There's no real transition here.

There were only a couple of things that really made staying there an inconvenience. One was the outhouse, which explains itself, and the other was the water. Since there was no well, the nearest place to get water was a natural spring, which was about a quarter mile down the dirt road. The first time I went there with Nannie, I was shocked to see just a hole in the ground. Where was the familiar "old-fashioned" well with a bucket on a rope? This was

Describe the outhouse a bit?

Nice use of a question.

an open hole with water in it. There was also a crawdad that lived in it, and it took quite a bit of convincing to get me to drink water that had things living in it. But the water was delicious and so cold it hurt my teeth when I took a drink.

What did you do until Sat. night?

The highlight of our weekend was the Saturday night auction. We'd all pile in the pickup truck and drive five miles to the place. It was nothing more than a glorified barn where all the folks around that area brought their stuff before the age of garage sales. We would sit in the bleachers and listen to the auctioneer selling boxes of this and bags of that. It was fun to buy a big box of stuff for 25 or 50 cents only to discover you had purchased some broken Christmas decorations, rope that wasn't long enough to tie anything, or a bunch of stuff that you really couldn't tell what it was or had been at one time. When we got restless sitting there, Nannie would take us to the "restaurant," which was in the next room. The smell of grease would hang in the air so thick. We'd have cheeseburgers and fries all around. They were the best I'd ever had; must have been the atmosphere.

This sentence is hard for me to follow.

Another amusing, light-hearted comment.

During the day, we'd go fishing or play in the woods that were next to the lake. One day we found some kind of vine hanging from a tall tree. After talking one of my younger cousins into being the safety "test pilot," we all took turns swinging on the vine and giving our best Tarzan yell. Other times, we'd play hide and seek in the cornfields.

Why are you now back-tracking to the daytime activities?

As Nannie and Papaw got up in years, they sold the cabin and moved back to Ohio. I was too young at the time to realize what was really happening. I'd like to go and see the place sometime. I've always wondered if my name is still on the tree where Daddy carved it for me. Someday I'd like to have the money to buy it back from whoever bought it and keep it in the family.

How long ago was all of this?

It's easy to see that, looking back, the cabin really mattered to you.

The ending is OK—but I didn't get a genuine sense of closure here.

COMMENTS

Ben: I could really get a feel for your grandparents' cabin here thanks to all the vivid descriptions such as the icy cold drinking water and the old dusty dirt roads. My grandma lived in a city, but I still remember visiting her when I was a boy, so I could relate to your special place. I liked the occasional humor in your voice (about the "atmosphere" in the greasy spoon restaurant and the construction workers building the lake without your help). Maybe you could develop that humor a bit more consistently as a way of tying the essay together through its tone, making it more of a humorous recollection of a fun place from your childhood?

Eleni: For me the best parts of the paper were the brief anecdotes such as going to the auction barn and being the first to walk in the cabin. Do you remember any other stories you could tell as well to give us a clearer picture of <u>you</u> at the cabin? Those stories make me think back to my own childhood; that's why I wanted to see more of you in action. I had some trouble following the flow of your essay. The essay seemed to jump around a bit. Were you interested in showing a typical weekend visit (because I only got a partial picture of that)? Or were you trying to show us how much you missed the old place? I think the last paragraph made me think you really missed the old cabin—is it gone now? has it changed? or have you? or both?

Lynn: The essay started slowly for me, but I got into it as you went on. It became easier to grasp why you missed this cabin with all of its happy childhood memories, so I understood your final paragraph. I liked the brief glimpses of your family too—your "typical Mom," your Dad carving your name on a tree, your Nannie and the ice-cold water, you and your cousins playing in the woods. However, I couldn't get a sense of how the paper was moving from one vivid description to another, from one anecdote to another. It almost seemed as if it could go on for several more pages with more recollections. Where is it going? Could you find a way to organize it more clearly? Maybe a recent visit to see what the cabin looks like now would work or a description of a typical weekend visit from start to finish?

 **A REVISION**

Vicki's peer group gave her sound, readerly advice and genuine readers' responses. They told her how they perceived the paper—as vivid but not

264 organized. They told her they could relate to her draft, but they wanted a better sense of where the paper was going. They asked her for more glimpses of the people and the place and both a stronger beginning and a stronger ending.

After listening to their responses, questions, and suggestions, Vicki rewrote her paper in the following way:

My Indiana Home

Now just past this hill there should be a curve with a road to the left right after it. There! Right there it is. Hey, they paved it. Last time I was here, it was gravel. I can't believe I can still remember all these turns after seventeen years. I guess it's like how birds know when to fly south. I just know where to turn. The last time I was here, I must have been around thirteen. It seems like nothing has changed, but everything has changed. Oh, there are a few more houses out here, like that one over there, but the little church here on the right looks the same.

Up ahead, over the next rise, there will be another road to the left, and there should be a little gingerbread-type house on the corner. Slow down; this is it. Well, the little house used to look like gingerbread. It sure is run down now. I hate to see that happen to a place, but at least this road is still dirt. We used to have so much fun riding down this road in the back of Papaw's pickup truck. We'd pretend the cloud of dust was after us. Hey, look behind us. It's after us now.

Papaw owned all this land through here. That soybean field used to have corn planted in it every year back then. We played hide n' seek in there for hours. And see those woods over in the distance? They're on the other side of the lake. We used to play in them too. Once we found a vine hanging from a big tree. We suckered my cousin into testing it out. Then we spent the whole weekend in the jungles of Africa, swinging from trees and hunting big game. No, we never saw any lions or tigers or bears. The biggest animal we found was the rabbit we scared up. He jumped and ran one way, we jumped and ran the other. It was so funny. He scared us more than we scared him.

You can see part of the cabin up ahead. See, there's the lake right behind it. This place sure has changed a lot. I'm glad the people have taken good care of it. I wonder if they would mind if we looked around. You'll really ask? That would be great.

We can?! Come on, I've got so much to show you. The first time I remember being here, they were just building this lake. I was probably eight then. I remember wanting to go watch so bad, but Mom wouldn't let

me. She said it was too dangerous, and she was right. Moms always are. **265**
I had to stay at the trailer that used to sit back over there. It had a big
grapevine behind it with the biggest purple grapes I'd ever seen. But anyway, I was so mad. I couldn't figure out how they could build the lake right
without me to tell them how to do it. But as you can tell, they did a great
job. Papaw stocked it with fish, and we used to go fishing all the time.
Amy caught a turtle one time. Right under its tail. We still tease her about
it a lot. Mention it next time you see her.

This is the original part of the cabin. They let me be the gofer and help
build it. You know, a "gofer." "Gofer" nails, "gofer" tools, stuff like that. It was
fun. Now I think they did it just to get me out of the way so they could work.
I wrote my name in the cement where the chimney is. And I got to be the
first one to walk on the floor when it was done. I thought I had really done
something. Guess I did, cause I still remember it. This part here has been
added on in the past few years. Guess the new owners wanted more room.

See that tree over there? Come on, I want to check something out.
Look right up there. You can barely see it. It says "Vicki." Daddy carved it
in this tree when I was little. I can't believe it's still there. Now these people
here know who Vicki is. There's the outhouse. I hated that place—it was
full of spiders and wasp nests. I bet there's inside plumbing now. I sure do
miss this place. I wish Nannie and Papaw had kept it instead of selling it.
Yeah, guess we better get going.

Wait, there's one more thing I want to see. It's on down the road about
a quarter mile. It's the spring where we used to get water. Yeah, we can
drive to it. We'd have to walk down here with buckets and take it back to
the cabin. The first time I came down here with Nannie, I expected to see
a well. You know. The kind with a bucket on a rope like in Kentucky. This
was just a hole in the ground with water in it. There used to be a little
crawdad that lived in it. Every time we'd come for water, he'd scurry back
under a brick. Yeah, I know. Sounds gross. I wasn't real thrilled about
water with things living in it, but Nannie talked me into taking a drink. It
was the best water I'd ever tasted and so cold it hurt my teeth. Oh, look
what someone did. They covered up my little spring. Why'd they put that
big cement cover over it? Guess you can't leave an open hole with water
in it uncovered any more. Yeah, I'm all right. I guess I just expected things
to stay the same. I'm not crying. My contacts hurt. It's just a stupid spring
anyway. Well, it used to be. Let's get out of here. Maybe the auction barn
is still there. Go back to the main road and turn left.

You really want to hear all these stories? OK, the auction barn. It was
terrific, the highlight of the weekend. We'd all pile in the back of the pickup
and head down there. It was just an old barn with bleachers in it where

everybody would sit. People from all over would bring their stuff there to sell before garage sales were heard of. It was fun to buy a big box of stuff for 25 or 50 cents and then find out that it was full of broken Christmas decorations, a hammer with no handle, or a bunch of stuff you really couldn't recognize. Nannie would take us to the restaurant, which was in the next stall. We'd have the best greasy cheeseburgers and french fries. You could smell the grease in the air. It sure was nasty, but the food was so good. It must have been the atmosphere. Yeah, right. It should be on the left somewhere through here. I don't see it. Maybe they replaced it with the flea market back there. This place has changed so much. Well, at least I remember what it used to be like. Gosh, I feel like my mom telling stories about when she was little. Am I getting old? I didn't realize just how much fun I did have over here when I was little.

Well, Nannie and Papaw decided to sell it and the house in town and move back to Ohio. They were getting up in years, and Mom didn't like the idea of them being so far away. It is a great place. It would have been the perfect spot to get away on the weekends. No phones, no TV. I really wish Mom would have kept it if Nannie and Papaw weren't able to. Ice cream? Yeah, there's one in Brookville about ten miles from here. Ice cream is just what I need right now. Thanks.

Obviously, Vicki found the peer group's comments valuable. She made major revisions in her paper, starting with a new view of how to write it, a view that responds to the reactions by Ben, Eleni, and Lynn. In her revision, Vicki has improved her paper significantly by converting her description into the story of her recent visit to the old cabin. Readers will have no difficulty following her revised paper; nor will they be surprised when it ends, since it concludes after Vicki has toured the entire cabin and local area and completed her visit. There is a sense of geographical movement over the land itself that helps readers keep track of what is happening in her story. As she spots a familiar sight, she either describes it or tells an anecdote about it. Notice that she has expanded the roles played by her family; she dramatizes her dad's carving her name on the tree and gives Nannie a bigger role in convincing her to drink the cold water.

The sense of loss is keener now too, as Vicki shows her readers how things have changed over the years. And yet she continues to show the light touch that her peer group praised—the greasy restaurant joke is heightened, the dust cloud is still amusingly alive, she was once a "gofer." In her vision, she has also remembered more details such as the purple grapevines, the spiders in the outhouse, the scared rabbit in the woods.

Perhaps the most significant change Vicki has made, however, is in recasting the essay as a dramatic monologue. She has added a character in her revision—a boyfriend—with whom she interacts throughout the visit to Indiana. Since Vicki is the only one in the story who speaks, it is a monologue. Yet her reactions and comments help us to see what her friend is saying and doing: he asks the cabin's new owners for permission to look around; he expresses concern that she is crying; he encourages her to tell more stories; he comforts her with an ice cream cone at the conclusion. By giving us a sense of the past and present at once, Vicki has succeeded in creating a double vision: We see the scene as she experiences it with her friend, and we see it as she remembers it from her childhood. We also get to know Vicki better in this draft, since we can see and hear her excitement at returning to the cabin, her disappointment at the changes, her sadness at her loss, her embarrassment over her tears. The revision has more of the author's voice and a greater sense of structure. Overall, it's more satisfying to read.

Although Vicki changed the structure of her essay in a remarkable way by revising it into a monologue, she might also have rewritten effectively by reorganizing her draft into a chronological recounting of her recent return to Indiana. Rewriting may require you to change your essay's structure. Rewriting does not necessarily require as dramatic a revision as Vicki's, but it often does. Because Vicki was willing to view her paper in global terms, looking at the entire paper, not merely the individual words and sentences, she has realized more of the essay's potential in her revision. Her subject was not only a rich one for her because of all of the memories she recalls, but it was also one her readers could identify with as well. She has now made it easier for readers to "get into" her paper. But that occurred only because of her willingness to rethink, reconceive, and restructure her draft.

The exercises in this chapter offer you an opportunity to work with sample student papers or a paper of your own that is in progress and revise it in the way Vicki revised her paper—thoughtfully, with an eye toward making the paper more readable and more organized.

 **SUMMARY**

Experienced writers know that they must first consider a draft as a whole when they rewrite it before focusing on specific phrasing. In other

268 words, they must take a global view of the draft before taking a local view of it. In the example in the chapter, Vicki wrote a draft describing her grandparents' cabin in Indiana. Vicki's draft was examined by her revising group; while the group members praised her detailed, emotional recollections of the cabin, they also pointed out that the essay seemed to lack a sense of organization, of a clear beginning and ending. Taking the group's responses into account, Vicki changed the structure of her draft into a monologue about a visit to her grandparents' old cabin. Because Vicki was able to take a global view of her draft, she revised her paper into a much more organized and powerful essay.

REVISING PRACTICE

Choose one of the following student drafts or a draft you are working on for class, and revise it so that it is more interesting and more readable. If your instructor allows, you may work in a peer group. Whether you revise a draft of your own or one of the exercise drafts, read through it thoroughly several times before you begin writing so that you can take a global view of the sentence structure, paragraph development, and ideas. Identify the strong points of the paper, those components or ideas you would like to keep. Consider what sentences and paragraphs need to be rewritten or replaced. Consider what should be the major focus of the paper and how you might develop the central idea through vivid supporting details. Consider the possibility of taking a different point of view on the material or establishing a different relationship between the writer and the reader. Then revise the original into a lively, well-structured paper.

Soap Operas

Soap operas, which usually portray a city and the citizens of that city, are becoming more and more popular each day. Whether it be mothers and fathers, grandmothers and grandfathers, high school age, college age, or even grade school age students, boys and girls alike, it takes only a few episodes to become attached to an afternoon soap opera. Most have tangled stories; just when the viewer thinks he knows the whole story, an episode brings a new and different disclosure out. Their days are planned around them—when they can eat, study, and even sleep.

Hank, who is on the brink of death, lies in the hospital bed with a 105° temperature while Ellen, his pregnant wife who used to be a prostitute, sits alone at this bedside watching for a change in his condition. Deliriously, he begins to talk to her, thinking she is his ex-wife, Consuela, and tells her how much he loves Consuela. Scenes like this from soap operas, which dominate afternoon TV schedules, attract millions of viewers daily.

Very prominent figures of the community usually have something they were involved in in their past but choose to forget. The only person in the whole world that knows the untold truth suddenly appears in town for no apparent reason after many years. And lately more topical issues have been appearing on soaps such as date rape and many others.

One of the reasons for their widespread popularity is even though they are sometimes predictable and hokey, they are never dull. As soon as things start going smoothly, another crisis hits. Jessica, an unmarried 18-year-old who is eight and one-half months pregnant, and Walter are at home alone during a horrendous snowstorm when she goes into labor. Her mother is out of town for the weekend, her grandfather is stuck in a snow drift, the phone isn't working, and the doctor who lives next door isn't home. This type of crisis is typical and would occur at least once in every episode.

Soaps are suspenseful. The shows are cut off at very crucial scenes, which, in turn, prompt viewers to watch the serial the next day for the spine-tingling results. Barry is grappling with the kidnapper to get control the gun when it goes off. The show is then cut, and the viewer is left in a terrific state of suspense. "Who got shot?" This strategy is used by the television writers daily to get the viewers to tune in for the next episode.

Whatever a person's reasons for watching a soap opera are, with their widespread popularity, it seems as though they will be around for many years to come.

Friends No More

Relationships are a special bond that two people share out of love and trust for one another. Friendships are types of relationships based on a special kind of love and respect which can also exist between opposite sexes. For example, Hugh and I were so close in high school that we were almost inseparable. We went through several years of high school with a best-friend relationship. However, now that we have both entered college and changed our ways of thinking, things are changing. We don't seem to be friends any more, but I don't really care.

Hugh and I had a very special relationship that was based on friendship alone. We behaved like a brother and sister and were always there for each other in tough times. It was a difficult situation to deal with because I was a female going through high school with a male best friend. Hugh and I met our sophomore year in high school, and certain people that did not know us very well always associated Hugh and me as a couple instead of friends. Our friendship was so strong that even when either of us was dating other guys or girls, we still managed to remain best friends.

Things are different now. It's a pain when Hugh calls me because it takes time away from homework. And we hardly ever see each other now. Since we go to different colleges, it takes too long to visit each other, even though we're in the same county. Besides, I want to meet different guys at my college while he ought to be meeting girls at his.

Hugh and I used to be alike, which helped to contribute to our strong companionship. Both of us played various sports and shared a lot of common interests. When we were bored, we used to call each other on the **271** phone and talk, talk, talk.

Having met so many new people and making my own new friends, I am not worried about our dwindling relationship. I think we feel the same way about making new friends and not seeing as much of each other. All of my friends had told me that friendships and relationships from high school never last in college. When two people go to different colleges, no matter how near they are to each other, they are bound to forget their old friends and make many new ones. This is the exact situation between me and Hugh. Hugh and I had been together for so long that it was time for a long break to explore new people, and college was the perfect place for this to occur. It is bad, in a way, to think back on all of the good times we had together and realize that is it over, but there are always memories to look back on. It is better, though, that we ended it in college so we could grow in our own ways independently. This is how sometimes the person that you're closest to for so long may not remain a best friend, no matter how strong the relationship might be. I'll always remember Hugh whenever I think of my high school days.

SUGGESTIONS FOR WRITING

 NARRATIVE TOPICS

In narrative writing, you try to tell a story so that your readers experience what is happening. Your aim is less to explain or to inform than to share an experience. For this reason, you will probably want to use specific, concrete, and (probably) personal details. Although most good stories do not have an obvious moral or lesson, they often have a point or a theme: they do try to say something about the human experience. Above all, a good story is interesting to read.

1. Tell a story about being afraid.

2. Tell a story about a time you apologized to someone and really meant it (or should have apologized but didn't).

3. You have just received a letter from this year's editor of your high school yearbook. She is asking you and several others to write a story titled either "A Great Day in High School" or "A Sad Day in High School" for possible inclusion in this year's yearbook. Write a story about a great day or a sad day that you remember from high school.

4. Tell a story about discovering that you—or someone else—had more guts than you had thought.

5. Tell a story about discovering prejudice or bigotry in yourself **273** or someone else.

6. Tell a story about an argument or quarrel—yours or someone else's.

7. Tell a story about one of the funniest things that's ever happened to you.

8. Tell a story about getting or being lost.

9. Tell a story about being rejected (by another person or by a group) or about rejecting someone else.

10. Tell a story about the last time you hit someone or someone hit you.

11. Tell a story about a time when you disliked yourself.

12. Think back to your years in elementary school, and quickly list (in no more than five minutes) whatever events and happenings you still remember. Then choose the one you remember most fully and most intensely, and write a story about it that you will later share with your family during Thanksgiving or Christmas vacation.

DESCRIPTIVE TOPICS

In descriptive writing, you present an object, place, person (or group of people), activity, or event so as to make your readers feel what you felt, sense what you sensed, and experience what you experienced. Good description often relies on showing rather than telling, so you may want to use specific and concrete details and illustrations. You may also want to get some action and motion into your description. Because description and narration overlap, you can write a descriptive paper on any one of the narrative topics.

1. Visit a local nursery school or kindergarten, and write a description of the children at play that will appear in the school's advertising brochure.

2. Describe your reactions to a work of art—a painting or a piece of sculpture—that you especially like or dislike.

3. Describe a place that is special for you—a roller rink or amusement park, an athletic field or playground, a cabin on a lake or

a bench under a tree, a farm, bar, or pizza parlor—to make your readers sense its specialness.

4. Describe what it was like to do something special for the first time—like driving, drinking, flying, waterskiing, hang gliding, or traveling abroad.

5. Describe a trip that you took by yourself or with others—to a city, to the ocean, to a national park, to a college, or to some other place.

6. Your kid brother is thinking about trying out for the wrestling team (track squad, school play, newspaper staff), but he isn't sure whether he'll like it or not. Describe a typical practice session to give him a sense of what it's like and whether he'll find it enjoyable.

7. Describe how you felt when you were forced to spend some time with someone you didn't like—say, on a blind date.

8. Describe the meeting of two people—friends, relatives, or lovers—who haven't seen each other for a long time.

9. To get along better with your parents (or sister or friend), describe for them an aspect of yourself that they've never really recognized or understood.

10. Describe a city or a foreign country you've visited so that others will want to visit it, too.

11. Take an object or set of objects that you once cared deeply about—perhaps a bike, a car, a set of electric trains, a doll, a pair of roller skates, a teddy bear, a set of baseball cards, a tree hut, a hat—and describe it to a friend so that he or she comes to feel how emotionally important it was to you.

12. Describe what happens on a holiday at your home to give an outsider a sense of the relationships among the members of your family.

 EXPLANATORY TOPICS

In explanatory writing, you try to explain to your readers something they do not already know. When they have read what you've written, you want them to say, "Wow, I never understood that before" or "Now

I see things much more clearly." But a good explanatory paper is interesting as well as informative. To create interest, remember to be concrete
and specific, and try at least occasionally to use narration and description
whenever they can help clarify, develop, or illustrate the central idea of
your paper.

1. Explain why so many people watch situation comedies (or tele-
    vision game shows).

2. Explain the effectiveness of any magazine advertisement that
    makes you want to run out and buy the advertised product.
    (Submit the magazine ad along with your paper.)

3. Write a paper explaining to yourself some question you really
    want to answer—like (a) why weren't you as popular in high
    school as you wanted to be? (b) why are you no longer close to
    someone who was once your best friend? (c) why do you feel
    differently about your parents than you used to? (d) why do you
    like certain kinds of music and not other kinds? or (e) why do
    you both like and dislike some of your friends?

4. Write a unified summary of your intellectual interests and
    achievements for the scholarship committee of your college.

5. Explain the reasons for the success of any musical group, single
    performer, album, or single song.

6. Explain how you have overcome a prejudice (racial, ethnic,
    religious, class, or sexual).

7. Explain in a letter to your high school principal (or teacher or
    coach) why (or why not) your high school experience ade-
    quately prepared you for college.

8. Explain what the toys children buy tell us about the adult
    world.

9. Explain why people swear (or explain what we can learn about
    ourselves from the kind of words we consider "dirty" or
    "obscene").

10. Explain in a letter to a close friend why you believe that sleep-
    ing around is immoral (or not immoral).

11. Explain why so many men are male chauvinists.

12. Decide what is your favorite book or movie of all time. Then
    explain to a close friend why the book or movie means so
    much to you.

13. Explain why people go to demolition derbies (or amusement parks, rock concerts, stock car races, or any other event).

14. Explain why a large number of Americans do not vote (or do not belong to either major political party).

15. Explain in a letter to your parents why you are going to change your major (or why you want to transfer to another school).

16. Explain in a letter to your parents why God has recently become more (or less) important to you.

17. Explain the emotional and psychological reasons for joining a sorority or a fraternity.

18. Explain why any television program, movie, or comic strip is funny.

19. A good friend is planning to visit a city (or other geographical area) that you know well, but he or she can spend only a day there. Explain to your friend how best to spend his or her limited time.

20. Explain in a humorous essay how not to do something—how not to go on a diet, how not to study for a final examination, how not to prepare for spring break at Daytona Beach, how not to choose a major, how not to exercise, how not to win the affection of the person who sits just in front of you in Sociology 101.

 ARGUMENT AND PERSUASION TOPICS

In argument, you try to convince your readers to believe what you want them to believe. In persuasion, you try to convince them to do what you want them to do. So both argument and persuasion depend for their success on moving readers from one position to another. You should assume, in other words, that your readers begin in opposition to your own position: your job is to bring them around. To do so, you usually have to accomplish two tasks: (1) you have to refute—or at least weaken—support for their position, and (2) you have to establish support for your own position.

1. Write a letter to convince your parents that you are sincere and serious in holding a moral, political, or religious belief that differs substantially from theirs.

2. Persuade a close friend to donate blood as part of a drive that **277** your campus organization is sponsoring.

3. Argue for or against the assertion that the abolition of the grading system at American colleges and universities would bring about an increase in learning.

4. Write a letter persuading a high school teacher (or coach) to change in some fundamental way the methods she uses to teach her class (or to coach her sport).

5. Argue for or against the proposition that sex education (or driver education, physical education, composition) should be a required course in high school or college.

6. Write a letter persuading a friend to try something your friend has never done before: jogging, organic gardening, transcendental meditation, scuba diving, or any other activity.

7. Write a letter persuading a roommate or close friend to drop out of school (or not to) or to change majors (or not to).

8. Argue for or against the proposition that the National League should follow the American League in using a designated hitter.

9. One of your best friends back home has been admitted to the school you are now attending as well as to a couple of other schools. Write a letter persuading your friend to attend (or not to attend) your school.

10. Argue for or against federal legislation that outlaws strip mining (or another other piece of legislation that relates either to energy or the environment).

11. You just talked to your kid brother on the phone. Some of his friends want him to start smoking pot with them, but he's not sure. Write him a persuasive letter.

12. You just got an unusually frank letter from your kid sister. Some of her closest friends are sleeping with their boyfriends, and she wants your advice whether to follow their example. The tone of her letter makes it clear that she will be strongly influenced by what you say. Write a persuasive letter to her.

13. Argue for or against the proposition that U.S. presidential (or congressional) elections should be publicly financed.

14. Write a letter persuading a pregnant, unmarried friend to have (or not to have) a *legal* abortion.

15. Argue for or against the raising (or lowering) or the drinking (or driving) age in your state.

16. Write a letter persuading a high school friend to live (or not to live) in a coed dormitory during freshman year of college.

17. Write a letter persuading your parents to allow you to attend school, instead of working, this coming summer.

18. Write a letter persuading the editor of a newspaper (or the director of a television news program) that there is a serious local problem that needs to be publicized.

19. Argue for or against the abolition of any rule or regulation currently operating at your school.

20. Write a letter persuading a prospective employer that you should be hired.

INDEX

Note: Page numbers in italics refer to the major discussion of the term.